WAITING
for the URINE

Reminiscences of a Scottish Transplant Surgeon

WAITING
for the URINE

Reminiscences of a Scottish Transplant Surgeon

David Hamilton

THE PARTICK PRESS : ST ANDREWS : 2019

Waiting for the Urine

Design by George Bowie

Created by Amazon KDP

Published in Scotland by
THE PARTICK PRESS
142 North Street
St Andrews KY16 9AF

www.davidhamiltonstandrews.com

ISBN 978-0-9510009-8-4
First published 2019

FRONT COVER: Jimit Medico Surgicals

Contents

ॐ

Chapter 1: Rothesay Childhood

Chapter 2: Move to Glasgow

Chapter 3: School Days

Chapter 4: Glasgow University

Chapter 5: Anatomy and Physiology

Chapter 6: The Corporate Life

Chapter 7: Hospital Teaching

Chapter 8: House Surgeon

Chapter 9: General Practice Locums

Chapter 10: PhD Student

Chapter 11: London

Chapter 12: Immunology Research

Chapter 13: Back to the Western

Chapter 14: Surgical Training

Chapter 15: Politics

Chapter 16: Travels

Chapter 17: Consultant

Chapter 18: More Politics

Chapter 19: New Writing

Chapter 20: Oxford

Chapter 21: Baghdad

Chapter 22: Wellcome Unit

Chapter 23: Itinerant Surgeon

Chapter 24: Gibraltar Locums

Chapter 25: Western Again

Chapter 26: The Sore Back Circuit

Chapter 27: St Andrews Life

Introduction

࿏

Whentransplanting a donor kidney to another person and the
stitching is finished and the clamps released, blood flows into
the grafted organ. The kidney changes from a deathly white colour but
there is often a pause before the urine starts to flow again. The surgeon
waits anxiously for the start of a new life for both kidney and patient.
The pioneer transplant surgeons had to be patient, often waiting for
days or even weeks for the poorly-preserved kidneys to revive. The
pioneers also waited for something else. Organ transplantation was
considered a lost cause, and had to wait for acceptance by the rest of
the medical world.

Doctors are traditionally reluctant to write about their life and
times, leaving such things to others, particularly those who have
scientific eminence, or who seek a popular readership. The rest of
us plead that we have nothing much to report, or, being willing, we
are constrained by confidentiality. This means a dearth of medical
reminiscences and those of us who take an interest in medical history
know how this hinders later reconstruction of events.

Accordingly, I now step up to the mark and report on the period
of unprecedented change in surgery in the second half of the twentieth
century. When I started in medicine, patients with chronic renal failure
simply died slowly and untreated, and heart surgery was in its infancy.
The surgeons of the day (all-male) stitched tissues together by hand,
and chain-smoked in the hospital. Their secretaries did the paperwork
with typewriters, using carbon paper for copies, and land lines
sufficed for communication. Outside the hospital, lethal city winter

smogs killed many, and for children, before the arrival of vaccines, the various childhood epidemic diseases were endured as part of growing up. Scottish society, largely run by men, was deferential and pious; sectarianism was rife and gay men risked imprisonment.

Just as we transplanters waited for the urine, some of us also waited and watched for other change, hoping for a fairer world, giving a nudge or two when possible.

I am reluctant to let these changes, both in surgery and society, slip away without a record. Accordingly I offer this personal account.

David Hamilton

ST ANDREWS 2019

Acknowledgements:

Many old friends, but particularly, David Purdie, John Boyd, Rona Black, Sir David Mason and some Year Club members helped with their own memories of some of these events, as did my sister Alison Mitchell. Michael Fry's *Glasgow* (2017) was a helpful social history of the city. Here in St Andrews, I had the devoted assistance of Julie Falkner in preparing the text and George Bowie has enlivened the book with his thoughtful design. My wife Jean not only helped greatly with comments on the text, but also got to know me better.

CHAPTER 1:

Rothesay, Bute

Guy Fawkes Night ... Difficult birth ... Family
Our garden ... Gas masks ... Rationing ... Poles and
Canadians ... Submarines ... The Big House ... School

I KNOW WHEN I decided to be a surgeon. Age twelve in 1951, I blew myself up on Guy Fawkes Night. I had fireworks in my jacket and rescuing some from another boy's on-fire box, I added his to my collection. But a fuse was burning, and they blasted through my clothes giving a full-thickness burn on my abdomen, about six inches across. It should have been painful, but it was not. As is well known, in serious injury, the brain has a kindly filter which kicks in. Instead of agony, all I felt was a need to get away from something unpleasant.

The adults wrapped me up and rolled me about in someone's coat to smother the combustion and then conveyed me to our family house nearby. It was still the era of house calls, and after our family general practitioner arrived, I was sent by ambulance to the Western Infirmary nearby, being just too old for the Children's Hospital. I required a general anaesthetic to clean up the ugly, charred burn. Before going under, there was a pleasant surprise. As children, we knew that the anaesthetic for any surgery, notably tonsil removal, used the dreaded mask, but the young anaesthetist announced that they had something new for me. It was an injection of pentothal into a vein, which put you to sleep without a struggle. When I woke up, the burned area was clean and painless, since there was no skin left to hurt, but I had to stay in hospital for a while for skin grafting.

The more I saw of the place, the more I liked the Western Infirmary. Always warm and brightly lit, it smelt like a hospital, having that characteristic sharp, reassuring antiseptic smell, now gone, which came from the solvent (possibly ether) used to clean the working surfaces. It was busy throughout the day and night and even at week ends, and I was in the company of caring, talented and attractive nurses. This was the place for me.

I was to be part of the Infirmary for the rest of my life, returning there as a medical student after school days, then training there as a surgeon, and after some travels, joined the consultant staff. I married one of the nurses. On retirement, age 66, after 54 years involvement, I felt like the oldest inhabitant. To add a sense of closure, the Western Infirmary was demolished a few years later.

But I run ahead; I had an earlier brush with death.

My mother went into labour in late June 1939, in the manse (the minister's house) in the town of Rothesay, on the Island of Bute, in the Firth of Clyde in the West of Scotland. There, my father was the new young Church of Scotland incumbent at the town's High Kirk. Although this was our mother's first baby, going to the mainland for hospital obstetric care was, perhaps surprisingly, not part of the *zeitgeist* of the day. In this pre-antibiotic era, city hospitals still had a bad reputation for serious postpartum infection, and home delivery was at least free from this threat.

As often happens with first babies, I was reluctant to appear and my head got stuck. In this well-islanded part of Scotland, some islands had one doctor, some had none, but we had two. Having two meant they could do surgery, still a feature of country practice, with one doctor doing the operation and the other giving the chloroform anaesthetic. Between them, they set fractures or took out tonsils, operating in the home, especially in the homes of the well-off, although there was a small cottage hospital in Rothesay. In the home, they used a small, firm kitchen table for carrying out such surgery. In this pre-NHS era, it paid them well.*

At the manse, I was making no progress, and our two-man medical team was needed, in obstetric mode, to get me out. Our Dr Howie, ready to act, reached the house first, bringing with him his obstetric forceps, doubtless reflecting that the first pregnancies of the wives of professional colleagues can be guaranteed to be difficult. Doctor Howie's immediate concern was a practical one. His partner, the anaesthetist, was not at home, and was out and about in the island doing house calls. The country practitioners relied on their wives, back at home, who, knowing the day's itinerary, could contact them. With the help of the local telephonist, famously also well informed, they could track their husband on his rounds. Meanwhile, my father recalls Dr Howie looking out the manse bedroom window, fretting at the delay in dealing with my deep transverse arrest. My anaesthetist was successfully traced.

When the forceps delivery was carried out, mother probably had a full stomach, since nutritious food and fluid would be well-meaningly offered during the long, exhausting labour. If they did not use the kitchen table, she would be on a soft bed, and bad lighting would increase the challenge for Dr Howie. Thankfully, after putting her under, I was pulled out, intact.

෨

These days, some doctors and others ask rhetorically if there has been any real progress in medicine, perhaps adding nostalgic anecdotes about the 'good old days' of medical practice. They might even praise natural childbirth. I'm not one of them.

As was usual after any delivery, mother stayed in bed for a week. The dangers of thrombosis were known, but it was argued that if you didn't move your legs much, clots would not pass from the legs to the

---

* In Rothesay, much earlier, we had a pioneering surgeon on the Island. In the Bronze Age, a skilled healer trephined a hole in the skull of one of the inhabitants, doubtless to 'let out evil spirits'. The famous skull is held in an Edinburgh Museum, and since the edges of the bone shows regeneration, the patient must have survived. In later times, Sir William Macewen (1848-1924), the famous Glasgow surgeon, had a home on Bute.

lungs. A nurse, Nurse Neilson, was hired to look after mother and baby for some weeks, as was usual in middle-class homes.

Mother, father, myself in pram and Blane our retriever on the Rothesay promenade.

Father was from the city of Glasgow in the West of Scotland and mother from nearby Paisley. Both graduated at the University of Glasgow, but details of their courtship were not passed on to myself or my sister, despite inquiries. Mother was the daughter of a civil engineer, active as an independent in local Paisley politics, and he rose to be Deputy Provost. He owned one of the first cars in the city. Mother attended the Girl's High grammar school in Glasgow, then became a primary school teacher. After marriage and the move to Rothesay, she did not work, nor was expected to work. Even if she had sought a teacher's post, the mood in the 1930s was against hiring married women as teachers. These posts were reserved for men at this time of scarcity of jobs. However, in Rothesay, as the minister's wife, she had duties and was expected to run the church's Woman's Guild. Much later, when studying the old *The Buteman* newspaper files, I noted that, to mark my birth, the Guild kindly presented me, the infant, with some National Savings Certificates. I expect I got them later.

Father's side of the family, a humble one, was a mystery. The three brothers did well at the (boy's) Glasgow High School, and one brother went to work in a Glasgow shipping firm. His young wife died of pneumonia in this pre-antibiotic era, and we nearly adopted their baby before he emigrated to America. The other brother, it emerged later, had robbed a bank (from the inside) and was jailed; this perhaps explains why there was little talk about father's side.

After his first university degree, father trained for the ministry at Glasgow University thus gaining the two degrees of M.A. and B.D.; they were on his notepaper and later, to me, this looked very grand. He then took the prestigious training post of assistant minister at Glasgow Cathedral, and from there was recommended for the vacancy in the church at Rothesay. Ministers of religion, then and now, could have a varied and interesting three-phase career. When newly qualified they sought a country parish, such as Rothesay, and with experience and a growing family, they might look for a move to a larger city church. With the family grown up, in a third phase, the ministers might return to a less busy, but still attractive, country parish. Other professionals were, and are, not so mobile. Lawyers, being fee-paid, must build up a practice, and starting again elsewhere is difficult. Hospital consultants with

THE HIGH KIRK OF ROTHESAY.

PARISH CHURCH

Sunday

Services—

11-15 a.m.

and

6-30 p.m.

Rev. James Hay Hamilton, B.D.

SEATS Reserved for Visitors.   ACOUSTICON for the Deaf.
BUSES leave Port-Bannatyne at 10-55 a.m. and 6-15 p.m., returning after service.

private practices were, and are, immobile. But salaried ministers had the ability to move and this sensible three-phase progression suited all, including the churches. In father's case he was at Rothesay until 1947, then to Hyndland Parish Church in Glasgow and then, much later, when my sister and I had left home, he moved back to the country parish of Colmonell in the south of Ayrshire.

My risky birth was just one month before the outbreak of the World War II, and Chamberlain's sombre broadcast came on Sunday 3rd September at 11.15 a.m. Father was already in the pulpit, but the beadle picked up the not-unexpected news on the radio, and notified father to announce this declaration of war. The choice of the first hymn for that morning, namely *Glorious Things of Thee Are Spoken* was, with hindsight, unfortunate since it was sung to the tune of the German national anthem.

Father was called up to be a chaplain in the Scots Guards. He had no combat role, but organised the usual sacraments and Sunday services, and took on extra responsibilities in dealing with the soldiers' many problems. This included counselling and appearing during army court-martials, acting as defence counsel for the accused. In father's absence, a retired *locum tenens* minister ran our parish, and the kindly, elderly Rev McEachern stayed with us in the manse.

My sister was born uneventfully two years later, and although we were regularly fatherless, I can't recall any sense of deprivation. When father came back on leave, towards the end of the War, he began to bring booty with him, including German army uniforms and equipment. We looked in awe at the murderous bayonets and returned with relief to our own weapons – bows and arrows and slings made from rubber bands. He also brought hand-made wooden toys and metalwork made by the impoverished civilians and bought from them as the Allies progressed through Germany.

Father's salary came in quarterly, and local shops and suppliers knew to wait for payment of bills. Our home, the manse, was the usual tied house provided for the minister, and we had Celia, a live-in maid/cook wearing a black dress and apron, and we had a golden retriever dog and hens. The Rothesay manse was, and is, a solid three-storey stone building, with mature trees and a rookery in the large garden which tumbled down towards the town. For us, there were birds' nests in the hedges and the climbable trees were my friends including a large old chestnut tree. In autumn, the chestnuts were eagerly awaited, and encouraged to fall by throwing up sticks. At the bottom of the garden, which adjoined the poorer part of the town, the Bad Boys occasionally invaded our space in numbers, and cause alarm to myself and my genteel boy and girl companions from the villas nearby. With these local pals, we had some secret ploys in the garden and one of them was smoking cinnamon sticks; another was exploring the mysteries of gender.

At play, there were the feared stings from wasps, clegs, bees and nettles and we got plenty of cuts and bumps which mother treated with Zam-Buk ointment, an unfailing remedy composed of paraffin, camphor and oil. Of my more serious injuries, one was a crushed thumb, caught nastily in a gate, and the scar remains. It was slow to heal and became infected, and at Dr Howie's surgery his wife, who, as well as being receptionist and telephonist, acted as nurse, soaked and removed the bandages gently. Following this, he put liberal doses of penicillin powder on the wound, the new miracle cure which had just arrived in the mid-1940s.

My tonsils were said to be a problem, and removal of these was an almost obligatory rite of passage for middle-class children, although my sister escaped. It meant a scary stay in a primitive Glasgow private nursing home and the ear, nose and throat surgeons of the day spent much of their time doing this operation. Before the NHS, they made a good living in private practice from this ritual removal of part of the body's defence mechanism. The only plus for us young patients was that after the operation, as promised, you got an unlimited supply of ice cream.

Above the town and the manse, was our golf course, famous for its views of the Firth of Clyde. During the War, to help animal grazing and save money, they cut the grass less often and put cattle on the course. I learned to play, and because new golf balls were not available, I hacked my way round with a badly-cut old golf ball handed over by father. One great moment for us was to find an abandoned golf ball in the wood next to the first hole, and, usually damaged beyond repair, peeling off the cover revealed the wonderful and seemingly endless yards of elastic thread inside. We had no golf tees instead using a pyramid made from sand from a box on the tee.

Rothesay Golf Course, close to our manse.

Our other sport was swimming. There were outdoor sea-water bathing pools on the promenade which filled at high tide, but we used these places to sail our model boats. The indoor, heated salt-water town Baths were an important part of our lives, and the Baths Master was an important local figure. We all learned to swim, particularly as exposure to salt water was regarded as health-giving. There was a mysterious poster on the Baths wall showing three similar men, or the same man. Someone, pulling my leg, told me they were the three patron saints of Bute – Ninian, Marnock and Blane. Instead, they illustrated the resuscitation of the drowned by the Holger-Nielson method, an ineffective strategy which involved flapping the arms; the more effective mouth-to-mouth breathing was yet to come.

Our live-in maid Celia was summoned to the upstairs rooms by call bells on the walls. She did the laundry by hand, helped by a hand-cranked ringer, and she, rather than mother, was the cook. but mother knew how to cook. Before marriage, it was the custom for middle-class young ladies to take instruction at the Glasgow 'Dough School' – the Domestic Science College – which published a famous cookbook, still in print. But mother's training was not only towards gaining personal culinary skills, since when married she was not expected to cook. Instead, she had to instruct the cook. The young Girl Guides of Rothesay also looked to mother for leadership, teaching them to cook and then sit their cookery badge. These hands-on events took place in the manse, and they allowed us children to taste the results. Making Scotch broth was a pass/fail item, and if the girls forgot to put in salt, they lost points.

There were many scarcities during the War. Hitler's strategy after he lost the Battle of Britain was to cripple Britain by U-boat attacks on our Atlantic shipping route with America. Even clothes were rationed and economical Utility national designs were available. 'Make do and mend' was the mantra and mother's Singer sewing machine was busy. Ration books controlled the weekly shopping, and to give balanced nutrition for the nation, the government brought in scientists like Boyd Orr to advise. The vitality of British youth was now a national priority, since the government had noted, with concern, the health and strength of the young Germans, a result of their 'welfare state'. Accordingly, for us children, important nutritional extras were handed out – vitamins (including rose hip syrup rich in Vitamin C), cod liver oil, orange juice and jars of thick, tasty malt (later sold as Virol).

Our day started with porridge, an eternally healthy and economical dish. We made toast at the coal fire using a fork, and butter balls were ready, curled by Celia with a special warm tool. Potatoes and fish were not rationed, nor were dried eggs, but meat was scarce and we had 'soup and pudding days' to eke out the rations. Food was also short for our dog, and scraps and dog biscuits often had to suffice. We had no sweets. The only oranges available were the seasonal bitter Seville marmalade variety, and when in season, they were a novelty and were made palatable by thrusting a sugar cube down into the core.

We knew about bananas, but I had never seen one. There was a memorable event when mother took me to visit a Rothesay neighbour who asked me if I would like a banana, pointing to a bowl apparently full of fruit. When I picked it up, it proved to be a china replica, and they laughed. I considered this to be a bad joke in poor taste. The first post-war cargo of bananas for Britain did not arrive until January 1946 and Bristol gave the boat a civic welcome.

Mother's sister had emigrated earlier to South Africa, and during the War, when we opened her Christmas food parcels on the Day, within there were exotic chocolates. Mother quickly sat us down to send an immediate thank-you letter, since our severe aunt would tick off mother if these letters did not arrive promptly. To pre-empt other complaints that we were an ungrateful lot, mother insisted that during our summer holidays we sent postcards to South Africa. My sister and I kept up this habit well into adult life, and, to our surprise, we were rewarded. When our aunt died, she left each of us a substantial five-figure sum which, divided by the estimated number of postcards sent, was an impressive investment.

Each morning there was a delivery to the manse of fresh, non-chilled, non-pasteurised milk. In our road, each household put out metal containers of standard size at their doors, usually pints or fractions of a pint, according to needs, and the milk was decanted into them from large churns on the farmer's cart. To speed up the service, we boys helped by pro-actively picking up the waiting empty containers on the doorsteps and, after filling, returned them to the house. There was competition for this early morning work and the farmer rewarded us with small payments, although the Big Boys usually got the job. The milk, when settled, had a thick layer of cream on top. Refrigerators were still to come, and we used the cream immediately, notably adding it to our morning porridge. This luxury contrasted with the otherwise simple fare in these hard times.

We had no car, nor expected to have one. Only the doctors had cars, and during the wartime rationing, to assist their house visits, they got petrol coupons. Instead, we used bicycles for any travels beyond the town and one expedition was to have lunch at the formidable Miss Dorothy Marshall's large country house. Despite a warning to behave, when the hare soup was served, to the embarrassment of all, I ostentatiously bent forward and suspiciously sniffed it.

Miss Marshall's career was interesting and reflected some assumptions in pre-war times. She was the youngest of three daughters born earlier in the century to the island's doctor, and his wife died when young. The older girls, Margaret and Sheena, went off to higher education, but Dorothy, as was expected, had to stay at home to look after father. Margaret trained as a nurse and became matron at Edinburgh's Royal Infirmary. Sheena became a zoologist and was the first women elected to Edinburgh's Royal Society, followed in 1963 by a fellowship at The (London) Royal Society. Dorothy, when their father died, used her much-delayed freedom to take up archaeology, and worked on high-profile expeditions with Mortimer Wheeler and Katherine Kenyon.

Although Bute, in the Clyde estuary, was distant from the Clydeside yards and the drama of the German air raids, the island was not peripheral to the War events. At the time of the Battle of Britain in 1940, if the Luftwaffe had prevailed, an invasion of Britain was likely

to follow. One possible German strategy was to move into Ireland, and then attack the west coast of Scotland, if only as a diversionary raid. To prevent this, on the west coast of our island, obstructions were put on the main beach to deal with landing craft and gliders.

There was a fear, lingering from World War I, that Germany would use poison gas attacks. Although delivery was difficult, and the gases had a very limited range, like the rest of Britain, we were supplied with gas masks. It amplified hostility to Germany and the adult version had a thick rubber head mask holding the heavy canister of activated charcoal. There were smaller versions for children, and special hoods for prams.

Britain expected bombing and later it had to be endured in Glasgow and the Clydeside shipyard towns. To deny navigational help to the German bombers, our town had no street lights and skylights had blackouts. We used torches to get about, and those in

Rothesay who ignored these matters had a rebuke from the Air Raid Precaution Wardens, or were to taken to court and exposed in *The Buteman* newspaper. One other local strategy to confuse air attackers was a dummy decoy town in the north of the island which did have lights. Poignantly, when the raids on the West of Scotland came, they took place on cloud-free, moonlit nights and the bombers could easily navigate using the visible River Clyde. The first German planes, guided by a radio beam, dropped incendiaries to cause fires and these marked the target for the following bombers. If these fires were extinguished promptly, it might frustrate the task of the following bombers, and to dowse the flames, we had a government-provided stirrup pump and hose. But we were far from any action, and its only use by us was for watering the garden, or for fun and games on a warm day.

Mass compulsory evacuation of children from Glasgow and the at-risk shipyard towns was arranged well ahead of the bombing. As elsewhere, all Bute households had to report how many spare rooms they had. Shortly after the declaration of war, nearly 1000 children arrived in Rothesay, each with a parcel of clothes, carrying gas masks and with a label round their necks. I learned about these events and incidents much later, and heard that we took some in to the manse, and that six went to Dr Buchanan's large house, our parents' friend. This influx to the town meant a culture shock on both sides, and the unhappy children, when the expected bombing was much delayed, soon pined for home. Though it was a fraught time for all, later anecdotes involving the evacuees were more light-hearted. One story was of Glasgow children from a deprived area who lodged with an elderly lady looked after by an ancient butler and a frail cook. One morning, one of the Glasgow evacuees spoke up:

'Where's my f**king breakfast?'
What did you say?' said the gracious lady of the house.
The urchin stood firm and repeated his demand.
'My dear boy,' said the lady, 'I've been wanting to say that for years.'

Bute was involved, often inconspicuously, in many other wartime matters, notably submarine warfare, closely described in Jess Sandeman's book *Bute at War* (2005). Submarines where our thing, and 95% of British submariners trained in the Rothesay depot ship HMS *Cyclops* in the Bay. This elderly mother ship arrived in 1940 from Malta (later replaced by HMS *Montclare*), and *Cyclops* had been so quickly restored and dispatched that it still had a Maltese crew. Some of them would marry Rothesay girls, introducing exotic names like Scibera and Scicluna to the island.

A more mysterious cosmopolitan influx to Bute was of 60 Polish gentlemen housed together outside the town in the Co-operative Society's pre-war holiday camp. The word on the street was that they were a Polish government-in-exile but a different explanation emerged later. They were indeed high-ranking exiled Poles, but were Nazi sympathisers dispatched there by the Polish government in Britain, and were being watched. These charming men were well-liked in the town and some successfully courted our local ladies. These marriages meant that Rothesay also gained Polish names, explaining why our church organist was a Mrs Mehalska. Canadians also trained with us before D-Day and had fun, being welcomed in the town for their supply of otherwise unobtainable items such as ladies' stockings. It is said that the incomers modified a traditional Scottish country dance to become the widely known Canadian Barn Dance.

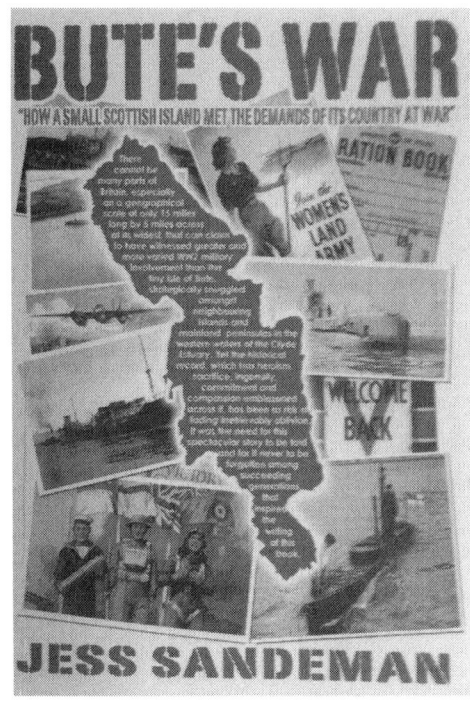

On the island, a few miles to the north of Rothesay, Port Bannatyne had a salvage company, with ocean-going tugs and a floating dock which were soon busy dealing with damaged vessels limping in after U-boat attacks on Atlantic convoys. Also at Port Bannatyne the requisitioned Kyles Hydropathic had a unit which trained the new midget submariners who carried out the daring, but risky, raids on the German battleship *Tirpitz* in September 1943.

In Britain, fears were encouraged that a 'Fifth Column' of Nazi sympathisers was in our midst, gathering information and working towards Britain's defeat, and accordingly, movement of 'aliens' was controlled and photography was forbidden. One group regarded with suspicion in the West of Scotland was the Italians, originally from Tuscany, who ran the cafes offering fast foods, notably ice cream or fish and chips. In Rothesay we had our well-liked Zavaronis and their family shop. The Italians were well-integrated in the community, and probably apolitical, but after Mussolini's pact with Hitler, many were deported to Canada, and some lost to U-boat attack.

If there was any sympathy for fascism in Bute, a possible source was the Big House of the owner of the island. Bute had a feudal structure and ambiance and was, and is, entirely owned by an aristocrat, the Marquis of Bute. At the southern end of the island their estate was a royal gift some time ago to an illegitimate son born to Scotland's King Robert II's mistress. After this start, the family had its ups and downs. The 3rd Marquis (1847-1900), who built Mount Stuart, their magnificent Mount Stuart mansion, used his money well as a patron of the arts, notably endowing, among other things, the Bute Medical School at St Andrews University and funding the magnificent Bute Hall at Glasgow University. The 4th Marquis, our man, was less impressive, and wasn't often in the island. I dimly remember him venturing out as patron of the summer Highland Games, and, said to have health problems, he died in 1947.

This Marquis admired the Spanish dictator Franco, and when the Marquis's brother Ninian died, his widow married Captain Archibald Henry Maule Ramsey (1894-1955) the Conservative member of parliament for Peebles and South Midlothian. Ramsey was an active

British fascist and, seen as a risk, was interned in Brixton Prison during the War with Oswald Mosley, the fascist leader. The rest of the Marquis's family, when war started, gave loyal service.

≈

The War won, age five, I went to Rothesay Academy, an excellent school, and Miss Funnel and Miss McCrone, our teachers, were a new dominant influence in our lives. I'm told they used the progressive 'look and say' method for instruction in reading. I reached school via a walk from the manse, and outside each house, the railings were missing, cut off at the base, and the metal taken away to use for armaments. The railings were only spared if they protected a descent into a basement.

My route to school down the road took me past the house of a former provost, marked outside by an ornate lamp post, past the house of the local official jailed for embezzlement, then past the house of the boy who got each new Dinky toy when it came out. At school I was deeply in love with the most beautiful girl in the class and I had a sign from her that she returned my feelings. Many, many years later, when back in Bute, I enquired cautiously after her, her name being ever bright in my memory.

'Yes,' our friends said, 'she is still here.'

'And …?' I asked.

The news was bad. She was obese and dying of alcoholism.

I shouldn't have asked.

≈

After school we descended back into the town. The pier was never dull and while we were content to fish off the pier with simple equipment for tiny suicidal fish, the Big Boys had better gear and could cast well out into the bay and bring in mackerel. From the pier, there was the shuttle boat taking Navy men back and forth to the huge depot ship, and in the inner harbour there were puffers, the famous blunt-nosed, flat-bottomed steamboats which could make five knots, delivering essentials, notably coal, for the island. The puffers were immortalised in Neil Munro's tales of the *Vital Spark*, and a Rothesay contact is mentioned.

The War ended on VE day, 8 May 1945, and I may have seen and heard the celebrations. Throughout the Firth of Clyde, ships hooted, pipe bands appeared, beacons were lit on the hills and church bells rang. Street lighting resumed. There was a political surprise in the election which followed, when the Conservative Party and Churchill were not returned to power despite his wartime leadership. Much later my father said darkly that our doctor friend in Rothesay had helped this defeat by disloyally voting for the Labour Party.

After the War, travel conditions eased. Professional golf resumed, and it was worthwhile for John Panton and Eric Brown to come across to a tournament in Rothesay. I had only seen my father play golf, and I marveled at Panton's famously long and accurate iron shots. The well-off summer visitors returned, recalling the earlier days when Glasgow families took houses for the entire summer in the towns of the Firth of Clyde. Father of the house then commuted to Glasgow on the fast steamers and enjoyed breakfast in the first-class lounge, served in style with silver service and silver cutlery. 'Doon the Water' to Rothesay was also returning as a favourite holiday choice for Glasgow working-class families, particularly at the time of the July trade holiday, travelling by train to Wemyss Bay, and thence by steamer to Rothesay. These famous boats included the *Duchess of Fife, Jeannie Deans,* and, above all, the paddle steamer *Waverley*, which has survived, just, as the much-admired last ocean-going vessel of its kind. On the boat to Rothesay, there was musical entertainment on the deck and on nearing the pier, the boats slowed and moved cautiously since the Bay was dangerously full of small rowing and motor boats hired by the half hour. On the pier, there were porters waiting with carts to deliver luggage. The boats carried no cars, as decreed by the Marquis.

During the holiday season, the street entertainment on the front included Punch and Judy booths, evangelism from the Band of Hope, and open air draughts played on large concrete boards. Close to the pier was an important concert hall – The Entertainers – in the Winter Gardens, which brought the best music hall acts down from Glasgow. The three cinemas in Rothesay still survived after the War, and they changed programmes in midweek. An A film and a B film sandwiched the patriotic Movietone or Pathé News, and you could enter the cinema at any time and leave at 'this is where we came in'.

The journey to visit our grandparents in Paisley was an adventure, starting on the boat from Rothesay, where, below deck, we inspected the paddle steamer's awesome engines, controlled and watched intently by engineers directed by commands from the bridge. The train from the elegant Wemyss Bay took us to central Paisley finishing with a tram car journey to our destination.

Grandfather was a severe man. I did not like his house, and was always glad to get back to Rothesay. Many years later, I had an odd *deja vu* experience. While viewing a French Impressionist painting exhibition, I was overcome with gloom, and later realised that it had stirred up memories of our grandfather's house. It turned out that during the War, the Paisley Museum and Art Gallery, to protect their impressive collection from air raids, dispersed the paintings to private houses. Grandfather, as a senior town dignitary, was one of those involved. Unknown to me, during these childhood visits to Paisley, I was surrounded by the works of Degas, Monet and Renoir.

In 1947, age seven, came the news that we were moving to Glasgow. They said I cried and cried.

&

CHAPTER 2:

Glasgow

City pollution … Epidemics … Skin grafts … Street life
Trams … Sundays … Street play … Food and Drink
Radio … The Scouts … TV arrives … Holidays

MY FIRST reaction to Glasgow was that it was dirty. Even the trees
were filthy. Back on our island, trees were my friends, but if you
attempted to climb or even hug a Glasgow tree, your hands and clothes
got grimy. In spring-time, there was a short period when the trees had
new green leaves, but within weeks they, like the bark, had a patina
of dark dirt. Glasgow, like all large cities, was blighted by the smoke
from the ubiquitous use of coal, used both at home and in the heavy
industries which made the West of Scotland wealthy in the past.

We were now in our new home – the manse of Hyndland Parish
Church in the West End. It was part of the solid red sandstone
terraces in the Hillhead, Kelvinside and Dowanhill area built during the
prosperous late Victorian era expansion of the city beyond and above
the unhealthy centre.* This speculative building, which often included
communal gardens, lasted until 1909, being curtailed suddenly by
Lloyd George's redistributive 'People's Budget'. With one war, then a
second one following, no more terrace houses were added and the city
continued its expansion west developing a large area of red sandstone

* See Nanzie McLeod's valuable *Tales of G12,* Glasgow 2010.

tenements, some with large flats, down the hill on both sides of Clarence Drive.

The larger terrace houses, like the manse, were now regarded as old-fashioned and were expensive to maintain at a time of tight budgets. Double glazing was yet to come and heating costs were high. When 'central' heating did arrive and replaced coal fires, the new warmth caused dry rot to emerge alarmingly in the old wood and caused dismay to the West End home owners. It was like having cancer in the family, and the sufferers behaved in the same way, concealing this problem to avoid its stigma. These large terrace houses were steadily sub-divided and converted into flats, though much later, the strategy halted and the few intact large family homes which survived in the West End showed sharply rising values.

Hyndland Parish Church's rural setting in the early 1900s, north-west of the present Crown Road North. Gartnavel Asylum (top left) was well outside the City.

Money was short, and with incomes for ministers failing to keep up with the inflation of the times, the clergy lost ground relative to other professions. We were aware of belt-tightening in the house, and our faithful maid Celia, who came with us from Rothesay returned home. Mother accepted that she would now have to do without help, other than a 'cleaning lady', and she returned to the kitchen and cooked for us. Mother was a good cook, offering traditional Scottish fare, within the difficulties of rationing, which continued into the early 1950s.

Father's new charge, Hyndland Parish Church, was originally out in fields at the west edge of the growing city, and was soon reached by the Edwardian terraces.* For the governance of the church, the Kirk Session's all-male elders met in midweek, and arrived at the church after dinner already dressed in black tie, the dinner hour being 6 o'clock. The elders dressed in morning coats for the communion service, but mother heard that some new elders hired the needed dress for the occasion, and after a word with father, the custom was dropped. At the church, each family had their own pew, and ladies wore hats, as they did beyond the house, notably at weddings.

For us children, it was still a time of epidemics and they had to be endured; vaccinations would arrive in the 1950s. Whooping cough was fairly mild for us older children, but mumps was unpleasant and gave you a sore face and time off from school, as did chicken pox. Measles completed the usual childhood infections. Bed rest was still an essential part of any treatment and you had a week in bed with your food brought to you on a tray. To help with the long day, mother bought me a new game, or a balsa wood kit to make up an aeroplane. A high point in the long day was when the doctor called to have a look and take your temperature.

Scarlet fever was rarer and more dangerous since heart and kidney damage could follow later in life. Polio visited Britain in 1952 and one boy at the school, a physician's son, had it, but no paralysis remained. Polio claimed a distinguished local West of Scotland victim, Nancy Riach, who held all the British records, and had been Britain's best swimming prospect for the 1948 Olympics.

Dentistry meant fillings and extractions, and we had to endure drilling with the slow, vibrating drills of the day and the dentists, paid by fees rather than salary, did well under the NHS. West of Scotland middle class teeth were, and are, notoriously prone to decay, and our mother eventually had false teeth. It is said that most of the Celtic football team who triumphed in the European Cup in 1967 were

---

* Hyndland Parish Church's architect was William Leiper, with stained-glass windows added later by William Wilson and Gordon Webster. Our Willis pipe organ was one of the finest in the UK, and we had a talented organist, Purcell J Mansfield.

edentulous and their dentures were kept during the famous game in a hat behind the goalkeeper, ready for a replacement for the photographs at the end.

For any serious family illness, father could call in a well-known, but frosty local Western Infirmary consultant physician, who was a member of our church. He followed the etiquette of not charging fellow professionals, like our father, for these private visits. His old-fashioned views gave him prominence in the hospital, notably opposing the use of steroids and other new remedies such as the anticoagulant warfarin, which he ridiculed, correctly identifying it as 'rat poison'. I developed an odd ailment which I still can't diagnose retrospectively, but I missed school for weeks with fever, nasty dreams and hallucinations. Our aloof consultant was again called in and after examination, without any blood tests, he pronounced that the diagnosis was 'anaemia'. He prescribed two bottles, one noted by my mother to contain very expensive vitamins, and I pulled through, after a while, with the help of the healing powers of nature. These same mechanisms were much relied on by our holistic consultant.

Grandfather came to live with us after his wife died, and shortly after, he suffered a stroke. We called in our consultant again and he did not suggest admission to hospital, but when grandfather deteriorated, he was moved to a private nursing home and died there. The middle classes still used these small, badly-equipped and badly staffed private sector establishments, often owned by the hospital consultants.

As mentioned earlier, I blew myself up and landed in hospital on Guy Fawkes Night in 1952, and I was in the Western Infirmary for a while. While my full-thickness burn healed slowly from the edge, I was the pet of the ward, being only 12 years old, and for me it was an agreeable place. The wards of the Western Infirmary had a 'Nightingale' layout with an unpartitioned row of about 15 beds on each side. Each ward was named after a local Glasgow Victorian philanthropist donor with their names etched on the large glass panels above the ward entrance. Above each bed, a plaque honoured smaller charitable donations to the hospital and below this was a ledge with a Bible and a glass container which held the daily specimen of

urine requested from each of us. No-one knew its purpose, but later
I realised it was a left-over from mediaeval uroscopy, namely that
inspection could reveal much about the patient's general condition.

The food was poor and to improve our diet, the family could
bring in eggs, and before boiling them in the kitchen, you added
your name in pencil to the shell. In the evening, the matron made a
speedy round of the whole hospital, looking for fault, and on Sundays
evangelists arrived and sang. Through the night, the nurses sat round
the coal fire in the centre of the ward.

A senior consultant headed each unit, and ours had two wards,
one female and one male, plus an operating theatre, all three opening
out from a busy central concourse. In the early evenings, I soon found
my way round to the theatre. After the day's surgical work ended, an
evening duty nurse remained there, and I helped her fold and pack the
swabs for sterilisation in the theatre autoclave ready for use next day.
Greatly daring, I could peek into the now-dim, high-ceilinged space,
rightly called a 'theatre', and its viewing gallery. To me it was a magic
place. Thereafter I had no other plan than to gain entry to this world
and its mystique. Mother was keen I should instead be a minister, but
when she raised the matter, I averted my gaze and changed the subject.

ॐ

One day, there was a buzz of expectation in the ward. The 'chief',
the consultant heading our unit, had made it known he would appear.
Until then, I had never seen him. The NHS was fairly new and for the
first time these senior doctors were paid a salary. Previously, they were
unpaid, earning a living from private practice, and though glad of the
prestige of a teaching hospital attachment, they were not expected to
attend the hospital regularly. But even after the NHS was established,
some consultants kept to their former habit of being 'visiting'
consultants, rather than basing themselves in the hospital.

Our absentee appeared with an entourage of my friends, the
junior surgeons and nurses. This thin, sad man, dressed in tweed, may
have been heading for the moors or the river or the golf course. The
medical and nursing staff treated him deferentially since their careers
relied on his patronage and references. When he came to me, our ward
sister removed the dressings from my burn, and without any greeting,

he just said 'skin graft' and moved on. I was not impressed with his bedside manner, and I never saw him again. Much later, when on the staff myself, I discovered that he was a reclusive alcoholic.

He was right about the skin graft and one of my young surgeon friends carried it out and it healed in nicely. Remaining with me still are the scars of the burn, plus the thin graft and slight markings at the partial-thickness skin donor area on my thigh.

The other medical influence was my 'uncle', our family's general practitioner friend in Rothesay, and they joined us on our Speyside July holiday, and we in turn visited them in August. I was interested in his lifestyle. Dr Buchanan had the traditional morning and evening consultations – 'surgeries' – in his house, and he not only owned a car, but such was the mileage he did on the island, he changed it every year. As an elder in my father's old Rothesay parish church he was a genial figure at the door, greeting the congregation as it entered. To add to this, I noticed that on Sundays he had a dispensation. Being 'on call', he could avoid going to church.

My mind was made up. Surgery was for me.

Winter could be a fraught time in Glasgow, with 'smog' – smoke and fog combined – on cold windless days, and year after year, this unhealthy pall could settle in, paralysing the city for days. Public transport suffered, and although the trams kept moving cautiously on their rails, buses got lost and entered side streets. Plans for dinners, dances, football matches and concerts were cancelled at short notice, and theatre audiences, even if they could get to the performance, could not see the stage. Chest ailments worsened, resulting in many winter deaths.

To deal with the public health problem, there was an obvious need for a reduction in use of coal, the main culprit, in the home and heavy industry. In December 1952, a lethal London smog lasted for four days, but in spite of calls for action, the politicians were reluctant to act. *The Times* complacently explained that this unpleasantness was not new, and recalled that when the Romans arrived, they met fog. The minister of housing, Harold MacMillan, regretted the new mood that governments could solve all problems, but set up a committee 'so we can be seen to be busy'. The heavy industries, being in decline, advised that they could not afford the costs of smoke control, and MacMillan's cautious committee report was buried. But in the following winters, smog-related deaths continued and eventually the needs of public health prevailed, leading to the 1954 Clean Air Acts. Later, to those of us working in hospitals, there was a steady reminder of the earlier lung damage; all post-mortems on Glasgow citizens showed diffuse black deposits throughout the lungs.

The polluted atmosphere and the related acid rain of the industrial city also affected Glasgow's houses, darkening the stone and obliterating any fine decoration. After the Clean Air Acts, city-wide stone cleaning could start in Glasgow, and it revealed that the grey residential dwellings, particularly the tenements, were, after all, made of delightful blond or salmon-pink stone. New cheerful vistas opened up, notably in the West End and in the Southside.

঺

In our West End, there was a daily reminder of the War – the 'bomb sites' – gaps in the terraces nearby. The bombs responsible were not aimed at us, but were misplaced 'creep-back' bombs intended for distant Clydebank and dropped on the West End by erratic navigation or released early by German crews impatient to get home.

There was another space beside our manse. When the speculative building of the early 1900s ceased, our terrace was left incomplete and the remaining gap now offered space to deal with the serious post-war housing problem in Glasgow. The solid stone tenements of the Gorbals could have been imaginatively refurbished, but in a response to Glasgow's poor national image, they were demolished.*

As well as sending the dispossessed to distant new towns, a quick solution to the inner-city problem was to use vacant plots within the city and place simple modular 'pre-fab[ricated]' homes for council tenants. Beside and behind the manse, a dozen of these one-level, 2/3 bedroom homes of simple construction soon appeared. Their cement block walls had a pebble dash finish, roofs of corrugated asbestos and

---

* Fortunately, the planners' wholesale replacement of the Victorian city centre by a concrete jungle was narrowly avoided, helped by protests from eccentrics like John Betjeman, to whom Glasgow was an admirable Victorian city.

the coal fire in the living room ducted heat to the other rooms. The fitted wardrobes in the bedrooms were a luxury, as was the small 'fitted' kitchen with a refrigerator. The bathroom and an inside toilet were also novelties for those coming from the older slum tenements, and all these pre-fabs had small gardens. Seen as a temporary measure to last for 10-20 years, they were remarkably robust. Tenants where so fond of them that they often later resisted final moves in the 1990s to Glasgow's new, but ultimately unpopular, East Berlin-style, high-rise, garden-less flats.

The first experimental high-rise apartments had appeared in 1953 at Moss Heights on high ground near the road to Paisley. Although only 10 storeys high, on Sundays, people made car journeys to admire them. The 'tall-is-good' strategy gained further support and lasted for decades but many of the least-loved tall buildings which resulted were demolished later.

The Rent Acts of the 1960s meant that the fixed private sector rents rose for the first time for decades, giving new pressure to buy, and private ownership increased. In another shift, the merchant middle-classes of the West End started a new migration, moving to places like Helensburgh further down the Clyde. Some of the well-off, instead of employing staff, moved into new blocks of 'service' flats with hotel-like support services. Locally, these included the two Art Deco H-plan luxury flats at Kelvin Court along Great Western Road, offering much gossip about the reclusive occupants and their finances.

All children need to get out 'to play' but the committees running our West End enclosed gardens were anti-sport and particularly anti-football. But play had to go on, sensed by children as needed for the maturation of mind and body. Denied the parks, we used another available space, now gone, for play. The car was not yet dominant, and in our quiet Crown Road North, we could play freely. Without parked cars and with only occasional interruptions by through-traffic, this allowed cricket in front of our house, bowling from one pavement across the road to the other, the wicket being the 'pig bin' on the pavement. This metal container gathered food scraps to go towards helping post-war bacon production. I can still hear the dull thump of the ball as it hit the bin and its rotting contents. This street now has parked cars on both sides, and continuous through traffic; streetplay is impossible.

Less well-off areas of Glasgow were even more car-free and street sport thrived. The future stars of Scottish football, often lacking football boots, or even proper shoes, and using a cheap 'tanner ba' or an old tennis ball, used this freedom to play. Young Alex Ferguson, the hero of Manchester United later, was honing his football skills on the car-less roads within the Govan tenements, also destroyed, across the river from us. The edentulous Glasgow Celtic football squad, winners of the European Cup in 1967, were almost all raised in the deprived East End and thrived in its street sport close to the club's stadium.

Our streets had other liveliness, now gone. Still lit by gas, a man came round nightly to light the lamps with a mantle. Visitors to our street included coal lorries, ice cream vans and summer Bretton onion sellers who landed at Leith on the east coast, and reached us by bicycle with loops of pink onions over the handlebars. Knife grinders came by regularly, as did beggars, who supposedly left signs on the house grading the inhabitant's level of charity. At election times, there was rival personal canvassing by the candidates and parties. But we had no concern about street violence. Glasgow was a safe city, contrary to its image, unless you got involved with East End gangland, now much reduced from the notorious 1930s. House theft was also unknown.

&

In the 1950s, our West End was served by the extensive Glasgow tram car network, earlier colour-coded to show the destination, but now numbered. Before the War, Glasgow's 22 mile tram route, number 14, Milngavie to Renfrew Ferry was the longest in the United Kingdom, and with a one penny fare for a child. The old trams had a lurching motion and made a grating noise on the bends, but the 'modern' streamlined yellow Coronation design, which came in from 1937 lacked the charm of the old square models. Near the manse, we had a choice of two routes going downtown from Hyndland Road.

The tramway system was part of old Glasgow, and to move forward, the city planners agreed that, like the Gorbals, the trams had to go, and the streets were surrendered to the car. But Glasgow was slow to get rid of our tramway system, perhaps sensing a mistake, or that parts might be usefully retained as a civic feature. In 1963, Glasgow was the last British city to abandon the trams, and the City celebrated their last day as a modernising event. If Glasgow had delayed much longer, we might have saved a bright feature of city life, offering a badly-needed tourist attraction. San Francisco hung on to their ancient trams and Edinburgh brought back theirs later, at huge cost.

On Sundays, we went to church morning and perhaps in the evening, plus Sunday School in the afternoon. We didn't go places on Sundays, since Sunday observance was widespread with most places shut. There was no golf or football, and since all shops were shut, the Sunday papers were sold in the Italian fish and chip shops or cafes.

During the church services, father's prayers included support for a long list of Royals, including Princess Margaret and he pointedly used the Prince of Wales' Scottish title 'Duke of Rothesay'. The Royals were prominent in our post-war lives, and the cinema newsreels and the press followed their many doings. A minor royal scandal arose in 1947 when Crawfie, the Scottish governess earlier to the princesses Elizabeth and Margaret, published her benign memoirs and harmless anecdotes in an American magazine. She was vilified and held up as a traitor, particularly in Scotland.

At Sunday School, occasional extra events enlivened the routine, and the Temperance Movement's itinerant speakers might arrive. These ladies attacked advertisements like 'Beer is Best' and rehearsed us to retort with the rival mantra 'Tisn't' (i.e. 'It Is Not'). 'Tisn't' we shouted from the car as we passed the relevant adverts. In the Gorbals, we heard that the same ladies, to enliven their talks, used a slide show which included one of a liver with cirrhosis. The kids got to know the liver anatomy so well that they hooted when the slide was shown upside down.[*]

*Recalled by Cliff Hanley in his *Dancing in the Streets*, Glasgow 1961.

Monday was father's day off and, after a busy week-end, which might add a Saturday wedding to his Sunday duties, he gathered for golf with his clerical colleagues – 'Minister's Monday.' In Glasgow, the Church of Scotland ministers had a special Monday-only membership at the well-known Glasgow Club at Killermont and this clerical group took the neutral name of the Glasgow North-Eastern Club. During the rest of the week, father visited the sick and made parish evening visits, calling at the homes of the church members. He arrived without appointment, although he had announced ahead on Sunday the street selected for next week's evening visits. Father liked to tell us how, the visit being unannounced, drinks might be hidden under a seat and if overturned, a wet pool then extended out onto the carpet. For further outreach, he held a week-day evening 'vestry hour', which probably offered counselling.

Our middle-class part of the city was respectable and presbyterian. Post-war Britain was a serious-minded and perhaps, looking back, a rather gloomy place. The old mantra for the middle classes taught that your name should appear in the press only three times – at birth, marriage and death. Divorce was almost unknown in the West of Scotland, but doubtless unhappiness existed. The economic cost of the recent war to a Britain hardly recovered from World War I, was serious, and we had again lost many young men. 'Who won the War?' my father would ask rhetorically, but did not wait for a reply. America, now the dominant economy of the Western world, lent and gifted us money in the Marshall Plan of 1948, not expecting prompt repayment. After the War, rationing did not ease up and got tighter, notably allowing less bacon. In 1948, a ship arrived in Glasgow bearing 450 tons of food, clothing and medical supplies, a thoughtful gift from the concerned Boston Chamber of Commerce and the welcoming party included local politicians, the Scottish Secretary of State, and Harry Lauder.

We used coal fires. In the morning, after clearing the ash in the grate, we lit the living room fire with sticks or twists of newspaper smeared with fat, or fired it up with little stone blocks soaked in paraffin. If a fire was reluctant to blossom, we encouraged it with bellows. To keep the fires on overnight, it was covered with 'dross', fine-particle damp coal, to let it smoulder beneath. Later we had a Baxi fire set into the sitting room grate which used air from below, reducing draughts and we emptied its large bucket of ash weekly. Coal in sacks was delivered by horse and cart at the back door, borne inside on the leather-clad shoulders of the delivery men and the sacks emptied in the basement. Father watched from the upstairs window, counting the number of sacks, since the men notoriously saved some coal for themselves. In our kitchen we had a modern gas cooker/oven, since mother had negotiated to replace the manse's Edwardian black range which used coal or anything burnable. We had a small coke boiler for heating water, topped up at bath time, and there were gas fires in most rooms.

Most things worked only for a while. New electrical devices might burn out if left on, and a wee man was called in to fix them. Refrigerators arrived as a blessing, but we had no dishwasher. After each meal, we washed and dried the plates and put them away, with these duties rotated among the family. In summer, there were flies and the necessary fly papers had a fragrant but sticky toxic surface with a fatal attraction.

The heavy Bakelite telephone in father's study used a rotating dial for local calls. Any rare long-distance calls were requested through the exchange, with brevity and economy encouraged by audible 'pips' at the end of three minutes. Father had no parish secretarial help but had a typewriter which was fun to play with and its different ribbons gave coloured text.

We still had porridge in the morning, (which my wife still makes for our family), but increasingly the graded, bottled milk lacked cream. Our grandfather stayed with us in his late widower years, and he liked to have a separate bowl of milk with his porridge. Tea rather than coffee was favoured. Few families had dinner at this time and instead high tea at 5 p.m. usually offered bacon and egg, with bread or toast, and cakes and tea to follow. There might be a snack later at night, perhaps toasted cheese and tea. There was no question of drinking wine with our meals, and indeed our mother held office in one of the Scottish temperance organisations. Wine was little drunk in Scotland, even in restaurants, being expensive, a tradition lingering from the special wartime tax added. On the few occasions when we had guests for dinner, the aperitif offered cautiously was a small sherry. Drinking gin was unthinkable. In the large houses nearby, after a dinner, the ladies would retire to a separate room and the men passed port round the table (clockwise).

Groceries came from a local shop close by on Hyndland Road and arrived in a large box weekly with a hand-written bill to be settled monthly. In the shop, butter and cheese was cut off large blocks and sugar weighed out into bags. In this cluster of shops there was a paper shop, and an ironmonger, but no cafes or pubs. There was a bank with the limited hours then normal and a Post Office down Clarence Drive. Beside one of the shops was our telephone box, with A and B buttons for connection or a refund. We had an award-winning celebrity hairstylist, Robert Hely, famously employed by Mae West during her visit to Glasgow in 1947. Occasional purchases needed a trip downtown on Saturday morning to the large Glasgow stores which shut on Saturday afternoons.

On Sundays, Scottish pubs were shut, but in the hotels, 'bona fide' travellers could get a drink, which led to evasive schemes by the locals. Scotland's licensing laws were slow to change, and when the Edinburgh Festival opened in 1947, incomers found that the Festival Club did not sell drink on Sundays. Our district in the West End of Glasgow was 'dry' and lacked pubs, since legislation from 1917 allowed each City area to vote by 'local option' to prevent public houses emerging and with our strong local West End temperance sentiment, we had none. This provision was withdrawn in 1957, without protest, and eventually our first pub appeared near the manse.

Many, many years later, our daughter lived in a student flat near our old manse, and she took me for a drink on Hyndland Road. With great difficulty, I forced it down.

For newspapers, during the week we took the Tory *Glasgow Herald,* a city institution, and the more heavily-illustrated *The Bulletin.* The front page of the broad-sheet *Herald,* instead of news stories, offered the traditional mass of classified advertisements including births, marriages and deaths. There were details of upcoming meetings, and small ads which sought staff, including cooks and maids. The big general stores downtown, like Pettigrew's, placed adverts, and all the Glasgow church services were listed on Saturdays. On Sundays, we took *The Observer,* and since the Sunday papers were printed on Saturdays this was acceptable, since it did not force others to work on the sabbath. We were one of the few homes not to get the popular *The Sunday Post,* hence missing out on 'The Broons' and 'Oor Wullie' cartoons. A kindly aunt handed in these pages to us during the week.

I was a Boy Scout in the First Glasgow Troop and we met nearby on Thursday nights. Our senior scout had been a 'conchie', i.e. a conscientious objector during the War, and some parents in the West End retained hostility to him. Some of my pals were not allowed to join the Troop.

Young boys, as ever, have to be careful of homosexual attention. At school we were safe, but there was a nuisance at the Scouts. All the young scoutmasters were beyond reproach, but an elderly district commissioner who came around had to be watched. His tactic was to supply kilts to us Scouts in his large Glasgow district at prices which our frugal mothers could not reasonably ignore. Once ordered, this involved 'measuring and fitting' sessions, as he called them, at his house in the evening. Extraordinarily, he carried out these sessions in a separate room from any parent attending, and we had to strip unnecessarily for the fitting. Trying on the kilts, he had to, as he said, 'pat down the bumps'. With the kilts ready for collection there was an second fitting session, and predictably he deemed that a adjustment was necessary, leading to a third visit. It was embarrassing, but it did not cause us lasting psychological harm. We were too worldly-wise to tell our innocent parents what was going on, but a few of the boys escaped by resolutely declining to have a cheap kilt.

For home entertainment, we had the radio, and these bulky 'wireless' sets had a set of glowing valves inside. Lord Reith, a severe Scotsman, who we were proud of, ran the BBC, the only provider of broadcasting content and he regarded radio as an educational medium rather than one for entertainment. The occasionally-devolved Scottish radio content was in the safe hands from 1933 to 1957 of Rev Melville Dinwiddie, a former Church of Scotland minister.

The all-male BBC radio announcers, unseen to us listeners, had a black tie dress code. The Home Service was speech-based, but in his Light Programme output, as its patronising name suggested, Reith permitted music and simple entertainment. Percy Edwards did bird imitations, Donald Peers sang, and glamorous Anne Ziegler and Webster Booth in (unseen) evening dress together offered 'We'll gather lilacs in the spring again'. From 1946, the BBC's Third Programme countered this frivolity by offering an evening diet of high-brow culture, serious music and the thoughts of literati and intellectuals like T.S.Eliot and Bertrand Russell. Later when this programme was at risk in 1957, a Third Programme Defence Society called on the BBC to stop 'pandering to the more moronic elements of our society.' But they failed to save the programme.

Nightly, during the week, at 6.15 p.m., the Light Programme offered the 15-minute adventures of 'Special Agent' Richard ('Dick' to his friends) Barton, which lasted from 1946 to 1951, prefaced by its famous 'Devil's Gallop' signature tune, used later by others. Barton, a public schoolboy intelligence officer, was assisted by Jock, his stereotypic Scottish assistant – 'Right, Mr Barton, sur' – and a deferential Cockney called 'Snowey'. Daily, the trio faced up to villains plotting to bring the nation

down, including sinister foreigners like Dimitri Melganik and Manuel Garcia. Each episode featured the nation on the edge of disaster with the outcome left literally up in the air. Next night, on the restart, 'with one bound Dick was free.'

The BBC leadership, never happy with the programme, replaced it with 'The Archers' in 1951. Post-war radio offered mid-week comedy, notably *Much-Binding-in-the-Marsh* and *ITMA*. *Round the Horn* followed and looking back, its subtle innuendo contained the first hint of the satire era to come.

Saturday evening radio listening had a ritual. We had Scottish Children's Hour at 5 o'clock, hosted for 32 years by the legendary Kathleen Garscaden. 'Attention all Shipping' followed with its compressed weather forecast, starting with any ominous warnings for mysterious places called Sole, Shannon, Rockall, or Malin. Then followed the national news and the football results, which Edinburgh-born James Alexander Gordon would later announce with skill for 40 years. These match scores had to be given at a stately pace, four seconds each, to enable listeners to check their football pools coupons. Punters waited with concern for 'Partick Thistle nil' (the wits said this was the club's name), then came 'Inverness Caledonia Thistle', the lingering tone of the announcer's voice indicating what was coming. After the results came the 'The McFlannels', a homely working-class soap, and then Scottish country dance music, offering a chance to learn how to dance.

For our board games, Monopoly was popular, and its attraction at the time is puzzling. The stock market was stagnant, entrepreneurs disliked, socialism in vogue and the private housing market at a low ebb. Monopoly involved land purchase and speculative developments, including building houses in poorer parts of London like the Old Kent Road or erecting hotels in Mayfair. There was the possibility of bankruptcy or turning up the 'Go to Jail' card, which acknowledged the sleazy dimension of this sector. Though far from our presbyterian way of life in a Scottish manse, this metropolitan capitalism was curiously appealing.

We didn't go out much in Glasgow. Our nearest picture house, the Grosvenor in Byres Road, had an 'ABC Minors' Saturday morning event, showing mostly cartoons, but despite requests, we were rightly not allowed to go. For music, there was the regular visit to Glasgow of the D'Oyly Carte Opera Company and the school organised outings to their Gilbert and Sullivan opera performances. It was all taken very seriously, and the satire directed at the Establishment in Gilbert's text went unnoticed at the time. The hero was the lead tenor, Peter Pratt, who had to endure endless requests for encores involving his funny walks. Downtown was the famous Empire Theatre, where the huge audiences knew what they liked, and it was known known as 'the English comics' grave'. We never visited it. But we did have a yearly visit to a pantomime. Glasgow was the pantomime capital of the world, and with an extended season over Christmas, New Year and beyond, it gave employment and encouragement to many emerging Scottish comedians. Indeed, there were so many, and since none came from Edinburgh, that you might think that Glasgow invented humour, and its content was, and is, based on local discourse. Of old, there was Will Fyfe, Duncan Macrae, Dave Willis and Jack Radcliffe, soon followed by Jimmy Logan, Rikki Fulton and Tommy Morgan. Then came Stanley Baxter and Billy Connolly, gaining international appeal, and Chick Murray, the comedians' comedian, was much admired for his exploration of words and their meaning. Another of our winter visits was to the Kelvin Hall Circus and Carnival and the joy of being given 10 shillings, which paid for rifle shooting and the thrill of driving the dodgems electric cars.

Kirk o' Shotts television transmitter opened up in 1952, receiving the national signal from Manchester and sending it out as far as Aberdeen in the north and Kelso in the borders. Television sets were few and the limited service, hardly more than two hours of viewing at first, started at 2 p.m. The service was clucky, and when there were problems, a soothing potter's wheel in action had to suffice. A surprise was that the BBC soon employed two female announcers, including Sylvia Peters, her name changed from the BBC-unacceptable Sylvia Lucia Petronzio. The strict BBC dress code for these ladies required neck-throttling tops and, below camera view, unseen, was a long dress. They both spoke like the Queen. Peters was judged to be 'too emotional' to read the news, but was allowed a small part in the commentary on the 1953 Coronation service.

A well-off neighbour, one of the few in our terrace to have television, invited us to watch the Coronation. Traditionalists like Winston Churchill had opposed allowing television to cover the event, considering correctly that it would erode the mystique of the monarchy. As a concession, not all parts of the occasion were covered and camera close-ups were not allowed.

Grandfather, when a widower, had come to live with us and passed on to us our first car, his 1930s red classic Morris Ten, almost-collectible even then. Of square shape, it had yellow trafficators which shot out from the body to signal a turn and in front, there was a thermometer perched on top of the radiator. We used it to reach our summer holiday destination, since like other city families, we rented a house, usually in Speyside in the Highlands, where the local owners moved out temporarily into smaller accommodation in the grounds. Our old friends, the Rothesay doctor, his wife and daughter Marjorie, joined us for this holiday month of July, and we returned to Rothesay for the month of August, restoring our contact. Marjorie married Lyn Bulloch, a Rothesay teacher colleague, painter and musician, and a stalwart in the island's organisations. The post of Deputy Lieutenant in Bute usually went, as elsewhere, to retired military men and the chieftain of the Bute Highland Games usually from 'the cream of the county.' But Lyn broke the mould and was the popular choice for both. He died in 2016.

For holidays, luggage, including bed linen, went ahead by rail in hampers and steamer trunks to be collected at the destination station. Motorways were yet to come and our car journey north was a heroic one, not only for the time taken on the challenging roads, but because well before the Highlands were reached, car sickness afflicted both of us children in the back seat. Petrol was still rationed and even an emergency journey to a distant vet with our sick and dying dog was problematic. In Speyside we had simple pleasures, including family tennis, occasional tennis tournaments, mountain walks, day trips and occasional golf (mother disapproved of more than that). I had a battered hand-me-down wooden-headed driver which was deteriorating, but I was fond of it. Father took me and the club to the multitasking professional at the local Kingussie golf club, a man who looked after the course, sold the tickets, gave lessons, stocked clubs and balls and mended clubs in his workshop. We left my driver, and when we collected it, he had sanded the face restoring bright wood and refreshing the plastic insert, then had cleaned and varnished the rest of the head. Returned to my hands, after this unexpected rejuvenation, it meant a magic moment.

Our ventures into the Cairngorm mountains commenced only if the weather was favourable and there was time to reach and return safely from the top. The upper granite massif could be reached starting with a journey to a car park at the bottom of the range. The walk-in, affectionately described in Nan Shepherd's *The Living Mountain*, was through pine and birch woods reaching the heather uplands with their streams of crystal-clear water. Mother knew

Speyside holidays in 1953 with my sister and (below) with the Buchanans from Rothesay. Taken by Dr Buchanan as his first colour photograph, father felt a bright red bowl was needed.

the names of the plants and flowers, pointing out bog myrtle, juniper, moss campion and blae berries as we passed. We occasionally sighted a ptarmigan and heard of the hares which turn white in winter.

The Cairngorms' impressive corries, pulled out by the north-running glaciers in the Ice Ages, now hold lochans and snow may persist in summer. There was rock climbing or scrambles in the corries, but not for us. On the plateau, botanists have found primitive vegetation surviving from before the Ice Ages, and there we paused and ate our packed lunch – rolls, boiled eggs and tea from a Thermos.

In these holiday evenings, after tea, in the living room lit and perfumed by the paraffin-fuelled Tilley oil lamps, father's admirable routine was to read a story to us all. The works he chose included the well-crafted John Buchan tales such as *The Thirty-Nine Steps,* and this one had resonance in Speyside. The action in the novel moved to a Big House in the Highlands, where powerful people from London decamped in summer and continued to run the country. Conditioned by these evening readings, in our movements around our valley, I imagined that in the big estate houses seen from the roads, the great and good were at that moment running the country. I was not entirely wrong at the time, but later everything changed when the Scottish Tory party and its style of politician went into decline.

We took holiday snaps with simple box Brownie cameras, and when back home you took the exposed black-and-white roll of film to the chemist who sent it away for processing, and prints from the negatives came back in two weeks' time. Smaller cameras with 35mm colour film came in slowly in the late 1940s and our gadget-minded uncle took up colour photography early. The film's very slow speed required a steady hand to produce the slides which, when developed, were best shown via a projector. In poor light, a flash gun using small, single-use bulbs was needed for colour photography.

In autumn, we took another family holiday at Crieff Hydro. Its hydropathic tradition had involved Spartan living, drinking pure water and temperance, but it had survived and developed into a family-friendly large institution with swimming pools and extensive grounds. Any drinking was done discreetly at a little hotel nearby. The Hydro's substantial endowments subsidised off-season stays for Church of Scotland ministers and their families, and we took this up.

If we had any thoughts of foreign holidays, which we hadn't, there was none possible until 1947. But with the economy picking up, by the early 1950s, such travel emerged with a limit of £50 to spend abroad. Cheap European package holidays by bus or plane came in later, and this new exodus to the sun and sand meant the neglect of the once-popular Clyde coast towns.

When rationing eased up, and foreign travel increased, Elizabeth David revitalised British domestic cooking and opened new vistas with her *Book of Mediterranean Food* published in 1950. Her recipes recalled the forgotten European gastronomy, but there was disbelief when she called for six eggs to start a sauce, nor were many of her ingredients generally available at the time – pasta, olive oil, peppers, herbs, figs and almonds.

In Glasgow, there was little eating out, and certainly not for us, with the choice limited to the older downtown expensive restaurants. Ethnic restaurants, offering Chinese and Indian cuisine, were still to come.

City life slowly brightened up and in 1949 George Square had a Christmas tree. Advertisements appeared on the trams, as did neon signs on buildings. We went downtown one night to view the new glamorous effect, notably the Central Station's wall with the animated non-white boy Ba-Bru, advertising Barr's Irn-Bru soft drink. The Station's large Hotel hosted distinguished visitors arriving by rail, and the showbiz celebrities were glad to offer a photo opportunity to the attentive *Glasgow Herald*. In 1954, there was one memorable image of the cowboy Roy Rogers and his horse Trigger both allegedly climbing the hotel stairs.

And for my sister Alison and I, there was school in Glasgow.

CHAPTER 3:

School Days

School ... Teachers and teaching ... The Classics
Literature ... Printing ... Evangelism ... Donald Dewar

I N GLASGOW, my schooling was at Glasgow Academy, and, for my
younger sister, at Westbourne Gardens School, both private, single-
sex schools who merged later. There was no problem getting in,
since these independent schools had difficulty surviving in the post-
war hard times and the financial travails of the middle classes. Many
thought these private schools were heading for extinction and with a
Labour government now in power, its ideological support and funding
suggested that the state schools would take over. This didn't happen.

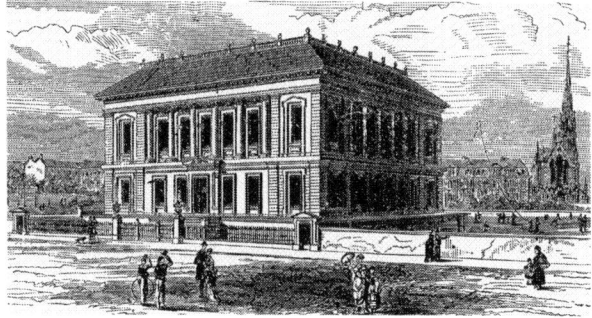

Glasgow Academy, founded in 1845.

Even though the Academy's maths entry test mystified me, they still took me in. My sister had a different problem since the primary teaching at Rothesay Academy was ahead of its time, and their 'look and say' system did not feature in her entry examination.

To reach my school from our manse, I took the 10A double-decker tram car from its terminus in a side road near the manse and we travelled sedately along Great Western Road's busy route into the city. Waiting for the tram to arrive, there were well-known diversions for us children. A penny coin put on the track could be bent through 90 degrees by the passing tram, and a half penny, properly placed, might flatten out to a fair imitation of a penny. The double-ended trams had identical drivers' cabs in front and back and we helped the conductor to turn round for the return journey by flipping the bidirectional seats to face forward. While doing this, we scanned the now empty car for discarded empty cigarette packets, hoping to find rarer ones, rather than those for the cheap Woodbine and unpleasant Pasha cigarettes.

On these journeys to and from school you had to behave and be dressed properly. My sister's school headgear was a beret in winter, changing to a Panama hat in summer; we boys had blazers and school caps. On these items, mother stitched in little fabric name labels made by the Cash company, and when it went into administration in 2014, many affectionate tributes appeared.

The Academy classrooms had wooden desks with sloping lids. The broad front edge had holes to hold china inkwells, and although fountain pens were coming in, ink and simple pens with replaceable nibs were available. The cupboards contained obsolete slates and slate pencils surviving from earlier days. The Biro pen arrived later in the early 1960s but it was messy and disliked, until better models emerged later.

Our school policy focused on teaching mathematics and the classics. Offering Latin and Greek still had support, since in the past, study of the humanities and use of these languages was alleged to produce an educated person, 'expanding' the mind and add precision to thinking. We had an enthusiastic young classics teacher, keen to defend the classics against any threats, and he taught as with the 'Direct Method', which used Latin in everyday speech in class. His enthusiasm was infectious, and we felt privileged, particularly having our own Latin name – 'Pistor' for me, nearly Latin for a 'miller'. The headmaster urged me to add Greek to my studies, but fortunately my father was dubious and got me out of it.

These embattled supporters of a classical education also advocated Latin as useful in everyday life, particularly in medicine. It would, they said, open up insights from the classical medical texts, notably those of Hippocrates, but also make sense of the Latin names of muscles, nerves, blood vessels and of many diseases. In addition, prescribing of medicines was still in Latin. But this strategy was faltering, undermined disloyally by the world of medicine then abandoning their traditional use of Latin. The state schools were first to decline to teach these languages and the classics examinations lost support.

The Sixth Form, Glasgow Academy in 1956. Myself on 'Baggy' Aston, the English teacher's right and Scot Nelson on his left. Donald Dewar is in the back row (middle).

The Academy was a public school, defined as one included in the annual Headmaster's Conference. This public-school status meant some snobbery within Glasgow, since we played rugby only against the other private schools, and not against the local state schools. Rugby was important for the school, but not for me. Neither heavy nor fast, I was an ineffective full back. Adult rugby in Glasgow was organised in the same way, with teams made up of former pupils of these schools – the 'Academicals' in our case. The rugby club ethos was Corinthian, and although 'unofficial' league tables based on match results existed, they were litle heeded.

But with good teams, open to all, emerging, like the West of Scotland and Edinburgh Wanderers, official leagues appeared and more rigorous training crept in. Near us, the Jordanhill Teachers' Training College team, coached by Bill Dickinson, a lecturer in physical education at the College, was playing well and disapprovingly called the 'Adonises', his team triumphed in 1969, winning the unofficial championship, and soon they had Ian McLauchlan, the 'Mighty Mouse', later a Scottish captain and British Lions player. Dickinson was appointed to work with the Scottish rugby team in 1971, but the conservative Scottish Rugby Union leadership balked at using the word 'coach' and instead titled him as 'advisor to the captain'. Immediately, Scotland won at Twickenham for the first time since 1938, and they did it again two years later in a centenary match at Murrayfield. It was also unthinkable then that any talented player would turn professional. Some talented Scottish Borders rugby players signed for professional rugby league teams in England, but they had a frosty reception when visiting home. Later, changing attitudes led to the unthinkable happening – Glasgow rugby teams started paying their best players.

☙

For physical education (P.E.) at the Academy, we had a splendid gymnasium lined with wooden bars and other items which could be pulled out from the walls. There was an unused vaulting horse and other complex extras, and their challenges were later revealed by the televised Olympics. Our gym teacher, said to have no testicles, on what evidence I know not, preferred to give us simple running exercises.

We put in more vigour into the playground play during the breaks, and played football with intensity using a tennis ball, or a bigger one if someone brought one. Playground football teams were chosen in an interesting way. Two natural leaders, acknowledged by consensus to be the best players, were the captains and the rest of us lined up against the wall for them to choose their players alternately. Those last to reach a team, like me, accepted our humble place in the cosmos. The goals were marked with school caps placed on the ground, and with this fuzzy target, there were inevitable disputes if a goal was claimed; the matter was decided by the strength of feeling in the rival teams. Many stayed behind after school to play football until chased out by the janitor. We had further play at home and even got some rough cricket on the 'dump' nearby. This time, the owner of the ball or the bat, was in charge. If displeased, he could deliver a threat – 'It's ma bat and my ba', and I'm no' playing' – a powerful ultimatum also used in the international negotiation between nations.

In school, at the morning break, there were crates of half-pint bottles of milk, available free to all, in and the rugby players downed a few bottles at speed. Free school milk had been brought in in the 1930s to deal with the nutritional deficiency in working-class children, but these problems had largely gone, and us middle-class children were in good shape. No-one dared end the scheme until Margaret Thatcher, as minister for education, did so in 1971. She survived the flak, won the argument, and ended the supply of crates of free milk.

In the individual subjects, the Academy had strength in French (Mr Varley) and mathematics, notably Mr Allman, and I loved the maths problem-solving. I did well in the maths exams, but no obvious career beckoned, and I was already determined to do medicine. History, as taught in Scotland, was moving away from being the history of the English Crown and our Mr Preston shared the new mood, as did Tom Johnston, the Labour Party's distinguished, nationalist-leaning post-war Scottish Secretary. He recalled visiting a Glasgow Gorbals school at examination time. He noted wryly that the deprived kids were attempting to answer a question on 'How did Henry VIII consolidate his position on the throne?' Johnston may have had the dark thought that questions on how Scotland dealt with disease in the past might have been more fitting.

I took geography instead of history when the choice had to be made, and our well-organised and respected teacher Mr Ogilvie gave us a check-list – the 'nine things needed for geography class' – and these had to be brought and declared to be present. He was ahead of his time. Such tick-box lists gained widespread use, with airline pilots first to use them in preparing for take-off. When the lists came into the world of surgery, notably when preparing patients for surgery, planning to amputate the correct leg, I thought of our geography teacher's lists.

In the English classes, we had to study Shakespeare, Dickens' prose and the English poets, including Chaucer, which gave most of us a distaste for the classics. Our English teacher trained us to be ready for the Highers exams with an analysis of one Shakespeare play and one English poem. If questions on the works of Robert Burns or Sir Walter Scott appeared, I do not recall them, nor were we ready for them. When our own sons reached this stage much later, at the same school, changes had occurred and there were questions on the work of Scottish novelists and even of contemporary Scottish poets. One of our boys studied the novel *Sunset Song* and then asked me to help with the analysis of a work by the Fife poet Douglas Dunn. Times had changed.

Though I disliked the classics, I was an avid reader, and favoured the juvenile magazines with sustained prose, notably the *Wizard, Rover* and *Hotspur* and, in books, I enjoyed the adventures of Biggles. This fare was deplored at home and school, but good, penetrating exam questions could have been framed on this literature, such as 'Discuss Biggles' attitude to foreigners.' This would have nudged us towards higher things in literary criticism. I later improved my taste, but, still cool about the classics, skipped eras to enjoy twentieth-century authors like Evelyn Waugh and Kingsley Amis.

I did however have an epiphany, much later. During a spell as a summer locum surgeon in a distant Scottish island I had, for once, not brought enough reading material. Heading back to the hotel at 5 pm on a Saturday, and with nothing left to read, and in despair, I called in at the local general store. Added to its main trade of selling envelopes, cards and Sellotape, on one shelf was a small collection of paperback Eng. Lit. classics. There was one copy of Trollope's *Barchester Towers,* just the genre I had rejected at school because of the force-feeding. With no escape, I bought it. At night, as they say, I could not put it down. I expected the elegance of the language, but the humour and satire was the surprise; at school, Eng. Lit. was a serious subject.

Unknown to us, while at school, a remarkable Scottish literary
revival was stirring in Glasgow's West End. Just a few blocks away, from
our school, Edwin Morgan, the Glasgow University lecturer and poet,
was on his way to fame, soon followed by other talented locals like Tom
Leonard, James Kelman, and Liz Lochhead. Local novelist Alasdair
Gray would produce his first work in 1968. Things were happening on
our doorstep.

Þ

In the basement of one of the school's houses was a printing
press plus plenty old-style metal type. Somehow we got elementary
instruction in the black arts and had a free run of this printing shop,
producing tickets and cards and also one large project. This was the
school rugby team's fixture list for the year, and once the type was set, it
was a simple matter next year to alter the dates and re-order the lines of
type. Our sturdy Arab printing press was in widespread use in printing
shops for small printing jobs but it was dangerous and all these presses
were eventually taken out of use, since if you were slow to remove your
fingers after inserting the paper, your hand could be crushed. At the
time, if there was this accident, the fault was yours, not the machine.
I enjoyed my printing and was to revive the interest later, first when
I edited the student newspaper and much later when I purchased a
professional machine and started a little private press, printing limited
edition works on the history of golf.

There was a religious and the military flavour at school, and we
started in the morning with Prayers at Assembly. We had our military
Combined Cadet Force, often called an 'Officers' Training Corps'
because it was assumed we would all be officers. At school, Friday
was Corps day, needing to don the stiff inelastic uniform, unsuited to
fighting, which, on the night before, needed attention from blanco and
Brasso. We paraded with rifles. One day the school announced that our
rifles would be locked away more securely and further enquiry revealed
that this was because of a terrorist problem in Ireland. This all seemed
dramatic and unlikely; it wasn't.

We had an annual camp at an Army base. When at Barry, beside
the Carnoustie golf links, I think I saw Hogan practising prior to his
1953 Open Championship triumph. Another camp was at Cultybraggan

in Perthshire, a former prisoner of war camp which had held the most committed Nazis.

For corporal punishment, the school still used the 'strap'. Lesser punishments were 'detention' after school and 'lines' of poems to be copied out many times, thus sadly linking Eng. Lit. to punishment. The straps (*anglice* 'tawses') came from Lochgelly, a small town in Fife, made there by saddlers who had diversified into this niche area. Their business closed in 1985 through lack of sales, and two years later, school corporal punishment was abolished, the first to do so being the state schools.

At this time of life, we had to learn how to dance, and the dances of the day, essential for occasional formal evening occasions, included the waltz and the quickstep. When older, we took dancing lessons downtown on a waxed floor at Warren's Dance Studio in the Albert Ballroom in Bath Street, one of the many smaller dance halls in Glasgow. Some of us in the West End, mostly the girls, took elocution lessons to learn how to speak like the Queen. Later the Queen changed to speak more like us. To add some social attainment, I had piano lessons, but sadly, I did not practice. If I had my time again, I would instead work hard at it.

Added to my steady contact with religion at home and school, there was an extra dramatic episode when a famous American evangelist arrived in Glasgow. The Church of Scotland, though it supported foreign missions, was ambivalent about local evangelism, i.e. whether to reach out and try to convert others in our midst. Others thought differently and in the centre of Glasgow, the Tent Hall, dating from Moody and Sanky's famous five-month crusade in 1874, continued to offer such meetings and outreach, as did the Church of Scotland's Seaside Mission run by Rev D.P.Thomson.

Rev Tom Allan, the Church of Scotland minister in the North Kelvinside parish, near us, also favoured evangelism, and to add to his radio broadcasting, he left his post to head the protestant evangelical 'Tell Scotland' movement. With unfortunate timing, Billy Graham, the American preacher, also planned to come to Glasgow and 'Tell Scotland' prudently agreed to work with Graham. They did so for six weeks in Glasgow's Kelvin Hall, from March to September 1955. This 'All-Scotland Crusade' attracted 15,000 nightly, with added events on Saturday afternoon.

Billy Graham, centre stage, at the Kelvin Hall, and, standing below, the converts who went forward after his address.

There was crusade fever in Scotland, with attendees coming in numbers from within Glasgow and from afar by train and bus. At the final meeting at Hampden Park, 100,000 attended, with 2259 converts resulting. Half the population of Scotland, it was estimated, had attended the meetings or listened to his relayed message. For his meetings, the Kelvin Hall was laid out as for a political convention, adding close-circuit television to overflow halls. The inspirational music and singing came from Glasgow's famous Orpheus Choir, put at the disposal of Graham's music master, who warmly recalled the partnership later.

Graham's message was gentler than that offered by most American evangelists or the fiery rhetoric of the local presbyterian firebrand Pastor Jack Glass. In Graham's 40 minute sermon, his message was that 'we had all sinned and had turned away from Jesus', and a decision for or against Jesus was urgent now, not later, and could not be postponed. He asked those convinced to leave their seats and go forward to the stage to signal their conversion, and once started, the trickle became a stream.* On the first night, 470 came forward as converts, and after giving their details, they were directed to link up with a local church. Graham was keen that school children should attend his meetings, and although we did attend his rallies, and were impressed, we were not invited to go forward, being advised instead to make an unspoken, personal decision.

The campaign was an immediate success, and it thrust religion into centre-stage for some weeks. The Glasgow University Union voted on the motion that 'Billy Graham is an undesirable immigrant' but it was rejected 190-187. But in the aftermath, the verdict was that, after the boost, regular church-going was not sustained. Afterwards, Allan returned to be minister at St George's Tron Church in central Glasgow and directed his energies to inner-city problems, using counselling and rehabilitation.

The Academy had some well-known pupils in a former days, notably the artist D.Y. Cameron, Walter Elliot the politician and the author J.M. Barrie who spent two years there. Lord Reith had a shorter stay and Jack Buchanan's obituary said of our film star pupil he was 'a more than average tap dancer'. Our generation contributed significantly more names – the MP Robert McLennan (an impressive Hamlet in the school play), the banker Sir Angus Grossart, Sir David Mason the Dental Hospital dean, civil servant Sir David Kerr, and the historians Norman Stone and Niall Ferguson. Jeremy Isaacs headed the Royal Opera House and Neil MacGregor took charge at the British Museum.

But no one did more for the reputation of the school than Donald Dewar, the 'father of the Scottish Nation' and the first First Minister in the Scottish Parliament later, which he had done so much to establish. The school at the time did not suspect that he would do well. Quite the reverse.

* R.D.Laing, the contrarian psychiatrist, then training in Glasgow, pondered on these revival meetings and concluded that Graham used the same methods, and had the same numerical success in bringing people forward, as did a stage hypnotist.

Donald was a bookish person, but inattentive to examinations. Two years older than the rest of us, having missed much school earlier through sanatorium treatment for tuberculosis, he was first in our group to get a driving licence and as an only child he was given much use of the family car by his indulgent father. His driving was erratic, and we had some hair-raising near-misses. His parents thought he should be more athletic and he started playing golf with myself and Scott Nelson in our year, and he joined the Balmore Golf Club where I was a member. But Donald was a lost cause. An unimpressive golfer, he lost balls so quickly that we could seldom finish. His father encouraged him to record his scores, thus charting his progress, and on returning home, father would ask how he had scored. At that point I averted my gaze.

After Saturday golf, we often had dinner at the Dewar's house and thereafter might go to the Scottish National Orchestra concerts, in the St Andrews Halls nearby, since another friend's father, owner of the famous Cosmo film theatre, had subscription tickets. Despite the post-war problems, the Orchestra was full-time from 1950. Karl 'Snarl' Rankl was appointed principal conductor in 1952, having had difficulties in his job in Covent Garden and he continued to be difficult in Glasgow. Hans Swarowski followed in 1957, since our cultural cringe assumed only another middle-European conductor would do, but shortly afterwards Alexander Gibson was imaginatively appointed in 1959, and under our home-bred leader, classical music and opera thrived in Glasgow.

Before going to university, four of us – Scott Nelson, later in insurance in England, John Park, later in business in Glasgow, and Donald – clubbed together and, determining to tour Europe, bought an old ambulance at a car auction for £60. It was not a good buy, and Donald's father, ever-supportive, brought in his garagemen to help with an essential make-over. We painted it and put in two more bunks in the back, giving accommodation for four.

After only mild parental misgivings, we set off for the South of France, and the ambulance first broke down at Hamilton, just south of Glasgow. Somehow a garage got it going again, and reaching and crossing the Channel, we then headed south. Nearing the Riviera, on a minor road, (no motorways then), one of the back wheels sheared off.

We got our vehicle off to the side of the quiet road, and since it was evening, we judged it best to hunker down. Walking along the road next morning, to our surprise, we found a village just around the corner and the garage mechanic not only arranged rescue of our van, but entered into the spirit of our venture.

'C'est un vieux ambulance' he murmured in admiration.

Off again, we enjoyed ourselves on the Mediterranean beaches in the south, but on the way back, the engine blew a 'big end', diagnosed by the loud hammering noise. The quick fix is to take the spark plug out of the affected cylinder, limiting the damage, but creating even more noise. After a hair-raising and noisy journey through the traffic of Paris, we needed an overnight stay. Parking in the service road off one boulevard near the Arc de Triomphe, we were woken during the night by a suspicious gendarme. Scott, our French speaker, gathered that the gendarme wished to know what we were up to.

Scott crisply replied 'Nous dormons.'

His confidence and command of French satisfied the man.

Next day food poisoning struck and my tour of Paris was now a series of hops between public lavatories. Halfway to safety on one of these quick sprints, I bumped into an attractive girl I knew from Glasgow, and she was clearly lonely. I had to make an excuse and leave.

Revving up the noisy van, we limped back to Dover, and sold it there.

Three of us four ambulance drivers left school that summer. But Donald was held up at the Academy for a second year in the Sixth Form, surprisingly being short of Higher exam passes. He had, unusually, not been made a 'prefect' in his first year in the Sixth, and now he was passed over for a second time, allegedly for lacking leadership skills. The snub may not have been entirely unmerited: Donald was older and could be awkward and at the school Debating Society he had suggested a vote of no-confidence in the teacher in charge. But we boys knew about his talents, and to soften his exclusion, though not a prefect, we made him an honorary inhabitant of the small prefect's room, which he used with enthusiasm. Improbably, the cricket team found him a role – they made him scorer.

> 11 Royal Terrace,
> Glasgow E. 3.
> 3 · 1 · 56.
>
> Dear David,
>
> I feel depressed. I am about to go out to tea with a retired teacher who taught me until I reached the great age of 8 and has not seen me since. Worse still the wretched woman knows my Scottish Nationalist aunt who thinks I am a kind of tame genius, well-behaved of course, I and I fear my hostess will also harbour this strange idea.
>
> You may remember that I promised to send you a New Year card. Well I did not, and that is the reason why. We had a marvellous New Year, (a tree fell on our car).
>
> Hoping you had a good time at Rothesay (or was it Dunoon?) and wishing yous you the complements of the season (trite again),
>
> Donald C. Dewar.

All of us who left school had just missed conscription – a compulsory two-year spell in the Army. Everyone agreed it was a waste of time, since the deadlocked Cold War war meant there was little conventional military activity.

I was off to Glasgow University, to do medicine.

∾

CHAPTER 4:

Glasgow University

Lecturers and lecturing ... Men's Union ... Sectarianism
Student Medical Society ... Religion

I SAT THE Glasgow University Bursary Competition, a competitive event offering a range of endowed grants for the top 100 candidates. Historically, it had enabled poorer students to get to university, and it still had a high-profile in Glasgow life, with the *Glasgow Herald* publishing the successful names. But by now, with the value of the grants falling and with the City paying the tuition fees of local Glasgow students, the competition was less important financially; state support had replaced philanthropy. The mathematics paper was not of the type I was used to, but I came in at number 99, which meant the chance of a modest bursary. Many were restricted to those proposing to study divinity, recalling the assumptions of earlier days, but my father had noticed a good award for the 'highest-placed candidate from the Island of Bute' and I got it. This helped our still-tight family finances, and also meant that there was no question of going elsewhere to university.

First year at Glasgow University was a disappointment, and I was unsettled. Medical education was stuck in the dreary assumption that a full year's study of physics, chemistry and botany was an essential start, and since two more years of anatomy, physiology and biochemistry followed, it was three years before you saw a patient. Clinical medicine, it was said, rested on a hierarchy of knowledge – for instance that physics led to understanding physiology and physiology explained disorders in disease, and chemistry via pharmacology underpinned medical practice. This dubious model of enlightenment underpinned the slow start and our lectures had little historical content, depicting a static, unchanging view of the natural world, almost hinting that little else remained to be discovered.

One of our four subjects – botany – did not fit this translational model. What was botany *for*? With any historical awareness, the reason botany remained in the medical curriculum was because of its important role in a former day. In the previous century, a knowledge of botany was needed ito inform medical practice, since plants provided a long list of the physicians' remedies – notably digitalis, quinine and morphine. Just as the military is always ready to fight the last war, botany survived in our course as a vestigial remnant. Unknown to us, the clinical teachers, particularly Sir Charles Illingworth, the professor of surgery, were trying to reduce the medical course to five years and to do so, wanted to cut back on much of this first year's teaching. After a long battle, the reformers later prevailed.

For our lectures in the Physics Department, we sat in alphabetical order in its majestic Victorian amphitheatre. A student called Dan Hamilton was understandably placed beside me – and more of him anon. The tiered rows of seats in the lecture theatre were almost vertical, and behind your head there was a number which in a former day meant the lecturer could detect if you were absent.

The daily lectures in each subject were given throughout the term by the same person in each department and the quality of lecturing was variable. Our charitable explanation was that the poorer communicators were perhaps famous scientists. One of these never-changing lecturers gave the impression he would rather be elsewhere, and the release he sought, it was said, was to escape and play the bagpipes. Later, he did have a successful career in our local College of Piping.

Most of my fellow students showed no impatience with the system and us cynics noted that these earnest students wrote down everything the lecturer said, probably including the salutation 'good morning'. I resisted such passive learning and had the dark thought that I could instead use the available excellent textbooks of the day and avoid the lectures. I was ahead of my time, because the mood later would swing against formal lectures. About 40 years later, Glasgow experimented instead with 'self-directed' learning, i.e. seeking knowledge for yourself from useful sources, with staff at hand for guidance.

I did however put an effort into the physics practical laboratory sessions and my lab book and report handed in at the end of term got praise and a good mark. Next year, a lazy student in the year below, later a fashionable Glasgow gynaecologist, begged it from me and copied it, also gaining a good physics mark. He passed it on, and 40 years later, a general practitioner near Dumfries wrote to me and told me that in his first year of medicine, when struggling with poor marks, he inherited my lab book. He copied it out, yet again, survived and blessed my name.

Unaware that my general discontent was justified, and feeling guilty, I often absented myself from the system and went off as soon as possible in the day, first via the little Papingo coffee shop nearby on University Avenue and thence to the student Men's Union close by. There, I mixed with some Arts and Law faculty students doing a minimum of academic effort, but keen on other agendas, including planning to become prime minister. John Smith would have made it, had he lived. Donald Dewar, still detained at the Academy, reached the Union one year later and started on his journey to head the future Scottish Parliament.

But there was one bright feature of that year's medical course. Zoology teaching was different. Anthony 'Sam' Barnett, our lecturer, had put aside that subject's usual formula, namely the hum-drum survey of the various groups of animals, and instead he taught human biology. While other medical schools offered their students the subtleties of the molluscs, he spared us these lists and charts and instead looked at the 'human species'. Based on his lectures, he published his textbook *The Human Species* and it was in print for decades. He permeated his lectures with social theory and introduced the risky liberal ideas of the time. Though telling us about genetics and chromosomes, he worked in that different human 'races' did not exist, only 'ethnic groups'. He emphasised that 'mixed' marriages, e.g. between blacks and whites – labelled 'miscegenation' by many – would not result in defective off-springs, a view widely held at the time. He also spoke out against racial discrimination in South Africa. It was heady stuff for us, but even the earnest conservative students in the front row wrote it all down. It must have been a difficult battle for him within the Zoology department, and the external examiners who did our oral examinations must have been warned that we knew nothing about worms, but had heard of eugenics. The departmental traditionalists did however have one success: we had to dissect a dogfish.

a Pelican Book 8'6
The Human Species
Anthony Barnett

Barnett had career difficulties later, rumoured to involve Californian-style experiments with LSD, and he also pressed his attention on a female student in our class. There was, however, a happy ending; they married and left, achieving academic success in Australia. He subtly affected the thinking of our generation of medical students.

The female medical students, then in a minority, were accepted and admired by us men, particularly by those of us from all-male schools. The University teachers were mostly male, and the city hospital staff even more so, and it was our girls who later 'stormed the citadel' and won the battle. There were one or two female lecturers in the University preclinical science departments and in our time, one of them married a biochemistry lecturer. She told us that, shortly after the wedding, her salary did not appear. The administration, when contacted, apologised, explaining they had assumed that after marriage she would leave work.

Tolerance regarding colour, ethnicity and religion within the University student body was impressive for the time. We had many non-white students from the Commonwealth, probably paying full fees and helping the University in hard times, and one of our African medical students, a football blue, took many of the prizes. These non-white students were unreservedly accepted by us, but outside, in the city, things were different, with much overt racism and sectarianism. At this time, I joined Arlington Baths, a private members swimming club, but on doing so, a committee member took me aside and warned me not to bring any non-white student visitors to the baths. This racist, after predictably saying he was not prejudiced, rationalised his prejudice in a convoluted and embarrassing way.

In the sectarian tension, the animus against Catholics outside in the city arose historically from their influx from Ireland during the mid-1850s famine, and on arrival they competed for work with locals. The hostility remained and was, and is, widely entrenched in society. Glasgow's larger legal firms did not employ Catholic law graduates until the 1960s. Sectarianism was notorious in sport, notably football, but also in golf. If Catholics applied for membership at the older golf clubs, the application form asked for the school attended and since the Glasgow school system was sharply segregated, this usually revealed their religion. But if the school attended was ambiguous, the applicant was then asked, 'What team do you support?' – i.e. offering a choice between Glasgow Rangers or Celtic football clubs. If that answer was of no help, the exasperated chairman asked, 'What team *would* you support?' Jewish golfers fared even worse, and knowing they need not apply to Glasgow's clubs, they established their own course and club at Bonnyton Moor to the south of the city.

The Men's Union was a useful antidote to the patchy medical teaching in my first year. Independent and run by the students, there was (and still is) a buzz about the building, particularly at lunchtime, not least from the massive information on the noticeboards, the text often adjusted by the Union wits. Announcements and summonses came over the porter's tannoy, intimating that so-and so was '*waaanted* in the hall'. A barber offered wet shaves, and there was economical, but unhealthy, food available and twenty snooker tables upstairs. At lunchtime, the film sessions included the latest slapstick Tom and Jerry cartoons to please their sophisticated fans, plus some mildly risqué movies. Films of surgical operations, notably on the eye, were unexpectedly popular and tough Union members might accept the challenge to attend and not faint. A more conventional offering was *Playboy Magazine,* kept in the Porters' box, and they took in a deposit of the Union diary to ensure its return; when returned the magazine's pages were counted.

We still had a few 'chronic' students around the Union. These older men survived because of an old University rule that if you got to the final year of your degree course, you could sit the final exams as often as you cared. Those who liked the student life, and wished to delay entry in the real world, could linger in the University, notably  the Union, for extended periods. Famous 'chronics' of old like Walter Elliot, the Conservative Party politician, and the playwright James Bridie (O.H.Mavor) had added colour to the Union. We had a few chronics, perhaps less talented than before, still hanging about.

Perhaps the most eye-opening encounter for us first-year students were the Men's Union debates, and, as described later, the Union's political scene showed considerable vitality. Looking down from the gallery at a Union debate in 1956, I was taken aback by what I saw and heard. A fresh-faced teenager of my own age was denouncing the Conservative government for their intervention in Suez. Coming from my background, I was shocked, not only at his views but also his temerity to doubt the wisdom and actions of our country's leaders. It was not something I could report to my parents at home.

Another unsettling incident followed. About this time a Church of Scotland minister, the Rev D.P.Thomson I think, held revivalist meetings in the Union at lunchtime. In his address, he explained one thing which struck home. He agreed that the existence of God could not be proven, and hence that belief in the deity relied on faith. I had been brought up with the word 'faith' which permeated church services and sermons, but had never realized the import. You either had this faith, a belief-without-proof, or you did not. As an aspiring medical scientist, I didn't do faith. I now lost my belief in God. This was an awkward development, while still living at home in the manse, but the matter never came into the open there.

The public status of ministers of the Church in Scotland was high, and any important civic or academic occasion required a Presbyterian, not a Catholic or Jewish, cleric on the platform. 'Our Church did not count' later recalled Glasgow's combative Catholic Cardinal Winning. Rev Neville Davidson at Glasgow Cathedral was always ready with comment for the press on the issues of the day, as was the left-leaning George MacLeod, minister in Govan, who set up the Iona Community. Other high-profile ministers included James Currie of television's 'Late Call' in the 1960s, a Rangers fan and an ebullient after-dinner speaker. In the University, we had the charismatic preacher Murdo Ewen Macdonald and later the bibulous Prof James Barclay, eventually Dean of the Divinity Faculty, a high-profile populariser, whose 17-volume *Daily Study Bible* sold well and widely, but failed to impress sophisticated theologians. We also had our popular Protestant university chaplain, sadly having to leave after difficulties arising from his occasional binge drinking.

We had our student medical society, the Medico-Chirurgical Society, and, at a time when scarves were in fashion, its members' long scarves were distinctive. We had an annual Ball, and our own magazine *Surgo,* but deference dictated that its articles should come from the staff. Meeting on Thursday nights in the dining hall of the Men's Union, a cheery room with an open fire, the lectures were also given by the staff.

But the first meeting in the first term had a different, dramatic format, aimed at attracting and enrolling all the new first-year students to our Society, the lure being that we would see patients, ahead of our long wait. But looking back, it was a grizzly affair, just tolerable within the *zeitgeist* of the day. The venue was Gartnavel Royal Hospital, the large psychiatric hospital in extensive grounds near the city. At the meeting, we students assembled in the concert hall, and after the eccentric superintendent greeted us from the platform, the show started. Gartnavel had some seriously deluded, but articulate, long-stay patients and these unfortunates were now paraded for our amusement, rather than edification.* Not long after, this opening meeting at Gartnavel was dropped.

Despite my unease, I managed to do well in the first-year exams, and I was selected, with others, to do an honours science degree, added on to the medical course, and I opted to do physiology. This allowed for extra, practical, hands-on experimental work and a research project plus more personal tuition. With extra summer work, this would add only one extra year to the medical curriculum.

My gloom lifted when this started next year. I realised much later, after a similar episode, that my 'black dog' problem in first year was reactive depression, secondary to the unstimulating passive learning. When I gained this insight into this unpleasant affliction, I knew how to avoid the danger, and managed thereafter, except once.

---

* R D Laing, the psychiatrist, who trained at Gartnaval, described this meeting sympathetically in his autobiography *Wisdom, Madness and Folly*.

CHAPTER 5:

Anatomy and Physiology

Anatomy ... Extra physiology ... Beer Bar ... Dances
Indian cuisine arrives ... Food and Drink

NEXT YEAR, our second year of medical studies, we reached the physiology, biochemistry and anatomy departments. Teaching was much better, since the staff in each department shared the lectures and some were established scientists. In anatomy, the dissection of bodies was a solemn business, but I can't say that we found this shocking or disturbing or led on my part to any deeper musings; perhaps it should have. We did wonder where the bodies came from, since there was no shortage, but took this curiosity no further.

We were warned that reverence was required in the dissecting rooms. One story at the time related that a medical student ahead of us had been caught skipping with a loop of intestines taken from a body, and he was instantly expelled. No one knew his name, but we had it on good authority. Later I learned that the same story lingers in every medical school, always passed on from a friend-of-a-friend, as an urban myth, one too good to be false. In the dissection rooms, which smelt heavily of the formalin preservative, we had teams of six students to each body with the male and female students segregated. Steadily, the body was explored, dissected and the fragments discarded.

Young 'demonstrators', newly-qualified doctors intending to be surgeons, supervised our work and carried out regular, body-side, practical examinations. They were a cheerful bunch, spending profitable time in the Anatomy Department, as a helpful strategy towards sitting the difficult first part of the surgical higher qualification. It also offered a chance to do research. We later met up with them ahead of us in the local world of surgery. Raymond Scothorne was the head of department and he and one of the demonstrators, Ian McGregor, later a distinguished local plastic surgeon, wrote an important paper on lymph node structure which would be much quoted in the world of transplantation. When I worked in this area much later, I could tell them, to their surprise and pleasure, how influential their work had been.

Many of us found that learning and memorising anatomy was irksome and difficult, and anatomy would not make much sense until we got into surgery. Indeed, practical surgeons had to relearn the anatomy of the areas of interest to them, particularly looking for the variants which do not feature prominently in basic anatomy texts.

My neighbour in the physics lecture theatre, Dan Hamilton, was necessarily still a neighbour in the anatomy room. He had growing obsessional traits which meant that his feelings of inadequacy about anatomy were total, welling up inside him when he faced an anatomy exam paper. He would get up and exit quickly from the exam hall. Though a bright student, he could not progress until he passed, and with his third and final attempt at the anatomy exam coming up, I made him stay at our home on the night before, and next day, I sat beside him at the examination hall. Prof Scothorne, alerted to the problem, understood and, keen to get Dan out of his department, had positioned himself outside the exam hall door. Before I could catch him, Dan, as ever, fled, but the professor stopped him and marched him to his office in the Anatomy Department nearby. There, he locked Dan into the room with the exam paper (and with plenty textbooks at hand), and told him not to come out until he had answered the questions. Nobody objected to this radical solution, and Dan moved on without further troubles, becoming a lecturer in physiology in Australia later.

I had a confusing time myself within the same examination hall, or rather the two halls. There was, and is, both a Hunter Hall East and a Hunter Hall West. Father, ever watchful, noticed an obscure University prize for 'Physiological Physics' and I entered for this special examination. I turned up at the Hunter Hall and they agreed that they had a physics exam on that day, but they didn't seem to be expecting me. In fact, there were two physics exams that day, one in each of the two halls, and I had chosen the wrong hall – West rather than East – or perhaps the other way round? I did my best with the tough physics paper, harder than the one awaiting me next door. Being the only candidate, I got the prize, and this cemented my reputation in the family as a dreamy academic. Much later in life, when suffering similar 'senior moments', I took solace from this early teenage lapse.

ᔓ

The extra teaching in physiology was good and the department well staffed. To support their research, each of the staff had a 'technician' assistant.

The salaries were paid entirely from the university funds; if there were any outside grants, we were unaware of them. One difficulty in attracting medical staff was the steadily increasing gulf between doctors' pay and those of university teachers. The university lecturers, like most other professions, including the clergy, were not unionised and later in the period of rampant inflation in the 1970s, they failed to keep up. A huge gap opened up between them and the doctors who had managed to get inflation-proofed salaries.

Physiology lecturer H.S.D.Garven in 1958.

The department was headed by then well-liked Prof Garry. As usual no other staff had that title. Keen on teaching, he encouraged his department's medical artist to produce useful images for teaching and these later appeared in a series of well-known illustrated medical text books. One lecturer involved in our honours course taught us to précis our essays, ending up with a small single sheet of paper with bullet points. My father, I soon noticed, used this same abridgement for his Sunday sermons and I took this useful habit on board. By the time of the final medical examinations in surgery, medicine and gynaecology years later, I had my summary notes written telegraphically with a mapping pen, on postcard-size sheets. Each subject was held together with a ring, and this assisted revision. When I started work in the hospital as a surgical resident, I had these surgical notes on my office desk and I commended and demonstrated this practice to the students who used my room. One morning my precious précis notes went missing. Concerned and suspicious, after the students had gone off for their ward teaching, I looked in their bags, and in one, found my notes. To give the student an honourable way out, I left the notes where they were and, on their return, asked if anyone had borrowed the notes, but had no response. I then privately confronted the responsible student, who confessed, and I got my precious notes back. Later, this ambitious and successful academic, could never look me in the eye.

The Biochemistry Department was impressive, headed by the stern Professor Davidson. He got a new building and to urge the builders on, he photographed progress, or lack of progress, regularly from outside and would not listen to any excuses. When the typed list of one of our biochemistry exam results appeared, it showed a correction by hand, swapping Dan Hamilton's result with mine. Our results had clearly been mixed up, and I mentioned this light-heartedly to someone in the Department. Davidson summoned me and told me I was wrong, such a mistake was not possible in his Department.

We students were not well off, many living at home and even travelling to classes from far, but even so, a few students married early. Rental rather than a mortgage for a home was the norm. The first mortgage we ever heard of was obtained by a student in our year, and our verdict was unfavourable. It seemed a crippling burden to pay back money to a bank for 30 years. On another occasion, when one of our senior professors heard of such house purchase by a young staff member, rather than rental, he was surprised and commented that 'You will have had to dip into your capital'. His assumption came from an era when the mostly middle-class young doctors had received inherited money.

Although I was busy with the extra studies, there was still some time for the life of the Union, notably the Beer Bar on Fridays. It did not serve spirits and the favoured beers on tap were MacEwan's Heavy (4% alcohol) or MacEwan's export (5%). The Real Ale Movement and lager drinking was still to come, plus the now-familiar Beer Bar drinking contests and speedy downing of pints. One of our medical students, Mike McDonnell, did murals for the Beer Bar, now gone, and when he later moved to Shetland as a GP his artwork was much admired. The Beer Bar, like all pubs, had a 10 p.m. closure and then, since the Friday night was young, there was the choice of the dance upstairs or adjournment to someone's house. Drinking and driving was risky and common, but we knew that, for a prosecution, the police station called a police doctor to do the assessment. We medical students considered that, if caught, we were safe, since the doctor summoned would charitably show some masonic solidarity within the profession.

The debating chamber was also the dance hall of the Union on Saturdays with tickets sold at the door. In midweek, the various student clubs also held dances raising money for the club funds. On dance nights, the girls were admitted at the front door, and upstairs the males congregated on one side of the dance hall with the girls standing on the other. The girls might or might not accept an invitation to dance and the two might or might not continue dancing thereafter. The Union's dance music was old-fashioned big-band ballroom fare played by a group of seasoned senior musicians headed by Bill Lambert. He offered waltzes and quicksteps but his music was considered to be impossible to dance to. Lambert survived satire in the student newspaper when their predictions for the New Year included that 'Lambert would play a new tune.' However, the music was perhaps not the priority. The Union on dance nights offered an area called the 'Squeezy' on the same landing across from the dance hall. This was the Union's Bridie Library during the day, but on dance nights the doors were left open and inside it was unlit. This privacy offered opportunities for all forms of courting.

There was (and is) a huge all-night event called Daft Friday at the end of the first term for which the Union, decorated with a theme, offered music and entertainment throughout the building throughout the night.

❧

Outside, in the city, ballroom dancing was still remarkably popular, and a dozen large dance halls flourished in the East End, plus other smaller ones elsewhere. The Locarno had support, but the Denniston Playhouse, which could hold 1,700 each night, had the most popular big band, headed by Louis Freeman. For private functions, the Art Deco Plaza Dance Hall with its steel-sprung floor and central fountain was favoured, with music from Jack Chapman; but no alcohol was served. All the famous Glasgow dance halls later died, long before the unexpected revival later of televised, free-style ballroom dancing.

Just as we wearied of Bill Lambert's offerings, something was afoot in youth culture. Impatient with conventional dance music, the new cult rock-and-roll was eagerly accepted. Bill Haley (almost-young at age 30) and his Comets visited Glasgow with huge success in 1957, but the *Glasgow Herald* was not impressed with Haley nor his hit song *Rock Around the Clock*. Jack House, Glasgow's favourite journalist, then aged 51, dismissed it as second-rate fare, opining that the craze would burn itself out. The famous East End dance halls agreed and banned 'jiving', but there was no way back for them.

Shortly after, another new sound was made welcome. Traditional jazz, based on neglected Southern American Dixieland rhythms, swept the country, offered first by Ken Collier, Chris Barber, Acker Bilk and other national icons. In this revival, we had Glasgow successes, notably the Clyde Valley Stompers and their singer Fiona Duncan, and these trad jazz bands were increasingly hired, instead of Lambert, for student club dances in midweek. Eventually, even the conservative Union board gave in, and weekend ballroom dancing's long reign ended. In turn the trad jazz sound faded in popularity in the mid-1960s, replaced first by Beatlemania, and then challenged by the anarchic Rolling Stones.

❧

Another revolution, a gastronomic one, was emerging just yards from the Union, when the first 'Indian' restaurant in Glasgow opened in 1959.

After rationing ceased in the early 1950s, new places to eat out in Glasgow had slowly appeared, but were mostly expensive downtown restaurants. About 1955, when I was at school, the first Chinese restaurant opened on Sauchiehall Street, and it took boldness to visit and pretend to know what you were ordering.

Green Gates, our pioneer Indian restaurant appeared at the top of Gibson Street beside the Union (the chefs were mostly from Bangladesh), and had been a traditional cafe. The new owner, Noor Mohammed, made a careful start, and for his cautious diners, concerned about the challenge of hot curries, he offered mild sauces and plenty water to drink. He knew that the Scots liked mince, and he headed his limited menu with curried mince with which he offered boiled rice plus a delicious stuffed paratha. I can remember the pleasure of this novelty still. One of the first to use Green Gates and show the way, was a medical student ahead of me who later became a famous hand surgeon in England. Taking his studies lightly at the time, and being on the Union Board, at lunchtime he had a pint or two in the Union before walking the few yards to enjoy this gourmet meal.

Noor's son soon opened the up-market Shish Mahal restaurant not far away down Gibson Street, and there, responding to the patrons' tastes, he was one of several British restaurateurs to claim invention, circa 1970, of the hugely successful chicken tikka masala. His cousin Rasul Tahir also set up the Koh-i-Noor nearby, making Gibson Street – Vindaloo Valley – the curry centre of Glasgow at that time. The enthusiasm spread, and the rest of Glasgow gave a welcome to this ethnic food as it had done earlier to the fast-food outlets opened by the influx of Italian restaurateurs. Soon Glasgow, Bradford and Manchester shared a reputation for the best curries in Britain.

❧

Conventional eating-out was also changing, led in Glasgow by a man with a classic immigrant rags-to-riches story. Reo Stakis had arrived in Glasgow from Cyprus, and after selling lace from door to door, in 1945 he bought a newly privatised downtown Victory Café, one of the former wartime fixed-price government eateries. With the end of rationing and the improving economy, he spotted a gap in the market and offered economical European menus. Stakis' Old World

Steak Houses were now the place to eat out. Soon, he had a network of restaurants, including one in Byres Road near the Western Infirmary, and they had an attractive, relaxed ambience with cosy cubicles. The restricted menu was predictable and reliable – prawn cocktail, sirloin or gammon steak (plus pineapple), chicken Maryland and Black Forest gateau to follow. He even offered wine. Until then, drinking wine was considered an expensive, distant European habit, but he offered the new low-priced labels, notably Blue Nun white or red Hirondelle which allegedly took up Austria's entire output of ordinary wine. Stakis also realised that Sabbatarianism's influence was declining and that eating out on Sundays might emerge. Since only 'bona fide travellers' could obtain a drink on Sundays, Stakis bought up off-licence shops and transferred the licence to his restaurants, allowing sale of Sunday drink.

Wine drinking was becoming more popular and tastes better informed, although French wines managed to retain their mystique. This changed when, in a blind wine tasting in *The Sunday Times*, to general astonishment, an Australian red came top. Next day there was a queue round block at the Australian Trade Centre, ending the French wine's dominance and signalling the acceptance of New World wines.

A pub near Stakis' Byres Road restaurant soon gained attention for a small feminist triumph. The local pubs usually comprised an all-male part, with a cocktail bar for mixed drinking, but one Byres Road institution, Tenants, was mono-gendered, and lacked such facilities. A female student group organised a bold sit-in, winning the argument, and the owner reluctantly had to insert a ladies toilet.

My next two years were devoted to hard work, the goal being the final autumn exam for my honours B.Sc. degree. The exams were just days before the re-entry into the fourth year of the conventional medical curriculum. I did well and when they were over, I felt drained.

ஃ

CHAPTER 6:

Corporate Life

Corporate life ... Debates ... Labour Club ... Guardian
newspaper ... Electioneering ... Sexual attitudes
The Dewar family ... Butler Rectorial

R EADY FOR relief from academia, after a tough honours year I re-
engaged with the so-called corporate life then at a high point in
its history. Centred on the two student Unions, these independent
institutions gave (and give) freedom, yet responsibility, adding
opportunities for developing interests and leadership not offered by
the University curriculum. The male students had, and have, their
Glasgow University Union, to give it its proper name, and the female
students had their own Queen Margaret Union. Both had single-sex
membership, but were open for dances and mixed debates. We might
be invited to tea with QM board members; I was made welcome since
my sister was on the Board.*

Built in 1923, the Men's Union, with its large debating chamber
which doubled as a dance hall, hosted three major debates each
term, with the six (all-male) political debating clubs taking turns to
be the government of the day. These events lasted all day and had an
impressive start at 1 o'clock watched by a full gallery which added some
heckling. Structured along parliamentary lines, the debate continued

* The QMU moved to a new building in 1969 and thereafter admitted male
members, but the GUU procrastinated and remained single-sex until 1979.

through to midnight, with an entertainment break at 10 p.m. The 'clerks' took notes, graded the speeches of the day, and posted their critique and a mark next day on the Union notice board. In the meantime, before running the country, there were the close-fought elections to the Union Board and the SRC. Other Union events included the Nixon/Kennedy debate watched closely and critically in a new enlarged television room organised by Jimmy Gordon, the President.

I had kept up links with my old Union friends, and they were now dominating the corporate life. Those doing law had an advantage, since after finishing their Arts degree, they had three more years of law studies, giving added time for Union activities. I soon stood for the Union Board myself and these elections meant canvassing in the building on the day. The election used a modern transferable vote system; after several transfers, I just squeezed in.

There were many interesting students around the two Unions, all linked with their political party or with the Athletic Club or the Student Representative Council. The Liberal Club stalwarts were Menzies 'Ming' Campbell and John MacKay, and, like some of the other debaters, both ended up in the House of Lords. Ming, like many of us, lived at home nearby and had attended Hillhead High School. President of the Union in 1964, and, unlike the indolent Board members, Ming was a serious athlete, breaking national sprint records and captaining the British athletics team in 1965. The Distributist Club, who used the terminology of G.K.Chesterton, had Roman Catholic students, energetically led by Jimmy Gordon. The Marxist-Leninists had their own Independent Club and we also had some Conservatives, small in number, and on the defensive, who acknowledged that in Scotland, for them, the end was nigh.* Teddy Taylor had been prominent in the Conservative Club earlier, as was Ross Harper, who went on after student days to prominence and controversy in Scottish Conservative Party circles.† Our endangered

---

* The student body however retained Conservative sympathies, electing Rab Butler in 1956 and Lord Hailsham in 1959 as student rectors.

† Harper's memoirs *Beyond Reasonable Doubt*, Edinburgh 2016 describe his student days.

student Tories were a civilised lot, unlike their huge national youth organisation, the Federation of Conservative Students. They had hate figures and after sporting 'Hang Nelson Mandela' badges, the organisation was shut down. Our Tories could only manage a half-hearted defence of apartheid in South Africa.

In national politics, Labour and Conservative took most of the vote between them. Electoral support for nationalist candidates did not come until the mid-1960s, but there was Scottish nationalist public sentiment which emerged well before it transferred into votes at the ballot box. One million people signed a Covenant seeking a devolved Scottish Parliament, and John McCormick, the nationalist leader, was elected as our student Rector in 1950. When some Glasgow students stole the Stone of Destiny from Westminster Abbey in 1950, it caught the imagination of Scotland, as if it had been football or rugby victory. The Scottish people continued to be touchy, and when the Queen took the title Queen Elizabeth 'the Second', rather than that of the first Elizabeth after the Union of Crowns, it met widespread criticism. School children scratched out the 'II' from their souvenir pencils and a new Edinburgh letterbox with her cypher was bombed.

There were influential nationalist students around and the Scottish Nationalist Club was well supported and respected. It centred round Iain and Neil, the sons of John McCormick, the nationalist leader, and we met their father at the family home nearby, though by then he was a sick man. When terminally-ill later, he was a patient in the Western Infirmary when I was a student and died there. The doctors flippantly said that they had the 'King of Scotland' in the ward; it was a sad end. Neil, later an Edinburgh academic, took the chair of public law at Edinburgh, and his brother Iain later captured the Argyll constituency for the SNP when the party entered its era of success.

I joined the Labour Club. Though nationally the Tories had been in power from 1951, forever it seemed, we felt that our cause was just and would prevail. Our discourse had a hint of religious morality and in my case, politics was probably a substitute for religion. With our deep longing for a Tory defeat, we had to wait until 1964, keeping warm our utopian hopes that Labour would triumph and bring in a new, fairer society. In policy matters, we had little interest in nationalising everything, or organising Paris-style student protests. No long hair either for us, unlike Gordon Brown in Edinburgh at this time. Union politics reflected traditional Westminster attitudes and were about preparing for power and gaining it

Our Labour Club invited Hugh Gaitskell, leader of the party in opposition, to speak at our annual student dinner and he charmed us all at the preceding drinks reception. During this, he turned to John Smith and asked what he should speak about after the meal and John said 'give them fairness and altruism'. Gaitskell looked puzzled and said 'Don't you want to hear about Clause Four?' We didn't.

Gaitskell, then in the thick of his struggle with the left-leaning Bevanites, insistent on keeping the clause in the Party constitution which required 'common ownership of the means of production, distribution and exchange ...' We despaired of this damaging internal debate, and pragmatic Labour Party policies were appearing, even at the debates. Donald was sitting beside John Smith on the front bench when a Tory rose to make a point of order. Donald liked to laugh and slap his right knee when listening to any Tory claims, and when the speaker bravely said that unless the big business thrived and made profits, there would be no taxes to pay for the NHS. Donald's hand stopped in mid-descent on its way down to his knee. Much later, in the Blair era, John Smith was given the task of leading the Labour Party into election-winning attitudes, and he headed the 'prawn cocktail offensive' trying to convince the City that New Labour was not anti-business.*

Although these leaders of our student Labour Club reached national prominence later, at this time in the late 1950s, they were in awe of the talented Leftist student group just ahead, notably Arthur Houston and J. Dixon Mabon, both local heroes and star debaters for the Labour Club. Houston, a mature student of working-class origin, was a candidate, as a 20 year-old student, in the parliamentary election at East Renfrewshire. Mabon became an M.P. in 1955, as the youngest member in the House. He joined the breakaway Social Democrats

* Andy McSmith's *John Smith: Playing the Long Game,* London 1993 has some material on this time.

later in 1981. Houston and other Union debaters contested The
Observer Mace trophy in 1955-57, and Houston fostered the younger
Labour Club hopefuls – John Smith, Donald Dewar, journalist Bob
McLaughlin, broadcaster Donald McCormick, and Hugh Macpherson,
a rare Bevanite and later a Tribune journalist.[*]

Of the other talent around, Derry Irvine, later Lord Chancellor
under Tony Blair, was not one of the regulars in the Beer Bar's Union
Board far corner table, concentrating instead on his studies. Meta
(gaelicised Margaret) Ramsay, older than our group, upset the received
opinion that a woman student could not become president of our
Student Representative Council. When she did, and should have been
ex-officio on the (male) Union Board, this was too much for the
traditionalist Board and, acting like a stuffy golf club, they declined to
invite her. Studying Russian at Glasgow, she was taken aside and after an
invitation to join the security services, she served in Helsinki, importantly
getting the KGB's Oleg Gordievsky out to the West. After gaining
promotion back home, she later became a political adviser to John Smith.

The Dialectical Society and other political clubs also held open
meetings, usually at lunchtime, and the best student speakers were busy
people. Our Glasgow University *Guardian* student newspaper reported on
the strengths and weaknesses of about two dozen debaters on this circuit
and it was hard to choose who was to go forward as our representatives
in the debating competitions, notably The Observer Mace starting in
1954. Doing well were Gordon Hunter, John Smith and Donald, and
they were picked. Humour in speaking was much-prized but our leading
debaters favoured serious-minded content, leavening it with dry humour.
To get to English venues for the event, they had difficulty, but could get a
lift by family friends at least to the edge of Glasgow and then hitch-hiked
from there, even to London, for the early rounds. The Union debating
teams won The Observer Mace trophy 15 times from its start in 1954,
and in 1995, after John's untimely death in 1994, it was renamed the

---

[*] Later, Glasgow contributed a Tory politicians in Liam Fox, who graduated in
medicine in 1983. The Union's SNP tradition continued with Nicola Sturgeon,
who started as a poor speaker, but toughened up at the Union debates. Other
notable students later were Brian Gill, Helena Kennedy and Nicholas Parsons.

John Smith Memorial Mace. The Union also won some international debating events.

Donald Dewar in full flight at a Queen Margaret Union debate c1959.

Donald loved to toughen up his political discourse and took every opportunity including a weekend meeting of the Glasgow Young Socialists at a holiday camp near Aberfoyle where John and Donald had a frosty reception and held tense discussions with the fundamentalists.

Nearer home, one Sunday, Donald decided that we should visit Turnbull Hall, the Catholic Students' Union near the Men's Union. He arranged with a Catholic student to include us in their Sunday evening discussion group, and Donald then provoked an argument on a theological point with one of the students. Out of his depth, the student summoned the Catholic priest with whom Donald continued to joust. As we walked home, Donald reviewed the exchanges, planning to toughen up his advocacy, ready for the next time.

Many of us at Glasgow University stayed at home, often caught between the two worlds of family and student life. The family life part shrank to weekends, with a separate Monday to Friday life revolving around the University and Union. Friday night was a highlight in this separate life and the Union activists and the Board members had our own area in one corner of the Beer Bar. On Saturdays, there was a smaller turnout, when the one or two of us on Board duty had to supervise the dance upstairs and then lock the place up. There was not much dialectical passion in our corner – instead the discourse mostly involved plotting the Union elections to come. On Friday, after 10 o'clock, one option was to go to the nearby houses of student-friendly parents – notably Donald Dewar's home.

The Dewar's house, just a few hundred yards away across the Kelvingrove Park, was not only the closest available, but the most welcoming. All three of the family had been ravaged by tuberculosis in the 1940s before treatment with streptomycin came in, and they needed sanatorium treatment. Donald's mother and father, a dermatologist at Glasgow's Royal Infirmary, doted on Donald, their only child.

To give Donald independence as a student, although he spent most of his time at the Union, his parents generously converted the basement flat of their large terrace house for his use. It even had a separate entrance from the street, which allowed him to come and go. As the only medical student in our group, I was seen as more respectable than the others, and Donald used me in a diplomatic role, sending me upstairs to speak with his parents in the gracious drawing room with its valuable Glasgow School paintings. They were a delightful, disabled, cheerful couple who loved talking about student affairs, and the medical school in particular. Also sent upstairs was Ming Campbell, who was useful in another way, since it did not drink.* One night, there was a minor rite of passage for me. Dr Dewar gave me my first whisky. A malt whisky, I think.

Downstairs in Donald's flat, for entertainment, he had a record player and his vinyl collection included the protest songs of Pete Seeger, Woody Guthrie and Bostonian Tom Lehrer who lampooned much, including the Harvard football team. At the time, public life and those in public life were treated with reverence, and hence Lehrer's clipped, steely voice and his attack on the conventional world was a novelty; satire was being born.

Donald's parents were ever-tolerant, but for middle-class parents, it was unusual, even deplorable, to belong to the Labour Club. This was unfair since we were not Trots, but Gaitskellites, and wished to change society by parliamentary means, not by outside action, nor was 'soaking the rich' a priority. Donald's increasing prominence in support of the Labour Party was noted in Glasgow Academy circles, and they viewed with disapproval this action by an 'Academical' former pupil. One Academical Club activist got word to Donald that if he tried to join the Club he would be black-balled. He didn't try.

* See Ming's memoirs *Menzies Campbell: My Autobiography* 2008.

The time had come for me to start speaking. The occasion was a debate on the NHS, and with the Labour Club taking its turn to be the government of the day, and with John Smith as the 'Prime Minister', the Speaker called me shortly after 1 o'clock. Fortified by a visit to the Union Beer Bar, I declaimed confidently, and was pleased to get increasing support not only from the floor but also from the noisy lunchtime gallery. My claim was that the NHS was underfunded and that the Tories, who had opposed setting up the NHS, should be ashamed of this and their lukewarm support thereafter. I had the house in the palm of my hand, and beside me, John urged me on. The Speaker was asked from the floor that I be allowed to continue beyond the allotted time, and to the noisy approval of the Gallery, unusually, this was granted. I won the Maiden Speaker's Prize that day.

From then on, I knew that I had unsuspected, latent powers of demagoguery but, considering myself to be a proto-scientist, I preferred to keep this deplorable skill well hidden. I let it out only on rare occasions, and indeed rabble-rousing can only work if you have a large, malleable audience. On one occasion later, when serving as chairman of the Scottish National Party Health Policy Committee, the debate at our annual conference, as it happens, was on the same topic. Unexpectedly called to speak, stirring up primitive emotions again with short sound bites, I got the delegates up and out of their seats wanting not only more from me, but also more money for the NHS. Afterwards I was taken aside and told that I was in favour with the SNP leadership – of which more later.

Toast List	
The Queen	
Toast to Charles James Fox	*The Chairman*
The Society	*Donald McCormick*
Reply ...	*John McKay*
Absent Enemies	*Gordon Hunter*
Reply ...	*David Miller*
The Profession	*John Smith*
Reply ...	*David Hamilton*
The Chairman ...	*Alastair McKinlay*

Toast list for Charles James Fox Club dining club dinner c1961.

Although I'd made a bright speaking start in the Union, I soon flopped thereafter, as the lead speaker in a lunchtime debate on abortion reform. I lost the audience by quoting heavily from worthy government reports. My cautious conclusion now was that matters, even public policy, should not be swayed by slick advocacy but policy should emerge after rational, evidence-based consideration, the strategy used by scientists. This was an unrealistic, naive stance and later, with neat symmetry, it was clear from my reading that bias-free science did not exist and that advocacy and rhetoric did feature. At the Union, I decided to keep quiet thereafter, but watch our world attentively with a journalist's role on our student newspaper.

At the start of that year I became sub-editor, then editor, of the Glasgow University *Guardian,* following on from Donald Dewar, and later I also edited the medical student magazine. Other student editors of the *Guardian* included Andrew Neil, starting work first with the *Paisley Daily Express* from 1971, later editing *The Sunday Times* for 11 years.* Having done printing at school, I was interested in the technology as well as the journalism.

As editor of the student newspaper, you had to write much of it yourself. But help came from the formal reports on the numerous debates and an excellent sports page handed in from the Athletic Club, notably from Craig Reedie of the Badminton Club, later a major figure in world athletics administration. I also got Student Representative Council news and some letters came in, usually grumbles about the SRC or allegations of 'graft' in the Union Board, such as their free private bar at the Daft Friday Ball. In my contributions, my spelling was always a problem. 'A man who cannot spell diarrhoea has no future as a surgeon' said a pompous consultant who advised us students. It ruffled me, since I had difficulty with much simpler words. Later, the computers' spell-checkers came to the rescue.

Our newspaper came out on alternate Fridays and on the evening before, I made my way down to a small printing business nearby on Great Western Road run by Mr Tidd. Mr Tidd's ancient flat-bed letterpress machine printed our broadsheet newspaper slowly, and there

---

* Other student *Guardian* editors also took up journalism – Donald Wintersgill at the *Manchester Guardian,* John Mullan edited the *Independent on Sunday,* Iain Martin worked at the *Sunday Telegraph* and was editor of *The Scotsman.* Much later, Fraser Nelson edited *The Spectator.*

was always some drama. His machine printed from Linotype metal text set by Mr Tidd's erratic compositor, a man with a drink problem, sacked from the *Daily Express* in downtown Glasgow, a rare event at the time, such was the power of the print unions. As Thursday evening went on, he became more erratic. Somehow, we got there, adding the pictures (metal plates on wood) and got the paper to bed and printed in the early hours of the morning. I always thought if war broke out, or a Royal died, we could insert the story and be first on the streets with the news.

I had two good ideas and two scoops during my time. The first success was a Career Supplement, an obvious idea now, but not then. Our mysterious student advertising manager, whom I never seemed to meet, silently took on the idea and presented me late in the day with about 50 large advertisements, many being full page, notably from banks and large British companies. This was unexpected and I now needed to pad out this now much-enlarged supplement with text between the ads. Though I presented the news of our monster paper early to Mr Tidd, we got only one third of it printed that Thursday night. Next day, Friday, Mr Tidd had to produce the *Newton Mearns News* (or was it the *Pollokshields Post?*) and we got back to tackling our albatross Career Supplement on Saturday morning. Mr Tidd and his wife ran a bed and breakfast establishment in Blackpool, so he shot off and got back to get the rest printed on Sunday night. It hit the campus on Monday morning.

A second idea came from two innovative students ahead of us, Ross Harper and Kenneth Fee, who ambitiously took over the services offered by the Student Representative Council, such as travel, and ran the ventures along business lines, calling themselves 'Student Enterprises'. Towards the end of my time as editor, they took over the hardly lucrative contract for our *Guardian*, and they told me that there was a new printing process coming in, and would I like to see it? I certainly did. We visited their printers and saw the earliest model of the small litho printing machines soon to change the world of printing for ever. Instead of hot metal – i.e. solid type – printing was now from a photographic plate. Kenneth suggested a trial run by producing an extra single sheet edition of our *Guardian* between the normal fortnightly issues. For our experiment, I cobbled together some text and joyfully we could paste photographs straight into the page. My mysterious advertising agent student found an advert or two.

The result was delightful. The single sheet, printed on both sides, had a modern crisp format with clear images. All that remained was deciding on a price. Most of the cost of printing of this single-sheet experiment had been charitably absorbed by Kenneth Fee and the adverts paid for the rest. So, I charged nothing. We left piles of our new idea around the campus, thus doing away with the usual problem of marketing and collecting payment. This naturally achieved the biggest penetration of our paper ever. It might have been the world's first free newspaper.

When the word got out that I charged nothing for it, I was taken aside by the SRC leadership, and asked what on earth I was up to. But my explanations were to no avail and I had to defend myself at a sceptical SRC meeting. Even a prominent Marxist-Leninist member spoke against me, darkly declaiming that 'everything has its price.'

Looking for scoops and stories over Christmas, I found that although money from the block grant given by the University to the SRC had gone to the six political clubs, the student Communist Society got none. I splashed this story, headlined as 'No Grant for Communists,' suggesting a self-evident prejudice. The Board at the Men's Union and the debaters saw this as an important issue and as a new chance to wound their old enemy, the SRC. Exhibiting rather synthetic indignation, they arranged an emergency Dialectical Society lunchtime protest debate in the Union.

When I looked further into the matter, the situation was more complex; all the *debating* clubs got grants from the SRC, and the Communist Society was not a debating club. However, the Union debaters, soon to be lawyers

and politicians, were still prepared to run with the story, accepting this difficult brief and trying to do their best with it. I saw how our would-be lawyers were rehearsing how to defend a serial murderer, or, as politicians, to hold the line on any tricky matter in their party manifesto.

Eventually, the Communist Society got an ad hoc grant. Immediately an Anti-Communist student society was formed called 'Rally' and announced it would also apply for a grant. But nothing more was heard on the matter.

The second scoop involved the retiral of the principal Sir Hector Hetherington. I asked a gossipy senior academic to brief me on the candidates being considered, and he helpfully added an assessment of their strengths and weaknesses. That issue of our newspaper was eagerly read in the Staff Club.

Some other single-issue matters were of interest. There was the new proposed Scottish university and the decision went against Inverness but in favour of Stirling. and at the Union we were huffy about our Glasgow's Royal College of Science and Technology becoming

Masthead and artwork for my Guardians were done for me by fellow students Martyn Webster and Jimmy Weir.

a university, though it did so in 1964. Proposals that the BBC should no longer be the only broadcaster, thus opening the way for ITV, caused dismay among the Leftist debaters.

Apartheid was an important issue. Chief Albert Luthuli in South Africa, president of the African National Congress and Nobel Peace Prize winner, had treason charges made against him, but when these were dropped, he was banned from travelling beyond 15 miles from his house. Our campaign to make him Lord Rector of Glasgow University in 1962 started in Donald's house. The students did elect him, with the nationalist McIntyre second and Edward Heath trailing in third place, ending the run of Tory rectors. But the Chief could not come to Glasgow for the award and the student body started a fund in his name to support a black student to study at Glasgow University. Luthuli died in 1967 aged 69 and the ANC leadership passed to Nelson Mandela, who came through Glasgow in 1994 and thanked Glasgow and eight other cities for making him a local freeman during his prison years.

Our intending politicians soon had career opportunities outside. With the national Labour Party increasingly split, the moderate Gaitskellites needed help. Donald Dewar and John Smith were soon courted, as was Jimmy Gordon, as possible electoral candidates by Willie Marshall, the respected, moderate secretary and organiser of the Scottish Labour Party. John Smith's first chance came when East Fife's member of parliament, Sir James Henderson-Stewart, died in 1961. Fife voters could be relied on to tug their forelocks on these occasions, and the Tory candidate was Colonel Sir John Gilmour, Eton and Oxford, Master of the Fife Hunt. The local Labour party chose our John as their candidate and his biographer says that John 'flooded the traditionally deferential constituency with exuberant party workers.' I don't recall it quite like that. On one occasion, five of us did set out in Donald's father's car for the St Andrews University Union, planning to rendezvous there with the local student Labour Club members. Entering the Union, there was no-one to be seen except a lone Sloane Ranger, elegant in a twin set and pearls. We asked her for help. She drew herself up in her red gown and announced with metropolitan pride – 'I don't believe there is a student Labour Club in St Andrews University.' She was almost right. St Andrews University was then a haven for libertarian free-market thinking, and many staff and English students later found their way into the upper reaches of the Tory Party and prospered under Margaret Thatcher.

John halved Gilmour's 15,000 majority, marking the beginning of the end for the Scottish Conservatives, and the start of John's political career. Donald Dewar, within months of qualifying as a lawyer, fought Aberdeen South in the 1964 general election. Lady Tweedsmuir ('Priscilla Buchan' to her friends), an impressive Tory politician, had held the seat for the Tories from 1946 and although Aberdeen appeared safe, Donald made inroads, cutting her majority by half to 4,000. Two years later, in 1966, Donald was elected at Aberdeen by 1,800 votes and joined John at Westminster. Later, the Tories lost North East Fife but it was our Ming Campbell who took the seat for the Liberals in 1987, and held it until retirement in 2014.

The Hillhead parliamentary constituency included the University, the Western Infirmary and our family home. Roy Jenkins, our SDP MP later, would claim it was 'the best educated constituency in Britain', and it was then one of the safest seats in Scotland for the Tories (now called Scottish Unionists). Indeed, the loyal *Glasgow Herald* called the Hillhead residents 'eyes-front-over-the-cliff Tories'. At the time, our M.P. was Tam Galbraith, son of the respected Member of Parliament for Glasgow Pollok. Tam had the misfortune to have been friendly in his government department with John Vassal, the homosexual Soviet spy, but Tam survived two investigations. As the Scottish Tory vote declined, eventually loosing all their seats, Hillhead was second last in Glasgow to go.

Many national events at the time caused discomfort in our respectable West End. The old certainties were fast disappearing and the middle class' deference to the Establishment was severely tested. The Cambridge spies Burgess and Maclean had fled to Russia in 1951, and Philby followed in 1953, leaving Blunt behind, protected from prosecution after confessing privately. The Suez Crisis in 1956, meant new cynicism about politics and the Profumo scandal in 1963 then rocked the political world.

We in the West End were brought up to respect the aristocracy and to 'love a Lord' but this deference was shaken when Lord Boothby was alleged in 1964 to have murky links with the underworld, although his long-running affair with Harold MacMillan's wife, well-known to insiders, was concealed from the rest of us. Scottish duchesses also lost esteem that year when the Duchess of

Argyll's dramatic divorce proceedings revealed her promiscuous love life. Nor did the devious Duke come out of it well. After Lord Denning's Report which dealt with these scandals, the London *Times* newspaper concluded that the Report revealed 'a society weakened by poor leadership, including that of the Conservative party'. But the *Glasgow Herald* was having none of it, and kept up a brave front: 'The serious and widespread rumours of immorality in high places have been shown to be without foundation.'

In this pre-Pill era, sexual attitudes and behaviour were cautious and careful. When the Edinburgh student newspaper bravely called for the Pill to be available without cost to students, their own Lord Rector Malcolm Muggeridge, with the support of the University Court, condemned the proposal. Related to this, the British Medical Association took the Scottish Office's Principal Medical Officer to task in 1963 when he declined to discourage pre-marital intercourse. Abortion was illegal, but was sought nevertheless, and we medical students might be asked for advice, always sought 'on behalf of a friend.' Homosexuality was still illegal, and although there must have been a small gay community, but it was not overt, nor has it been revealed in retrospect. The Wolfenden Committee of 1957 proposed to decriminalise homosexuality, but Scotland remained unimpressed and the one dissenting member, opposed to reform, on the Committee was a former procurator fiscal for Glasgow. When he spoke at the General Assembly of the Church of Scotland he had support. The *Glasgow Herald's* stance on homosexuality was that 'the dividing line between socially abhorrent behaviour, as a sin and as a crime, is exceptionally hard to draw ...' It called for research to discover a cure for homosexuality.

The student corporate life suffered a disaster about this time. The occasion was the University's Rectorial Address on 21 February 1958 given by the University's new Rector, Rab Butler, the respected Home Secretary and deputy Prime Minister. Butler had prepared the thoughtful address expected of him, but a civil servant perceptively warned him that the proceedings 'might be arduous and undignified.'

The ceremony was at the Glasgow Corporation's St Andrews Halls. At the doors, those who had not thought to bring any suitable missiles obtained supplies of ageing fruit and bags of flour, said later to have been provided by the hostile Union Board to rain on the SRC's parade. The Hall had balconies at the sides of the main platform and hence it was also possible to lob these missiles not only up from below but also down onto the packed platform party, entertained up to this point by an ad hoc student jazz band. Butler started, and the barrage started. Butler soldiered on, even after the direct hits with flour which gave joy to the press photographers. It is uncertain if Butler finished, since his remarks were inaudible. The event was then abandoned.

The damage to the good name of the University was clear next day when the national newspapers united to condemn the student behaviour, adding the iconic photographs of the whitened Butler. Principal Hetherington received angry letters. An irate Glasgow graduate in Kansas disowned his alma mater, and, in case Hetherington had not seen it, enclosed a press cutting from the *Kansas City Times*. Parents of Glasgow students were also embarrassed and made this clear to their off-springs. The Glasgow disorder coincided with the then-current political controversy over the cost of student grants to the taxpayer, and the Glasgow disturbance seemed to confirm that tax money was going to unworthy hooligans.

An investigation was needed. The secretary of the Union Board, Jimmy Gordon, was summoned to an uncomfortable meeting with the Principal which was also attended by the much-disliked, anti-student Professor Christian Fordyce, who favoured disciplinary action. Gordon acknowledged the disaster and agreed in his written apology that 'irreparable damage has been done ... our graduates will find the path through life more difficult.' The necessary Senate Investigation Committee also summoned Donald Dewar and he came back down to the Union and told us about mass of press photographs laid out on the Committee table. Fortunately, he could not recognise anyone shown in the action, except the jazz band players.

Butler himself took the matter well, perhaps too well, and his non-judgemental verdict blamed the 'high spirits of youth'. His critics, notably the 'hangers and floggers' in the Conservative Party noted his tolerant stance and took it as further evidence of Butler's lack of resolve on crime and punishment. Butler's biographers have concluded that his charitable response to the Glasgow episode affected his future in the Party. In the wider world, the University of Glasgow had to live under the shadow of this disaster for a while, not least because the events chimed in with the negative, violence-prone image of the city.

But the set-back may have energised the student body. The student leaders were put on the back foot, and in siege mode, denigrated by the staff, their parents and the taxpayers of Middle England, this may have given our group a new ambition to succeed. Derry Irvine, later Lord Chancellor, famously said to his pals at the time that he was off to England to 'get in among them' and show them that Scotland, after all, had talent. The two student leaders who had taken most of the criticism survived and soon gained respectability. Jimmy Gordon, far from being job-less as he feared, founded Radio Clyde, soon reached the House of Lords and ironically later served on the Glasgow University Court. Meta Ramsay, the Secretary of the SRC, who had hosted Butler during the Rectorial events, was also ennobled after her successful career in MI6.

Much later, the University leadership erased memories of the event and found that they could, after all, be proud of that generation of students. The Memorial Gates on University Avenue now display two names from these times – Smith and Dewar. The student organisations of those times are now seen in their best light, as a nursery of talent and part of a golden age of student life at the University of Glasgow. But there was that one day that all would like to forget.

For Professor Fordyce, the classicist, who had sought to punish the Rectorial riot students, things did not go well. Shortly after, he produced his long-awaited life's work, namely his translation and commentary on the Latin poems of Catullus. Readers familiar with this famous and often erotic text could not believe what they found. Fordyce had left out the naughty bits, deeming them to be 'unsuitable'. This gave local detractors an opportunity for wounding gossip, and Fordyce's distant colleagues in the little world of classical studies deserted him and, in their book reviews, rose to the occasion with wit and sarcasm.

I enjoyed this involvement in the student life, perhaps indulging in it too much. By springtime my regular absence from the fourth-year medical teaching was noted. I was summoned to the Dean.

ॐ

CHAPTER 7:

Hospital Teaching

Teaching and teachers ... Women staffing ... The Unit system
Pattern of surgery ... Holistic physicians ... Casualty work

THE DEAN was informed by two departments that I had gone missing and had poor marks in their mid-year exams. I had hoped to bluff my way through the new subjects including pharmacology, but failed. My Glasgow University *Guardian* cartoonist Martyn Webster, later a prominent plastic surgeon in Glasgow, was also enjoying the extra-curricular activities, and had a comparably bad performance. The Dean, a tolerant man, listened to my 'burnt-out' alibi, and seemed reassured when I told him that, with a burst of speed in May, I would assuredly catch up. I managed this sprint, and I did catch up on the last lap.

We were, at last, into clinical studies.

Glasgow's clinical medicine had a revival at this time. Between the Wars, Glasgow had little in the way of an academic surgical reputation, and our College of Physicians and Surgeons, then called the 'Faculty' was little more than a club for those in private medicine. Its fellowship and membership diplomas had no national status. After WWII, with some skilled negotiation, a Royal Charter was obtained and the renamed Royal College now had exams of status equal to those of the Edinburgh and London colleges.

At the University, the basic biomedical science departments had always been good, but now after WWII, the clinical departments improved greatly, helped by the relative absence of private practice, and this new vitality was evidenced by the local output of textbooks and the arrival in Glasgow of postgraduates, even from America. With full-time staff, and with specialism encouraged, large units like the regional plastic surgical unit and the neurosurgical Institute with its 'Glasgow Coma Scale' would take the city name out to the international surgical world. In the Western Infirmary, Ian Donald, the obstetrician pioneered the use of ultrasound and one floor below, Sir Charles Illingworth trained many academic surgeons. It was almost a 'Second Enlightenment' resembling Scottish medicine's eminence in the 18th century which rested on the assumption that scholarship, not private practice, was important and that medicine could thrive as a science.

Our morning student teaching in fourth year was at the bedside from 9 – 11 a.m. and the size of the city meant there were many general surgical and medical units. Orthopaedics, chest and heart surgery was still done in general units, as was the small amount of blood vessel surgery. At the Royal Infirmary, specialty medical units were emerging, notably for kidney and blood disease, but the physicians at the Western Infirmary resisted the new idea, claiming that the only real physicians were those who could manage all human ailments.

The general units usually had three consultants and perhaps three or four juniors at various stages of training. The two-ward unit was known by the name of the 'chief' – the senior consultant – 'Mr So-and-so's unit. At the Western Infirmary, you were said, semi-seriously, to have arrived if you were a consultant there, an elder at a West End presbyterian church and a member at one of the exclusive West of Scotland men's golf clubs. Few Catholics and fewer Jews reached the consultant ranks at the main Glasgow teaching hospitals and although increasing numbers of doctors from abroad now took the junior posts. promotion to consultant posts was yet to come,

There were no women consultants in the medical and surgical units of the teaching hospitals, and women first got their place in the specialties, being promoted in surgery last of all. Rona MacKie, from our year, was the first woman professor (of Dermatology) in the Glasgow Medical Faculty. With this growing success of women in the formerly male world, the hunt was on locally to find the first female consultant in the Glasgow teaching hospital world. In the University's Arts Faculty, a very senior, disliked staff member was on the case and she concluded that Glasgow's Victoria Infirmary had apparently led the way by appointing Ivy Mackenzie to a consultant post in the 1930s. Failing to consult any local doctors, she published the history of Ivy's triumph in a man's world. If she had asked, we all knew that Ivy was very much a man. The University wits made the most of this blunder.

The Glasgow hospital wards still had an unreconstructed Nightingale design, with rows of perhaps twelve or more beds up one side and down the other, without partitions. Though the arrangement meant no privacy, the best that could be said for the design was that any crisis in the ward was immediately noticed by the nurses or neighbouring patients. Above each bed there was a wooden ledge. Few knew what this was for, but I did. When I was in the Western Infirmary age 12, as described earlier, a specimen of urine from each of us was placed there for inspection. This ledge was now empty or perhaps had a Bible.

It was a time of large ward rounds, headed by a consultant plus the ward sister, with the three layers of trainees below. The patient had a humble place in these exchanges. After the round, some ward chiefs kept up the older style by leaving the building promptly, and requiring the resident doctor to accompany them to their car. Although there was not much private practice around, it was still sought, and there was rivalry. When one of the city gynaecologists employed a chauffeur, his rivals put it about that he was going blind.

These large ward rounds featured in *Your Life in Their Hands*, the television programme which started in 1958 and, still in black-and-white, it was transmitted live. The series was an important event in television history since it helped demystify the medical world, then still largely mysterious. The BBC announced that one of the episodes, for the first time, would feature a surgical operation and this created considerable adverse comment. M.P.s asked the Postmaster General to intervene and block the BBC's plans, and the British Medical Association was also opposed, saying that opening up medical practice 'would increase the number of neurotics and stimulate fear of hospital treatment.' Privately they feared that removing the mystique of medical practice would be a mistake.

In choosing which clinics to attend for our teaching, we applied ahead to the Dean's office, and after our preferences were noted, about ten of us were allocated to each unit. Since this was a beauty contest among the units, the chiefs were flattered if their unit was known to be popular, and if student requests were low, hinting at poor teaching, then the Dean would have a word. There were plenty of patients, surgical or medical, to use for teaching, and they came into the wards for a while before surgery and lingered on afterwards, since the accepted paradigm was that rest was essential before and after surgery. Particularly interesting cases were brought in for longer periods to be used for the student or postgraduate exams, and the unit chief took pride in having a range of interesting cases on show. Obtaining advance permission from the patient for teaching was new and beginning to appear, and was never refused.

We attended each morning's teaching which was shared by all the staff during the week. We students, because of the many clinics in different hospitals, knew much about the personalities in the medical school, and we were less charitable than the *Glasgow Herald*, who could always be relied on to give a laudatory obituary. Only occasionally would they use code that 'his reticence, often mistaken for arrogance, instead concealed a shy and caring personality.' Some of the older consultants were not pleased at the rising number of female students, and the students knew that the Western Infirmary was more tolerant in this matter than the Royal Infirmary. They tried to avoid one unit chief at the Western who insisted that the girls should not wear short-sleeved dresses, even in summer.

With the curtains drawn round the bed, which gave enclosure and a false feeling of confidentiality, the ward rounds were also in progress at this time and they passed by outside the curtains. During the teaching, possible diagnoses were discussed in depth, which often needed euphemisms, notably avoiding the word 'cancer' since these patients were never informed about this diagnosis.* The staff of the unit took it in turns to teach and a clinician with empathy might impart good communication skills. The patient often gained more insights than were offered to them during the large ward rounds.

The patient's history was taken by one of us and a physical examination by all followed. This examination of the patient, still central to medical practice, was emphasised and with disease presenting at an advanced stage, there were clamant physical signs. We were introduced to examination of the chest, and, proudly owning a stethoscope as a rite of passage into the clinical world, we had to listen for various diagnostic noises – creps, rales and rubs. There was also the difficult, arcane matter of heart sounds, 'murmurs' of all kinds, since valvular disease was still common. But things were to change and clinical signs were steadily downplayed preferring evidence from the increasingly informative radiological techniques. Diagnostic authority was moving from the clinician to the radiologists, and in chest disease, all was revealed by imaging. Cardiologists would soon prefer their scans and pressure measurements, and downplay the murmurs heard. The stethoscope was heading for extinction.

The pattern of surgical disease at the time was different. Blood vessel disease, notably aortic aneurysms or poor leg circulation was not yet a problem. Cancers presented late. Heart surgery was on the increase and use of by-pass, after a slow start, becoming routine. Regular dialysis and organ transplantation for kidney failure was yet to come, and we had no intensive care. Tuberculosis could now be cured and streptomycin therapy meant that sterile lung cavities remained and these needed surgery. Some chest physicians in our region, seeing their specialty contracting, re-trained as chest surgeons.

We were almost part of our teachers' unit for a term, and during bedside teaching, they assessed each student's abilities and, with an added clinical exam at the end of term, the staff could make a fair assessment. You got your first medical jobs (six months as house surgeon or house physician) from getting known to the staff at these units.

* The newspapers were also silent, notably about breast cancer, since both words were avoided.

❧

But among our older physician teachers, there was occasionally puzzling behaviour. Some were very keen on the 'quality' and 'tension' of the pulse at the wrist and we found it difficult to detect these almost mystical parameters. These physicians were also not keen on the laboratory measurements or special tests which we scientifically-minded young student expected to hear about. They were hesitant or even hostile to the use of new remedies, such as steroids and anticoagulants. These men enquired particularly closely about the patients' lifestyle and avoided making a precise organ-based diagnosis. They might broaden their discourse by alluding to the life and works of Hippocrates.

One revealing vignette sticks in my memory. We joined one of these physicians at his outpatient clinic and he was dealing with a young man complaining of indigestion. The physician ordered no tests or x-rays, nor made a focused diagnosis. He moved on quickly to treatment which was not pharmacological and was restricted to lifestyle changes, in particular recommending 'more exercise'.

'But, Doctor,' the man said, 'I run from my house to the office every day and then run back home in the evening.'

'In which case,' said the physician, hardly shifting gear, 'you should rest more.'

At coffee time, we concluded that our teacher was comically old-fashioned. But light dawned years later. We were witnessing leftover thinking and management from the 'holistic' 1930s, when illness was blamed on a lack of 'balance' in the body, rather than arising from any particular organ. The treatment was to seek to restore health by encouraging the body's powerful self-righting mechanisms, using a learned physician's skill and suggestions for changes in diet, exercise and climate. This holistic medicine had almost disappeared in our post-war scientific era and we were catching the last glimpses of this different medical system.

Adding to our training in the areas of general medicine and surgery, we went around to other specialty clinics. At the famous Rotten Row maternity hospital there was impressive production of babies and plenty complicated labours. There was a large operating theatre with huge outside windows, and it had a particularly large balcony viewing area to watch the action on two operating tables side-by-side. Caesarean sections or forceps deliveries were done in this theatre, witnessed by ranks of watchers and two cases might proceed simultaneously.

We also attended the famous Children's Hospital but our verdict was that we were treated like children, particularly by the authoritarian, talented professorial head of the academic unit. On Friday mornings, the young patients discharged that week were reviewed and case sheets were passed along a line from junior to middle grade to the most senior and after reaching the professor, he solemnly entered the diagnosis in the box on the outer sheet. Woe betide anyone who had already filled in the box. The infectious disease hospitals were also isolated from the steady liberalisation of attitudes proceeding elsewhere. The senior physician at these hospitals were also the medical superintendents and very much in charge. At lunchtime the medical staff had to gather for lunch, and he dispensed the soup to all from a tureen.

My attendances signed off by heads of Units and Departments, also showing a two week student locum.

❧

Our experience in practical surgery started early, as students, and we slipped gently into practical surgery in ways not possible later. One way was by attending and helping out in the Casualty (later renamed Accident and Emergency) Department. These departments had a low status and were manned by very junior doctors before they moved off to surgical or other posts. There was loose supervision by seniors and any mistakes were treated with charity. The most famous department in Glasgow, possibly in Britain, was, and is, the Glasgow Royal Infirmary Gatehouse, which, as the day progressed, dealt with an increasing load of the sick and injured from the surrounding deprived East End area of Glasgow. There were plenty cuts, bumps and fractures, but Glasgow's famous razor slashes from inter-gang feuds were gone, stamped out by good police work and long sentences handed out by the judges. Instead life-threatening stab wounds were appearing, and this change was a source of confusion to the police. Accustomed of old to measure the gravity of the assault by the length of the razor's skin wound and the number of stitches inserted, the officers were disappointed at being told of the tiny size of the stab wound. They would urge the doctor to inflate the dimensions a bit to assist adequate justice later in court.

Friday night, payday, was busy, but the highlight of the year in the Gatehouse was Hogmanay, when, starting about midnight on 31st December, the consequences of the heavy drinking during this semi-pagan festival began to be seen at the Royal. The flow continued well into the next day, and we students were welcome to help with the influx. We would simply arrive, roll up our sleeves, find a space and get to work, since much stitching was needed. A local anaesthetic was usually given, but not always required. Outsiders, notably journalists, might come to watch and one who witnessed the scene shrewdly noted that as the events of the festive night and following day unfolded, the patients seemed to take over the Gatehouse and made it their own, such were their numbers and their jovial unawareness of the passage of time.

As I got better at simple suturing at the Gatehouse, I acquired some more sophisticated surgical techniques. Some memorable lessons included one from Alistair Mack, then a newly-qualified doctor at work in Casualty, and later one of the better-known Glasgow consultant surgeons. He showed me, when single-handed, how to stitch a drunk's bleeding tongue laceration, awkwardly located well back in the mouth. Attempting to freeze the ever-moving tongue with local anaesthetic merely provoked further withdrawal of the tongue and more bleeding and choking. Alistair showed me that you first anaesthetise the tip of the tongue, then put a long stitch painlessly through this frozen tip and putting a heavy forceps on these threads, it would pull the tongue nicely out of the mouth. The once-inaccessible laceration was then frozen using added adrenaline to stop the bleeding and confidently stitched.

Many of these surgical techniques in Casualty were, and are, enjoyed by the operator. They suit and satisfy the surgical personality. Someone comes in with a problem and leaves, fairly soon after, without it. In dealing with a dislocated shoulder, the immediacy of a prompt reduction is deeply satisfying. One intervention soon needed in the casualty department is almost miraculous and biblical in its success. Heroin overdose can be fatal, but if the purple-faced, hardly-breathing sufferer reaches hospital, and the antidote narcan is given intravenously, recovery is immediate. Some of the surgical techniques can be elegant in their simplicity. Rings on fingers can get tight and the finger swells and tuns blue. The ring need not be cut off and instead, after winding a thick thread tightly round the swollen finger beyond then under it, the precious ring can be eased off. Even retrieving foreign bodies from the eye or ear is rewarding. In these cases, the surgeon is indispensable. Holistic or alternative medicine is silent on the matter of marbles stuck in the nose and chiropractors wisely stay clear of managing dislocated shoulders. Surgeons like doing these simple procedures, though the older you are, less chances are offered.

Soon we students could add ward work to our experience by doing weekend locums for the 'residents', the house surgeons and physicians. This meant living-in from Friday night to Monday morning, and the resident might or might not give us a small reward. We were busy and, astonishingly, looking back, one of these week-end tasks for the surgical resident was to organise matched blood ready for any necessary transfusion during any planned surgery on Mondays. Our Haematology Department gave an emergency weekend transfusion service, but declined to support blood matching for planned Monday surgery, and I was shown how to do this when I reported for a weekend's work. Included in other likely tasks was immediate certification of death.

I gained some other personal surgical experience. Drew Kay (later Professor Sir Andrew Kay) was an elder in my father's church and he arranged for me to help on Saturday mornings with his famous gastric secretion tests. This measured the patients' stomach acid by sampling it through a stomach tube each half-hour. To add to this, every fifth Saturday was 'receiving day' for his unit and I started to hang about after my duties with the tests were over. When the senior surgeons went home, there was just myself, the resident/house surgeon, and the junior surgeon in training (SHO), as the front line. The residents were glad to stay in the wards and get on with the paperwork, leaving me to help the junior surgeon as his assistant in the theatre for any cases. I stayed on into the evening and into the night, until the action was over. I saw a lot of surgery.

During this time, I was still living at home in the manse, but kept in touch with the Union corporate life. I felt I had hospitality to repay and our parents reluctantly agreed to let me have one party, just one, in the manse. I had ordered a small barrel of beer to be delivered, and it arrived a day early. This would not normally have been a problem, but that day my mother was holding a committee meeting. It was not a meeting of the Scottish Women's Temperance Association, as the wits who later spread the story around alleged, but a meeting of the Women's World Day of Prayer Committee, admittedly an organisation which overlapped with the Temperance activists. During the opening prayer given by my mother, the doorbell rang and she signalled to one of the ladies to answer the door. She came back with the hushed message, namely that 'There's a man at the door with a barrel of beer.'

࿐

Another less dramatic, but also uncomfortable matter, at home was the rise of satire on television and it attacked some of the attitudes we were brought up with. Satire came in with vigour in response to the problems of the Establishment, particularly the faltering Tory government, damaged by the Profumo affair. 'Beyond the Fringe' launched in summer 1961 at the Edinburgh Festival, *Private Eye* emerged shortly after and 'That Was The Week That Was' followed in late 1962, headed by cheeky young David Frost.

Our parents initially did not know what to make of the programme's irreverence, but I was relieved to find, glancing at my father, that he laughed occasionally. The BBC received many complaints from government, the Army and the churches.

Archbishop Makarios in Cyprus complained about his portrayal, deeming it a 'gross violation of internationally accepted ethics'. Pressurised by the great and good to curb Frost and the others, the Postmaster General Reginald Bevins threatened to intervene and 'do something about it', but prime minister Macmillan disagreed and nobly decided that they should take their medicine.

Three years of medical student clinical life passed quickly. Then there was the Final Year Dinner and production of our Year Book, a rite of passage, funded by events throughout the years. Of our year's total of 120 students, 40 were women. The two final year dinners were segregated – and the girls wanted it that way. For their dinner, only 40 male staff were invited and those favoured with invitations made known this nod to their popularity.

Then loomed the three-week ordeal of the final examination, and when they were over, we were almost out into the world. Almost, because for the next year we were imprisoned in the enclosed, cloistered world of the residencies in surgery and medicine.

~

CHAPTER 8:

House Surgeon

Hospital Units ... Working hours ... Emergencies ... Porters
Pattern of surgery ... Medical resident

MY FIRST job, starting in the summer of 1963, was working for six months as a surgical resident or 'houseman' – a term recalling the older all-male medical world. Our Western Infirmary had five general surgical units and every fifth day – 'receiving' day – we dealt with emergency surgical cases, admitting them to our unit directly and using our operating theatre next to our wards. This was the 'unit' system (called a 'firm' elsewhere), now gone, and it encouraged teamwork and instilled loyalties. It even encouraged competition within the hospital which was sometimes on show at the Saturday hospital clinical meeting. If picked for the resident's job at one of the better-known units, we felt privileged.[*]

Each surgical unit had one resident house doctor to look after the 30-40 beds, and our Mr Fraser's Unit had 50 beds, the extras being for chest surgery – lung cases and (closed) mitral valve surgery. At the professor of surgery's unit, he had brought in some elementary human rights and managed to get two residents instead of one. But the

---

[*] For a useful account of surgical residency, see Colin Douglas *The Houseman's Tale*, Edinburgh, 1975.

hospital wits unfairly said that his Unit needed two residents because all his patients required two operations – the original one and then the re-do for complications.

The dynamics of the now-forgotten unit system are worth recalling. The resident(s) were/was on call all the time. The junior SHO or registrar worked 9 a.m.- 5 p.m. daily in the Unit and covered the 24 hours work on receiving day, perhaps getting home to sleep if all was quiet. The senior registrars also worked 9 a.m. - 5 p.m. and might be called in for any difficult case on receiving day. For any difficulties arising in the Unit's patients at night on non-receiving days, the resident would request that someone should come in.

Our unit's three consultants shared five full day's theatre work each week, with the lists often extending into the evening. Throughput was rapid since the simpler anaesthetics methods meant quicker turnover, and the patients returned to the adjacent wards without a recovery stage. I can't recall any serious immediate post-operative trouble, and I would have known. Two experienced sisters ran the theatre, and, very much part of the unit, they did not leave until we finished the long lists. The consultants, since they did no private work, were always in the hospital, either in theatre or on the ward rounds or at the busy outpatient clinic downstairs. There, all the patients arrived at 9 o'clock; clinic appointments were yet to come.

On the ward rounds, our formidable older ward nursing sister took charge, giving quick resumés of each case from her Kardex, and she made herself available to meet relatives each afternoon. Cancer diagnoses were given out to the family, but not to the patient. Some Western Infirmary sisters were legendary, and one, although only five feet tall, ruled the elite Gardner Institute. Junior doctors on arrival were encouraged 'to think positively because she can smell fear'. In our tiny staff room, there was an 11 o'clock gathering and our faithful ward maid brought in tea and coffee and provided tasty sandwiches made by splitting toast and filling the interior with chopped boiled eggs saved from surplus patients' food. The theatre team, putting on white robes, joined the rest of us who had just finished the ward round and this convivial gathering coordinated the work of the unit.

Continuity of care in the unit was impressive and no one seemed to go on holiday, or indeed left the building, and nobody was ever ill. We had one capable, young unit secretary, who was also always there. She typed our letters and reports, and up to four carbon copies were possible. Later, in a drive for centralised efficiency, our records officer introduced a secretarial pool system for the hospital typing, withdrawing the unit secretaries, but illness rates soon rose and a mountain of case sheets and un-transcribed tapes accumulated. The unit secretary system was restored, with relief.

There was only one house officer in each of our surgical units, meaning a working week of 168 hours i.e. 7x24 hours. We had fewer blood tests and fewer 'drips' to put up, but this used metal needles put into the vein, and they didn't stay open long. Radiology was much simpler than later, and the diagnosis, particularly in abdominal emergencies, often had to await surgical exploration. Blood gas measurements could be done as a favour by a tedious method available in the Surgical Departments' research labs. For laboratory tests, steel needles and glass reusable syringes had only recently been replaced by disposable versions. In the biochemistry laboratory, they still used tedious hand chemical estimations; the Autoanalyser was yet to come. Our irritable consultant biochemist railed against the increasing demands for tests and checked each request on arrival. He would pour the specimen down the sink if he disapproved of a request, famously sending a message to 'tell Professor Illingworth that the urea and electrolytes were normal two days ago, and that should suffice'. This 'Canute' attitude was part of understandable concern for the hospital budget since times were still hard. But others in the labs had more political skill and encouraged the flow of requests for tests, pressurising the administrators for more funding.

With no nights off, social life was minimal. No handovers existed since we didn't do handovers. I didn't fall asleep while driving, because we didn't drive anywhere. Though on-call continuously, we might go out for a pint at 9 p.m. for an hour, since the nearby Byres Road pubs shut then at 10 o'clock. Before leaving, you checked with the newly

Handing over to the nurses' night shift using the Kardex, at the ward's central fireplace in 1966.

arrived night nursing staff at the ward fireplace (no longer using coal), that all was well, confirming with them that the resident in the unit on-call for emergencies would cover our brief escape. We learned later that the 'Permissive Society' was in full swing outside, but we hardly noticed. However, Christmas time was fun in the hospital, with the traditional morning visit to the wards by the entire medical staff plus families. On the day before Christmas, we had the Urology Department's party which featured their consultant's jazz ensemble and the tight outfit worn by their Infertility Clinic's glamorous secretary.

We were entitled to two weeks' holidays, but, like others, I didn't take them, because. even if I found a senior medical student to do my work, our cardiac and lung surgery was tough. They paid us quite a good salary of £360 per annum. A medium-sized car would cost about this sum. There was no charge for our room beside the wards, and there was a small spartan dining room for us residents where we were quickly served free food to get us back to the ward. One innovation was that our inventive Regional Physics Department had constructed an experimental 'bleep' system, one of the first of its kind. Using a wire loop around the outside of the hospital, a signal activated the little device held by the resident on call for emergencies. When called, you went to the nearest phone to find out from the switchboard who needed you.

We felt no grievance at the conditions, indeed quite the reverse. It had always been thus, and all the surgical staff above us had been residents earlier. Having been invited to be a member of a close-knit unit, there was pride in coping with this first important career challenge. All our generation looked back to their resident's year with affection, and when reminiscing at reunions, like war veterans, we wondered how we survived. After the residency, we emerged with considerable surgical experience, perhaps not of operative surgery, but of diagnosis and management.

My bankbook from 1966 showing the hand entries, in sterling, of my first salary cheques.

But complaints about young doctors' salaries and conditions of service were rising. We had the British Medical Association, then a feeble version of a trade union (using that name was anathema to them), but it was a metropolitan organisation, largely concerned with London hospital consultants' politics and private practice. The BMA, responding to any requests for action from junior staff, took the line that when they were young, they had survived these primitive conditions, and so could we, This lack of BMA interest in junior hospital staff (and general practitioners) led to revolts by both shortly after. A free-standing JHDA – Junior Hospital Doctors Association – emerged to push for better salaries, shorter hours, better contracts and better accommodation, which came in later when the BMA eventually took heed.*

ॐ

* Much later, the European Working Time Directive cut down the junior working hours even further and the new shift work meant the end of the unit system. The unit's teamwork was replaced by ever-changing complex rotas and there was concern about continuity of care and impaired surgical training.

'Receiving' day, i.e. admission of emergencies every fifth day meant a busy and hardly civilised 24 hours work. These days, wards or even hospitals close because of 'lack of beds', but we coped, and took in all cases without discussion. When a ward was full, as often happened, we crushed the beds closer, and the porters brought more beds up from the basement. When it became difficult for us to get between the beds, we started a new row down the middle of the ward beyond the fireplace. The post-receiving ward round next day threaded its way through, or even over, the crush of beds and in the next few days, we recovered, ready for the next influx four days later. We knew no other way.

The pattern of surgical emergencies was different. There were many head injuries from drunkenness and road traffic accidents (pre-seat belts), we had plenty breast abscesses, obstructed hernias and perforated duodenal ulcers. There was the steady arrival of alleged cases of appendicitis, many of which went unnecessarily to theatre, a decision usually supported later by a charitable pathologists' reports on the specimen. Intensive care was still to come, and resuscitation was not attempted, although an oxygen tent might be offered. During terminal deterioration, it was thought that the heart was the weakest organ, and we gave heart stimulants. An unexpected collapse of a patient in the ward in the early 1960s meant an attempt at external cardiac massage without ventilation. If that failed then the chest might be opened and direct heart massage carried out – in the ward. Some survived and the doctors responsible were local heroes.

Our porters had an important role. All emergency patients arrived at the front door and the porters did the triage, sending them to Casualty or the medical or surgical receiving unit of the day. The porters had their own typology – including the intriguing 'condition of lower body, Doc' – as they would announce on the telephone to me on our surgical receiving day. These conditions below the umbilicus were indeed for us, most of the time, and above this level, the heart and lung problems were for the physicians.

The hospital porters had, besides their expert triage, a sensitive role in collecting the 'Ash Cash', as we called it. After a death, if the relatives chose the cremation option, the head porter met the family and arranged for us junior staff to sign the documents. He returned the papers to the relatives and on our behalf collected the fee which was two old-fashioned guineas, i.e. two pounds and two shillings. The head porter would then find you, and as he proffered the money, the two pound notes were visible, but his thumb anchored the two shillings. It was a reasonable commission and relieved us of the burden of collecting money from a grieving family.

But our Western Infirmary head porter once overstepped himself. At coffee time one day, the news spread around the hospital that our man was wearing a Glasgow Academical tie, one restricted to the former pupils of the local private school attended by many of the consultants. Hurried consultations about the matter in the corridors followed. They nominated a spokesman to investigate, and he reported that all was well; the porter had bought the tie at a jumble sale – for sixpence. After a whip-round, to which even the meanest of the consultants contributed, they re-purchased the tie (with the usual 10% premium) and saved the honour of the school.

Next door to our surgical wards was the Ear Nose and Throat Department. Twice in the week, there was a pathetic line of children in dressing gowns and bathing caps sitting silently in line waiting for the morning of mass tonsil and adenoid removal. 'Sniff the perfume' – i.e. chloroform on a mask – was still the method for this short operation. One of the great achievements of evidence-based medicine later was dispelling the belief that tonsils and adenoids needed regular removal. Looking back, it was an almost mediaeval barbaric ritual, but it had support from public opinion. These lymphoid organs served a purpose and there is evidence that the operation in the long-term caused some damage to the defence mechanisms. The ENT department also had a hearing aid clinic run by the necessarily-loud and formidable Miss Fortune. One of the ENT consultants had a Rolls-Royce, bought from the proceeds of removing middle-class tonsils in private practice. Visiting American surgeons enjoyed being photographed beside this stately car.

In the last week of my surgical resident job, we had the death of a young man. He had a chronic gastric ulcer and was sent for surgery to our unit from a hospital near Glasgow because his physician there, who had treated him for years, had no confidence in his local surgical colleagues. At operation, a large, long-standing stomach ulcer was found, not only stuck to the liver, but the base of the ulcer was liver substance. It was an unusual situation and our chief felt that, as well as removing part of the stomach he had to shave off the diseased liver tissue. After a few days, the young man started to deteriorate and eventually died. A post-mortem showed that bile had leaked from the raw liver surface into the abdomen. This happened over my last weekend in the surgical unit, and, deeply involved in the events, I was shaken. I had always thought of surgery as a career, but now had doubts. Fortunately, I was never involved in a equally tragic case.

My six-month medical residency followed at Stobhill Hospital and it was a doddle in comparison, with two nights off out of three and proper accommodation. Our chief, Stanley Alstead, was a kindly man and the Unit's leisurely ward rounds were a change of pace. Medical treatment was largely expectant and in dealing with a heart attack or stroke, we watched and observed; without scans or any interventions. A patient, with atrial fibrillation, lost an arm when a clot from the heart lodged high in the main artery, since no surgical intervention was then available. There was occasional drama when treating diabetic coma and in one other area the mood was changing. Our helpful Stobhill biochemist, who gave a service in the north of the City, was on the alert for acute renal failure and would advise on fluid and calorie intake. In a few suitable cases, he had even arranged for the first Glasgow patients to go to Leeds for treatment by Britain's first artificial kidney.

After that, like most would-be surgeons in Glasgow, I took time out in a basic science department, preparing for the difficult first part of the surgical examination, and doing some research. But the university term did not start until October, two months later. Apart from playing some golf again, there was a way to use these months well; I did some general practice locums in the north of Scotland and Northern Ireland.

CHAPTER 9:

General Practice
Locums

Lossiemouth ... Malt whisky ... Harris ... Northern Ireland
Kinloch Rannoch ... Prescribing skills ... House calls

'THERE'S SOMETHING we haven't told you,' explained the Lossiemouth doctor, about to take his holiday. I had arrived at this small Moray Firth fishing and holiday town.

Now qualified in medicine, during the summer gap I could do general practice locums, i.e. serve as relief during the doctor's holidays. My father, after retirement as a minister, had also used this method to see the world, and, being on the Church's Colonial and Continental Committee, he got his pick of attractive short locums and mother joined him. They helped out in Church of Scotland churches in many parts of the world including Gibraltar, Paris, and Jerusalem. Father was doing the Rome locum and staying in the commodious Church of Scotland manse in Rome when Pope John Paul I was enthroned on August 1978. The manse was full, with added extra beds for the influx of protestant clerics, and after the elaborate ceremony, they all went away. But the new Pope died shortly afterwards and they all came back for the traditionally prompt funeral. Father had earlier also done an imaginative swap with an American Presbyterian minister in Asheville, North Carolina. Though this was not a success at our Glasgow end, the American congregation was glad to have our genial father for a while.

When general practitioners needed a locum, they advertised in the medical magazines. There was plenty of choice for me, usually offering £50 a week, and I organised a varied itinerary for the summer, with some golf in between. It was still assumed (wrongly) that the medical school education prepared you to cope with general practice immediately after qualification. This meant a steep learning curve, and you quickly learned some lessons. An early home visit was to a boy with measles, the first (and last) case I'd seen, and the mother had helpfully diagnosed it, there being other cases around.

'Would you like to wash your hands?' she asked before I left.

While I did so, I thought it best to clean the thermometer as a signal of further cleanliness and I put it under the hot tap. The liberated liquid mercury nestled briefly in the basin and then disappeared down the sink. I didn't confess; liquid mercury is not toxic.

'There's something we haven't told you,' explained the Lossiemouth doctor.

'We have left our dog … do you mind?'

I certainly did not mind.

'It's a blind dog' he added. Still no problem.

Lossiemouth (Moray) Golf Club clubhouse with the doctor's house behind.

The Lossiemouth doctor was a keen golfer and had moved house over the years, getting ever nearer to the championship course. He finally purchased the impressive stone house nearest to the first tee with its fine view of the bay and the marvellous sunsets. I would do his locum several times thereafter, and he and I became friends. He was a reader of the drafts of my books later and I had the same role when he was writing his three books.*

It was a time when GPs still worked from home and did house calls, even in the towns. The Lossie morning surgery was from 9 to 10 a.m., followed by house calls in the morning and afternoon, followed by the evening surgery consultation from 5 – 6 p.m. At the end of my first evening session, the old dog pushed his way through the surgery door on the hour and indicated that I was to follow. Off we went. The dog moved decisively to the first tee and, making sure I was following, went down the first and then the second holes. But it was not to be a full walk-round. He cut across to the 17th tee then back up the noble 18th hole, and we were home. Clearly, the good Dr McConachie's evening routine after the surgery hour was to do four holes and then back for dinner.

He had an interesting practice which included the Royal Air Force base and the well-known Gordonstoun School where he had rather nervously given the Prince of Wales his immunising injections. For his practice, Dr McConachie had rules. He made it known that his patients had to phone for a house call before 11 a.m., and as the locum, I was not to deviate from this.

One call came in at 3.00 p.m.

'I'll be round tomorrow,' I said firmly.

It turned out that the patient was the wife of the RAF base commander and when I visited the next day I found she had a patch of pneumonia at the left lung base. When Dr McConachie got back, I confessed about this embarrassing delay.

'Well done,' he said.

---

* John McConachie's books included the Lossiemouth Golf Club history, the story of the Northern Open Championship and the fate of the Aberdeen student soldiers in WW1.

But there were occasional urgent evening and night calls which did need a visit. One came from Elgin three miles away at an unhelpful time on the night of a big televised European football match. I now had a second-hand MGB sports car and I made good time on the fast, famously-straight road between the towns. The child was unwell but the diagnosis was easy since a look in his mouth showed pus coming from both tonsils. There was penicillin available in the doctor's bag and I was back for the start of the match.

Dr McConachie taught me about single malt whiskies. Elgin nearby was, as now, the centre of the Speyside malt whisky world. In the Lowlands, we knew only about the well-known brands like The Famous Grouse and Johnnie Walker. We were not interested that these were blends, mixing expensive single malts from the North with cheaper factory-produced Lowland grain whisky. Knowledge would spread later about the single malt whiskies and their mystique, and Dr McConachie's tuition gave me a flying start. The main local malt whiskies vied with each other for supremacy and the top two were, and continued to be, The Glenlivet and Macallan, and although the Lowlands knew of Glenlivet, no-one talked of Macallan. Dr McConachie favoured Macallan, as did the Lossiemouth golf club, who bought a barrel each year as their club whisky, leaving it for ten years to mature. Macallan whisky soon became a cult, fetching remarkable prices at auction.

Years later, visiting Pittsburgh, a surgeon took me out for an Italian meal. He seemed to have a close relationship with the waitress, a Sophia Loren look-alike, and after they exchanged private greetings and nudges, he introduced me by saying

This is my friend from Scotland. He will be drinking whisky, of course.'

She replied

'I'm afraid we have only Macallan and The Glenlivet.'

I was impressed, and when she went off, I remarked that she seemed to be a talented lady.

'She sure is,' he said, with a faraway look in his eye.

Another locum took me to the south end of the Isle of Harris for a week. The doctor's house was at the edge of Northton, a ribbon of crofts on a dead-end track towards the Toe Head wilderness and bird sanctuary beyond. He was into wildlife photography and he showed me the new lengthy, Japanese telephoto lens which had just come onto the market, and which had revolutionised distant study. Our local telephonist lived in the village and since she dealt with the requests for house calls, and then saw you passing on your visits, she always knew where you were. The local villagers were all strict Free Church members and on Sundays, as I drove past their houses, they, dressed in black, watched me closely.

A curious thing that I and other travellers noted when in these parts of the Islands was that their house clocks were always ahead of real time, even leaping half an hour ahead. I used this strategy later on my watch as an antidote to being late; it gets you there on time.

ॐ

That summer, I did another holiday locum in Northern Ireland, in the large county town of Lurgan. Before The Troubles, we in the rest of Britain knew nothing of the local tensions, even naïvely assuming that this part of Britain was entirely Protestant. So, it was a surprise to find I was working in a Catholic practice and indeed the senior partner was well-known in the republican movement. My education improved further when I found that their Catholic patients lived in an enclave at one end of the main street, close to the surgery. On arrival, I noticed a drumming noise in the evenings and they told me it was part of the rehearsal for the Orange Lodge March at the weekend. The event proved rather scary for us in the Catholic enclave, as the march took a deliberate and provocative loop away from the main street into our streets. I was learning fast. Even in the West of Scotland, within sight of Ireland, we did not understand what was going on; years later we would.

One afternoon there was a call about a possible heart attack and I made my way on foot to a cul-de-sac within our Catholic area. Concerned family members and others had gathered inside and outside the house. Inside, I made my way up past those on the stairs to find more gathered in the small bedroom, grouped round a very ill-looking lady sitting in a chair. She had had heart attacks in the past and now had more chest pain. I found she had a frighteningly slow pulse and hence the diagnosis was of heart block, perhaps secondary to a new myocardial infarction. I had a diagnosis and the management was clear.

'Off to the hospital,' I said.

The solemn group in the room conferred, and shook their heads. Realising I was a stranger, one of the family then explained to me that the Protestants ran the hospital and hence it was best that I treated her at home.

Reflecting on the challenge, I knew that the doctor's black bag, passed on to me, was deficient; indeed it held only a prescription pad. I had only a hazy recollection of how to treat acute heart block, if indeed there was any. Those gathered in the room expected some action and noted my hesitation.

But there was now a murmur from those lining the stairs. One of the other doctors in the practice, passing by, saw the gathering and decided to investigate. I was glad to see him, as were the others in the room. I explained the diagnosis to him and the impasse following the refusal to go to hospital. At this point he delved into his bag, brought out a syringe and an ampule, and rather theatrically injected the lady's arm. Shortly afterward she professed to be feeling better and looked better. We left down the crowded stairs, their much-loved practitioner getting most of the pats on the back.

As we walked back I asked what he had injected.

'Not sure,' he said, 'might have been water. There wasn't anything we could do.'

'My boy,' he added, 'always do something.'

In this Catholic practice I was necessarily involved in obstetrics and home deliveries, and one night there was a call to a distant house in the Irish countryside.

'Straight on, you can't miss it, there will be a swinging light' were the brief directions, and I found my way. It was baby number ten for mother, and the midwife, who had also arrived, took charge. Out the boy popped.

But I got some credit; the family had run out of baby names.

'What's yours, doc?'

I sometimes wonder what happened to young David Hamilton Murphy.

ॐ

Back in Glasgow and settling into research, as described later, over the winter I also did regular weekend locums at Kinloch Rannoch, on Loch Rannoch in the Highlands, about an hour's drive north of Glasgow. The doctor's lovely house was to the west of the village perched on a cliff overlooking the Loch and he was a fisherman and fished the loch. On the water, he was out of touch, but if needed, his wife would hang a blanket on the washing line. After noting this signal with his binoculars, he would row for the shore.

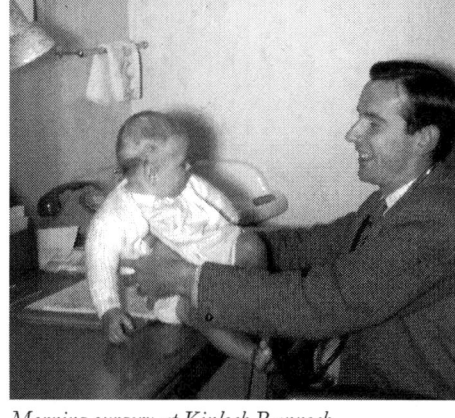

He held the usual morning surgery and his home visits followed, going

Morning surgery at Kinloch Rannoch

clockwise around the loch one day, then going anti-clockwise next day. Dr Byrne's routine included many social calls on disabled or isolated persons, checking that all was well, and delivering any medicines. These country practices were often run as 'dispensing practices' if chemists' shops were some way away. For this, they held a range of medications in the surgery, not only handing out pills, but making up liquid mixtures from impressive, decorated stock jars with taps. There might be four or five large containers, elegantly engraved with Latin names starting with '*Mist*' (for mixture) plus the name. One was *Mist Kaolin et Morph* – chalk and opium – a cure-all for most gut troubles, including winter norovirus, and there was *Mist Expect* for chestiness. A tilted drip tray ran beneath the row of taps, and any spilled fluid drained off to one side and into a container. In the little world of dispensing practice, their black humour tells of a perceptive GP who knew the art of prescribing (which differs from the science of pharmacology) and kept this drip tray overflow for his use. Labelling it *Mist Omnia*, it was celebrated as a sovereign remedy among his patients.

My travels in the world of primary care revealed more of the art of prescribing. I encountered several patients getting monthly Vitamin B12 injections, the treatment for the rare blood disease of pernicious anaemia. Preparing to give their injection, and looking up their records, there was no mention of pernicious anaemia. I was tempted to stop the mysterious treatment, but a perceptive GP warned me that this was a well-known strategy when dealing with the 'difficult', 'never-well' patients who haunt their surgeries. After giving a vague diagnosis of anaemia, the doctor would start the monthly injections, whereupon requests for appointments on other matters ceased. B12 injections also give a mild general boost; it also makes racehorses run faster.

I was always opposed to doing private practice, and I only ever had one private patient – at Kinloch Rannoch. In my private cases, I can claim 100% success and satisfaction; I quit while I was winning.

The patient was a London financier and owner of a sporting estate nearby. He came in to the evening surgery and wondered if I could help with his deafness in one ear which was bothering him while out shooting on the moor. He explained he did not normally use the NHS, but patronisingly encouraged me to do my best. Even looking at the ear from the outside, there was wax filling it to the entrance. I scooped out much and syringed out the rest. Delighted, and rejoicing in the unexpectedly prompt return of hearing, he asked about my fee. I first thought of charging 10 shillings, but had the presence of mind to recall his familiarity with Harley Street practice. I charged 10 shillings and sixpence, half a guinea, and he paid cash.

Over the hill from Kinloch Rannoch, Dr Walter Yellowlees worked in Aberfeldy in the famous practice run by Jack Swanson, a prominent British Medical Association politician. Yellowlees, an early enthusiast for a healthy diet and lifestyle, also wrote his book *Doctor in the Wilderness* and it valuably recorded much about country practice now forgotten. At Aberfeldy, their routine for house calls was similar to the Kinloch Rannoch pattern, going up-river (the Tay) on Tuesdays, Thursdays and Saturdays and down-river on the others. If urgent calls came in, the doctor's wife-assistant would phone a post office on his likely route and they would alert him by placing a large envelope in the window. Yellowlees' book shows that in 1950, they did 14,000 home visits, shared between the three partners. This fell to 4,000 by 1980 and has probably now reached close to zero. As home visits declined throughout the country, it had another effect. To host the patients now attending the surgery, they needed larger rooms. Eventually, health centres followed, with receptionists taking over the work of the doctor's wife.

Some things have been lost with the decline in house calls, regretted even by the doctors who bowed to *force majeure* and welcomed the change to health centre consultations. On a home visit, the illness is seen in its social setting and the doctor can also make many informal observations on the family and the home circumstances. This background can assist later during any further clinical or administrative contacts with the family. For the doctors, getting out and about was also therapeutic. A daily circuit of Loch Rannoch, in all its moods, can lift the soul.

There was also time for golf during these summers and I could create a circuit, reminiscent of The Tour, since in summer you could go agreeably from one big amateur holiday tournament to another. These lasted a week, starting with practice days, qualifying rounds (scratch and handicap) with knockout in the days to follow. After Montrose, in the North you had the choice of Nairn, Tain and Dornoch. If you didn't make it to the weekend, as they say in Tour circles, then there were Saturday or Sunday tournaments nearby, often of 36 holes. Although I had little success, it toughened you up, and on return, your handicap dropped gratifyingly at your home club.

On the golf circuit in the North, one highlight was playing at Dornoch, enlivened by staying in the astonishing Carbisdale Castle youth hostel, the last castle built in Scotland. The Dowager Duchess of Sutherland erected it in 1917 after she fell out with her Sutherland relatives across the river to the North, and she put a clock face only on three sides of the impressive tower so that, without a north-facing clock, she did not give them the time of day. It was a haven for King Haakon VII of Norway during the Nazi occupation, and then a youth hostel from 1945 to 2016.

Taking my golf seriously, coming off the course, one evening, I resolved to study the effect of alcohol on golf. The club was Nairn and outside the clubhouse, there are was, and is, a fine putting green. I went round in level 2s then partook of a pint. So it went on and my scores seemed to improve, but well into the experiment, it had to be terminated. As dusk fell, I lost my ball. A path with round white stones surrounded the putting green.

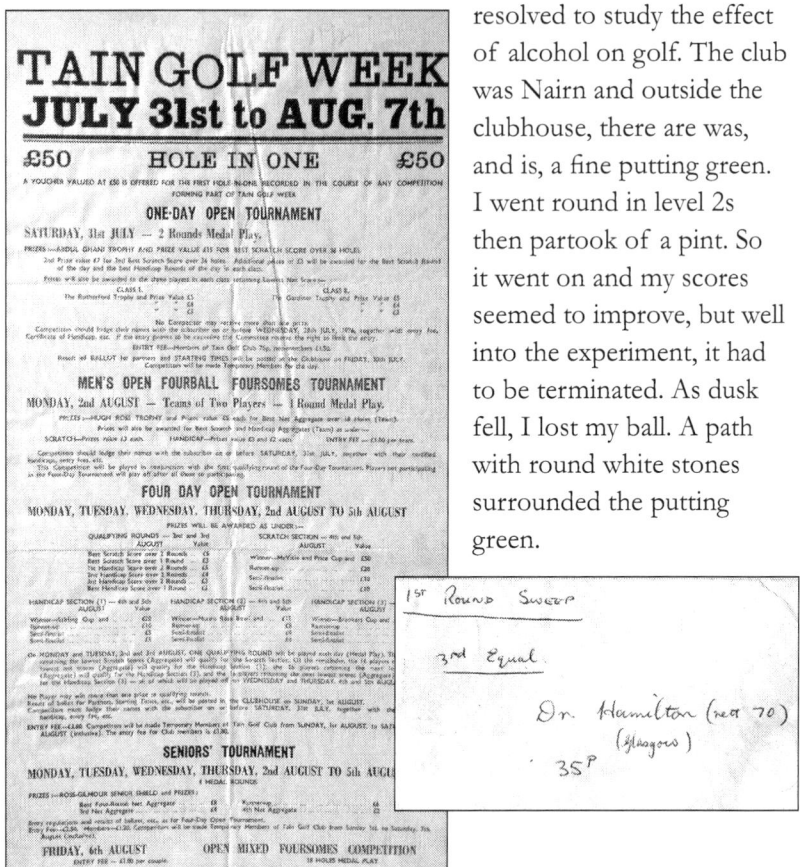

In October, I started work on my PhD degree in the laboratories of the Physiology Department of the University of Glasgow.

CHAPTER 10:

PhD Student

Early lesson ... Bad data ... Vivisection ... Pathology training
Roddy MacSween ... Cram class ... Sir Charles Illingworth
An old problem ... Edinburgh fellowship

'YOUR TECHNIQUE is not good.' I had to agree with him, since. I was no chemist. Doing long chemical manipulations does not fit well with the surgical personality.

It was common then in Glasgow for those intending a career in surgery to spend time in the University's Anatomy or Physiology Departments, or less commonly in Pathology. This strategy offered time to study for the difficult first part of the surgical fellowship qualification offered by the Royal Colleges. In this way, these departments gained young staff to help with their teaching and research. I would spend the next three years working on a PhD degree split between the Physiology Department and NHS work in the Pathology Department in the adjoining Western Infirmary.

My research was based in John Gillespie's group in the Physiology Department. I had done research under him as an honours student and was grateful to him for an early lesson in the scientific method, perhaps the most important one of all. There are mysterious cells in the gut lining – the enterochromaffin, granule-containing cells – and he wondered if the nerves to the gut controlled the cells. I stimulated the nerves to gut tissue in an organ bath for a few hours, and after fixing and staining the tissue, I counted the number of cells still containing the granules and compared it to unstimulated tissue. Triumphantly, I reported that. after stimulation, the granules were gone from half the cells. Gillespie asked if I knew which tissue, stimulated or control, I was looking at when I did the counts, and I did know. His technician then masked the slides and when I did the count blind, to my chagrin, nerve stimulation showed no effect. Your brain is ready to let you down.

My project involved measuring nor-adrenaline (the hormone produced from the adrenal gland) in the cat spleen and tracing the location of hormone added from outside. It can be measured after treatment with chemicals which changes it to give bright blue fluorescence in UV light. First, as a baseline, I needed to measure the normal amounts in the spleen. My supervisor was a young lecturer working under Gillespie who I did not like and he had been using the fluorescence method for a while. But my measurements of normal spleen nor-adrenaline showed mysterious and serious variation, and he suggested that my technique was not good. I readily agreed with him.

The problem persisted. But light began to dawn after simple detective work. Mixing the chemicals alone with no tissue extract – the controls – instead of having no fluorescence could also show readings in the fluorescence detector. In despair, at last I found that putting distilled water alone into the special quartz measuring tubes often gave a reading. Something fluorescent was coming off these cuvettes. Looking at the technical manual describing the detailed operation of our machine, it turned out that these little cuvettes, after use, required a wash in acid and then a rinse in distilled water. Our otherwise helpful lab technical staff had not been told, or forgot about this step, and instead washed the tubes in the usual way with soapy water and then dried them. Detergent can give fluorescence. At times I was only measuring Tween.

Although this was a triumphant epiphany, I needed to be cautious since others in the lab might be affected, including my rather shifty supervisor who used the same method and same tubes. I managed a quick look at his lab results book and it showed the same irregular readings, and worse still, during this time, he somehow published his results.

When I gave out the bad news about the fluorescing cuvettes, I expected a high-minded response. But I was taken aback that, despite the sanctity of science, nothing more was said. Life just went on. But, with clean tubes, overnight my problem had gone and after this waste of time, nice results came through. Even so, I soon moved, with relief, onto a better non-chemical phase, looking directly at tracing added nor-adrenaline in tissue sections with fluorescence micrsocopy.

For animal experiments, each University department ran its own animal house, regularly visited by the Home Office inspector, a fierce ex-military man, who could call in unexpectedly. We regarded him as a nuisance and telephoned news of his arrival around the campus to warn the others. But, looking back, his oversight was important to the standing of experimental science, since we were beng watched by the antivivisectionists, and they were gaining parliamentary support. Militant groups also attacked university animal houses and any incident would have weakened the case for animal experiments. The zealous inspector was on our side.

Combined with this research, I did routine work in the Pathology Department of the Western Infirmary close to the University. The pattern of work involved reporting on the surgically-removed specimens and doing the post–mortems which were helpful if there had been difficulty with the diagnosis. Later, as years passed, and particularly when the new radiological techniques became successful, fewer surprises emerged at autopsy. In the 1950s, almost half those dying in hospital were examined by post-mortems, but the number of these examinations then dwindled. In America, hospitals formerly needed a high percentage of autopsies after death for their accreditation, but this regulation lapsed.

On my first day in the Department, I was made welcome by a young pathologist. After greeting me and before moving on, he briskly added 'Heard you play golf. See you at Leverndale tomorrow after the hospital meeting.' The pathologist was Roddy MacSween, later Sir Roderick. Someone overhearing our conversation then explained to me what he meant, and that the hospital golfers drove over to the car park of this psychiatric hospital on the south side of the river. Linking up, we took a smaller number of cars down to the Glasgow Gailes golf course, a links course playable throughout the year.

Roddy enjoyed his work and his life, and made research look easy. When he joined the Department, he and another had the choice of the two expanding specialties – liver disease or thymus/immunology – and Roddy got liver. It was difficult work then based on the end-stage findings at post-mortem, but when liver biopsies became routine soon after, interest in liver pathology blossomed and Roddy then joined an international group who met from time to time in agreeable places, bringing their slides and sharing interesting cases. Taking the initiative within the group, he organised and edited a multiple-author book on liver pathology which became the standard work, and he later held high office in the Royal Colleges.

In our golfing group and the hospital golf club, he organised us and made sure we entered for the competitions and he pioneered the use of a metal-headed driver. We got to know each other well. Roddie was our best man when Jean and I married later. Roddie and Marjorie owned a cottage at Southend in Argyll and there they developed a friendship with Angus MacVicar, the author, and his talents as a storyteller are found in his memoirs of life and golf in Southend.[*]

---

[*] In Angus MacVicar's huge output of books golf is prominent in his *Golf in My Gallowses* (1983). His son Jock became a distinguished sports journalist.

The Pathology Department was in good hands of Prof John Anderson and the routine was agreeable. The three-month rota involved one month dealing with the surgical specimens, then one month on post-mortems and then one month of research, which I spent in the Physiology Department. Reporting the surgical specimens was enjoyable and these tissues arrived throughout the day often already in formalin. At 4 p.m. we examined the tissues further, sending samples for fixation and staining. The prepared slides arrived through the hatch from the preparation room into our small square room with its benches and microscopes around three sides. The compact seating arrangements assisted discussion of the slides without having to move. Slowly we juniors became confident with making a diagnosis and we were helped by the seniors in the more difficult cases. A stressful service offered during this month was to report on frozen sections required during breast surgery and after removal, the lump passed to us for immediate diagnosis. If cancer was present, further breast tissue had to be removed. The senior pathologists took on this responsibility, and I don't remember any mistakes made. We gathered at a weekly 'projection' meeting for discussion of difficult or interesting cases.

At this time, four of us set up a little 'cram' course preparing candidates to sit the first part of the surgical fellowship exam. One of us taught anatomy, one did physiology and I did pathology. We usually enrolled about six or eight would-be surgeons, usually from overseas, some of whom, having failed the tough exam already, or even twice, and were understandably concerned for the future, being limited to three attempts. Starting a new course one autumn, we arrived for our first session in our rented room in the local public hall and saw a mass of turbaned young men queuing outside the hall. We thought our fame had spread; instead, a pop concert by the 'Great Sikhs' had brought in the crowd.

We got most of our candidates through. One young man later became a highly regarded surgeon in the West of Scotland and much later, when I attended his retiral dinner, he made a point of publicly thanking us for this help at this time of crisis. Another success was with a Royal Air Force trainee surgeon coming up to his third and final attempt. We got him through and when we retired to a Byres Road pub after the results came through, he somehow managed, using the pub's coin box telephone, to phone his wife in the RAF base in the middle of the Indian Ocean.

ॐ

Over in the hospital's ward block, our talented head of the Department of Surgery, Sir Charles Illingworth had now retired. During his tenure, he built up an academic department where none existed before, and, putting Glasgow surgery on the map, he sent out a stream of surgeons to head academic departments in Scotland, England and Wales.

But he was still making his presence felt in retirement. He noted the new interest in postgraduate training and established his *West of Scotland Postgraduate* magazine and I soon got a taste of his tough management methods. For any new scheme, research or administrative, he would summon a group of those who might be interested to contribute. On this occasion he included me because of my experience as a student editor. With us gathered round the table he then asked each of us what we could contribute to his new magazine. Because of his quiet authority and fame, all wished to impress him, and all enthusiastically offered articles.

At the end of the meeting, Illingworth carefully agreed on a date for the next meeting. Soon after came an unwelcome reminder from him about what you had agreed to do, adding that he hoped to have the article before the next meeting, which was already fixed. You alone suggested the idea and were stuck with the obligation. At the next meeting, there were fewer people, but he had allowed for wastage, and he steadily dumped those who could not deliver. Doubtless, he used this method in the past to identify and foster surgical talent. I lasted for a couple of cycles.[*]

But after a bright start, the Health Board withdrew funding for Illingworth's magazine. He famously used it to criticise the Glasgow 'Heathrow academics' allegedly neglecting their departments by instead seeking preferment in the London-centric medical establishment.

* See David Hamilton 'Is the M.D. out of date? *West of Scotland Medical Postgraduate* 1966.

But during this time in pathology, I noticed regular bouts of low mood and inability to function properly, recalling the similar slump I endured in my first year. Soon I found the pattern. It was towards the end of each of the research periods, every three months, that the gloom descended, and I realised it was clinical depression, of the reactive type. Relief came immediately when starting on the next month's daily routine work. After its unfailing appearance in these cycles, the cure was clear. I needed to be busy. Significant involvement in full-time research, though attractive, and which suited others, was not for me. Having insight into my problem, I could avoid it and was never troubled again, except for one period later, when I was trapped. Though people said kind things about my research, the surgical life offered problem-solving during a busy week plus the pleasure and challenge of the technical manipulations of surgery. I now planned to get back to the wards when I finished the PhD.

❧

Nearing the end of the three years, having passed the first part of the surgical fellowship exam, a once-and-for-all opportunity opened up to sit the second, final, surgical part for the fellowship of the Edinburgh College of Surgeons. At that time Edinburgh allowed you to take the exam three years after qualification, irrespective of your experience during these years. The regulations would change, and even though I had done no surgery, I could enter under the old regulations. It was a no-lose situation, and I made no special preparations, relying only my precious precis notes on surgery for the final student exams.

On the day, being good on surgical theory, my written papers in Edinburgh posed no problem. The only fear was the clinical and oral exam when my woeful lack of practical knowledge might be revealed. My clinical case was of breast cancer and was easily dealt with, and my hope for a surgery-lite fellowship looked good. Reaching the last hurdle, the oral examination by two examiners, it started well, but when the second surgeon took over halfway, my heart sank. He was a tweedy Edinburgh type, and he asked me about fractures at the ankle joint. For our student final examination in surgery, orthopaedics was excluded and hence my precis notes on this specialty were deficient. From student anatomy days, I knew there were two bones at the ankle joint, namely the tibia and fibula, but not having used this information since, I was hazy on which was which. I needed to decide quickly, having a 50/50 chance of success, and having taken this plunge, set off to bluster and perseverate. I had chosen wrongly. But the examiner was mostly looking out of the window, understandably bored after a good lunch, and perhaps wishing to be elsewhere. Only after a while, did he start to listen more closely to my bluster which had a strange pattern – my swop of the tibia for the fibula. He was working out what was going on when mercifully the bell rang.

Saved by the bell, I escaped and I was through. I now possessed the useful, indeed essential, FRCS (Edinburgh) qualification, but I never held that honour in great regard thereafter. Many years later, I obtained the equivalent FRCS (Glasgow) qualification, with even less difficulty. The then-president obtained a list of Glasgow consultant surgeons lacking the Glasgow diploma and invited us down individually to the College. Over a cup of tea, he told me that the College would be glad to have me on board, and passed over a standing order for me to sign. I was now burdened with two subscriptions. Others took on even greater outgoings, since ambitious surgical trainees at the time might also add a third fellowship from the London College. I felt that one was enough, and I managed to get rid of the Edinburgh surgical qualification, as explained later.

I returned to the Western Infirmary's basic surgical training armed with an unmerited Edinburgh fellowship and they made me welcome in the wards. Glad to be back, I started a year of surgical training. Although there were openings in Glasgow, I wished to see more of the world of medicine and went off to London for both surgical training and surgical research.

CHAPTER 11:

London

Restaurants … Emigres … Hampstead Golf Club
Hospital life … Private practice

I OBTAINED SURGICAL work in London and then, landing on my feet, got a research grant to work there on organ transplantation with Sir Peter Medawar, the Nobel Prize winner.

Arriving in London clutching a copy of the *Good Food Guide* presented to me by my ever-thoughtful sister, I settled at the Lambeth Hospital, one of the St Thomas' group, south of the river. Looking at the map of the restaurants, there was only one entry nearby, since the sophisticated London foodies at the time took the view that nothing much happened south of the Thames. This isolated restaurant was Crispin's, well-thought-of by the *Guide*, and I gave it my immediate patronage. Our Scottish habit was to eat at five o'clock, and, not wanting the label of a country boy, I went round at 5.30. After sitting for a while, a puzzled cook looked out from the kitchen and asked if he could help. I said I would like to order, and he nobly provided a menu, and, greatly daring, I ordered an exotic item, coq au vin. By this time, I felt that heather was perhaps growing out of my ears. As I was leaving, the first diners appeared.

In London, our Glasgow University Union emigres were there

in numbers. Donald Dewar and John Smith were newly-elected MPs and among other Glasgow students, there was Donald's sister-in-law Mamie, a radiologist, and Pat Gordon, a QM Union Board member, working at the King's Fund. David Miller, a Liberal Club activist, was into London publishing. We caught up regularly, including use of the cosy *salon privé* at Crispin's, though later in the evening. Much later, after retirement, Jimmie (Lord) Gordon organised a regular London dinner for us 'Jubilados', i.e. those of our era who were around the Union and had survived beyond the age of 70.

I had hardly arrived at the hospital when a not-expected phone call came from Sir James Howie. Howie had been the professor of bacteriology at the Western Infirmary in Glasgow and was a family friend from Speyside holiday days, and he now headed the Public Health Laboratory Service at Colindale in the north of London. He was a keen and competitive golfer. Even on holiday, he had supposedly claimed the first hole from a minister of religion who left his clubs on the tee while driving off, a technical infraction of the small-print of the Rules.

Howie told me to appear at Hampstead Golf Club on the next Saturday and join him for lunch at the long table there. This small nine-hole club was, and is, a very private one, although neither wealthy nor snooty. Celebrated as Prime Minister Harold Wilson's club, he played there with his general practitioner friend and security guards. Howie told me that although the members usually sat down in order of arrival, I was to have lunch beside 'The Admiral' and take an interest in the man's naval career. After lunch, Howie took me aside and told me I would shortly be a member of the club, proposed by himself and with The Admiral as my seconder. Howie phoned two weeks later and said that, although things had gone slowly, I was in. He blamed the Club's sluggish secretary.

We fixed our first game for the following Saturday, and it was a gloomy, ice-cold November day with added overnight snow. London winters are unpleasant – when the Romans arrived, they moved on. My phone rang at 8.00 am and it was Howie, just making sure that I intended to play that day, and on arrival, I found him tut-tutting that the clubhouse was shut with no lights showing. Since the ice and snow did not cover the entire course, we went out into the gloom and on the treacherous surface had a close game in the ancient Scottish winter match-play tradition. As we came up the ninth and last hole, I was seriously cold and my hands were refusing to answer my brain. To my pleasure, I saw there was now a light on in the clubhouse, and we would get a shower and perhaps some food. Our game finished all square in front of the clubhouse. To my astonishment, Howie did not advance for the customary handshake but headed off to the first tee again, intent on a full 18 holes, and off we went again. When we returned to the clubhouse, the lights were off.

In the London surgical world, I did not like what I found. It was as bad as we thought in Scotland, and I shared A J Cronin's verdict in his novels, notably *Hatter's Castle,* which deplored the decadence of London commercial medicine. Our Scottish tradition and assumptions arose from our salaried service, the absence of private practice and our links with universities. For surgeons in training, London meant access to money, not an opportunity for scholarship. And more than money was on offer. London, being the capital, offered prestige and patronage from royal, aristocratic and political contacts. Getting involved in research was unattractive and unremunerated, and the bright London students, beguiled and diverted, did not use their brightness. In the wider world of science, London had impressive credentials in biology, chemistry, physics and much else; in clinical research, the capital failed to pull its weight. The academic surgical departments were small and unimpressive, headed as the cynics said by 'someone to teach the students after failing in private practice.'

These small London medical schools had all-male staff and students and selection might be based on non-academic priorities such as the-rugby-team-needs-a-prop-forward. As late as 1989, when one of the London medical schools started admitting women, the consultant surgeon honorary president of the Rugby Club accused the Dean of 'destroying the medical school.' The Dean continued the policy and later wryly remarked that after the girls came in, the rugby team still thrived, and his medical school's women's hockey team was all-conquering. The school's orchestra and choir were also much improved, a fact, he observed, which was perhaps unnoticed by the rugby players.

London hospital work had a strange pattern. In the big London hospitals, the consultants were not expected to be called in at night. To relieve them from doing this emergency work, the hospital's most senior trainee lived in the hospital and did the work. In return for this enslavement, they promised the trainee, getting old by this time, the next consultant job. Another difference was that London consultants had puzzling appointments to several hospitals, working for a day or two each week at two or even three hospitals. The reason for the multiple appointments was that it increased the consultant's contacts with general practitioners and hence widened the net for gaining private patients. These hybrid appointments meant they seldom followed up their NHS cases post-operatively leaving it to the local trainees, who also did the emergency work.

Shortly after my arrival, my consultant phoned me one night, saying he'd seen a patient outside and was sending her in. His diagnosis was appendicitis, but I was to 'make up your own mind'. Examining the patient, I didn't think there was a problem but, since he thought so, and it was best not to disagree, I started to take the girl to theatre. Fortunately, a nurse took me aside, knowing I was new. She said that this was obviously a private patient, and what the consultant meant was I was to welcome the patient on his behalf. The consultant would operate and charge the patient. Later in the evening, the patient went to theatre, and this did not involve me, which seemed odd. I hung about. Soon after, I met the consultant emerging from the theatre with a stranger.

'How nice,' the consultant trilled, 'to have her family doctor involved in her operation.'

The stranger was the general practitioner who had referred the patient to the consultant, and the consultant brought him in as an assistant, doubtless a nervous one, at the private operation and he would get the assistant's fee. This was 'fee-splitting', or near it, a cynical reward to the GP for referring the private patient, and this would encourage future referrals. Fee splitting was, and is, unethical.

The removed appendix was not diseased, I heard.

There was more. I assisted this consultant when doing some private cases outside, and one day he took me to a private clinic in Harley Street to assist him operating on a patient with a breast lump. The private clinic's rooms were elegant enough, as was the décor of the anaesthetic room, but once inside the theatre, it was primitive, with wooden rafters visible above.

We started. The miserable ambience was heightened when, after he started removal of the entire breast, someone arrived with the patient's chest x-ray, taken at the last minute, and it showed secondary tumours in the lung. The extensive surgery, now beyond recall, was unnecessary. My consultant mulled over how to spin his way out of his blundering management and got a story ready.

And, though difficult to believe, worse was to follow. The anaesthetist was an older, blue-nosed, burly figure who exchanged forced public-school chat with the surgeon, mainly about tennis parties. He used an old-fashioned mask for the anaesthetic, rather than the modern way of passing a tube down into the lungs. Rubber straps round the head held the mask in place, and they could need adjustment to keep the airway open. As he fiddled with the mask, at first I thought he had this airway problem. But he continued to fuss during the two-hour operation, half-opening the mask to one side and putting his face close to the gap, as if inspecting a problem. As I watched him, a more sinister explanation appeared; I realised he was probably sniffing the gases. This was a recently described addiction to a new anaesthetic gas and some anaesthetists had got hooked, as did the glue-sniffers in the community. He would not do it in his NHS work, since there were too many people around in theatre. Here, alone, in Harley Street, he was safe.

These dark incidents aside, our hospital life was agreeable. The all-male students and other junior staff were a cheerful lot. Across from the hospital was the hospital pub and no-one minded if you had a pint there while on duty, reached by a direct telephone line.

Before I left Glasgow, I had got a research post at Mill Hill in the north of London. The money had come from a retired St Andrews historian via our professor of pathology in the Western Infirmary and she stipulated that it be used for tissue transplantation research. They hoped that I would bring back to Glasgow the experience gained, and I was glad to plan for this.

ॐ

CHAPTER 12:

Immunology Research

Medawar ... Mill Hill ... Av Mitchison ... Conferences
Naomi Mitchison ... Mice ... Northwick Park

BRITAIN HAD a great tradition in tissue transplantation just after WWII, despite the hard times, or perhaps because of them. We had not only Nobel Prize winner Sir Peter Medawar but also Roy Calne's pioneering surgical work, and he had wisely escaped London's poor academic surgery environment by taking the chair at Cambridge. The National Institute for Medical Research at Mill Hill, where I was going, was at the height of its fame, and as well as Medawar there were a famous group of immunologists, including Avrion Mitchison and John Humphrey.

Just before going to Mill Hill, tragedy struck. Medawar, with whom I would work, suffered a catastrophic stroke while reading the lesson at a church service at a meeting of the British Association for the Advancement of Science. His life was at risk in the short-term and although he was to make a very slow recovery, it left him partly paralysed, and he eventually stood down as director at Mill Hill.

With Medawar absent, our group was leaderless for a while, but there was help at hand, and Avrion Mitchison took an interest in my work until Medawar returned. At Mill Hill, everybody worked late and some, bachelors like myself, stayed really late. The Mitchisons had a tied house nearby belonging to the Institute and on Saturdays, Mitchison scooped up anyone who had come in to work and took us over to his house for lunch. During the week he might also gather up those working late, again providing a simple dinner in his house.

After starting the research work, I had a new problem – insomnia. Often I couldn't get to sleep at all, and struggled into the lab late, accepting it as part of the new pattern of evening work. Then another possibility dawned, because after dinner in the evenings, Mitchison offered little cigars with coffee, but when I declined these, it made no difference. Then light dawned. The after-dinner coffee at 9 o'clock was responsible, and, the culprit thus identified, sleep promptly and blissfully returned.

I have avoided caffeine thereafter, and the syndrome is well known. The sufferers are not born sensitive to coffee but something changes in your mid-thirties, probably caused by loss of an enzyme. Coffee then hangs about in the system and you avoid it after seven in the evening. Vigilance is essential, since there is caffeine in Coca-Cola and related soft drinks, and even in chocolate and some teas. There can be occasional slips at dinners when, halfway through a late coffee, there is the sinking realisation that a sleepless night will follow. However, this coffee stimulation can be useful and morning coffee gives a useful boost to the brain. Surgeons and anaesthetists use the same strategy when at work, steadily neutralising falling concentration with regular cups of coffee.

Having solved that new personal problem, my old one – the 'black dog' of depression when in full-time research – did not emerge. To prevent it happening, I had arranged for some clinical work, but soon realised that my daily experimental surgery sufficed. Mouse skin grafting was my thing, and I was also skilled at removal of the mouse thymus, and the bone marrow transplantation which followed, involving intravenous injection of marrow cells into the mouse tail skin veins. My project was exploring the empirical finding now noted in human transplantation, that while graft rejection is common in the first few months, later acute rejection is uncommon. Some patients can stop taking their antirejection treatment and come to no harm. I studied a nice little model of this 'adaptation' phenomenon. I added to the challenge by studying xenografts – grafts from one species to another – and soon could get indefinite survival of grafts even across wide species gaps. My healthy, lively, mice with luxuriant tufts of hamster hair no longer requiring treatment were much admired. I could also get survival of chicken skin which then grew feathers, but after the word went round, I declined to show off this tasteless, almost freakish, success.

Medawar returned slowly to work. Our lab neighbours were Mitchison's talented team, and a huge boost to immunology came when Martin Raff in this lab identified the T lymphocyte. The significance of these different lymphocytes was being worked through by him

and others across the corridor from us. These talented 'Young Turk' immunologists were politically active and the Americans among them, opponents of the Vietnam War, held a blood donation session at Mill Hill with the plasma sent as a gift to North Vietnam. They also felt curbed by the policies and leadership at the stuffy British Society for Immunology and mounted a successful revolt. Their call for more democratic selection of papers, and display of poster versions of the papers not selected for presentation, was successful.

In Medawar's group, we attended international transplantation conferences, but these were getting to be large, unwieldy affairs. In science, good news travels fast and it can be old news by the time of the big gathering. Medawar was known for his reservations, preferring to support meetings of small groups of knowledgeable insiders. The social side of the big conferences could be awkward. At one meeting in Paris, we arranged to meet a celebrity American transplant surgeon at a local Paris bar. When he eventually appeared, although we were thirsty, his idea was that 'since we are in France' we should order a bottle of expensive cognac. It came with 12 thimbles, which hardly sufficed for our needs on a hot day. This surgeon, said to massage his research data, was a nuisance in other ways and, taking an attractive girl in our unit aside, invited her to a private party. The girl knew of his reputation, and he was disappointed when she brought me along for safety.

Dinner at the Medawar's house meant an impressive evening since he had some influential friends. His wife Jean was a great cook and my job, Peter being disabled, was to pour the wine which came from the first magnum bottles I had seen. Medawar was also interested in scientific method and his library had early editions of Francis Bacon's works, notably his *Novum Organum* (1620). It was Bacon who had urged understanding the world by observation rather than speculation. In the lab, Medawar noticed I had a copy of his own book *The Uniqueness of the Individual* and begged it from me, since he had none left. I swapped it for a signed copy of his latest work, which I sent to my sponsor in St Andrews, to her delight. Later, although I would make little impact on the world of immunology, I contributed some writings. Medawar had further strokes later, and when blind, I was proud to hear that Leslie Brent, his former colleague, read aloud my book *The Monkey Gland Affair* to him. I also paid Medawar back in a small way for his training and support by writing a book on the history of organ transplantation, published later after Medawar's death. When it came out, Av Mitchison said nice things about it and that 'Medawar would have approved.'

When Medawar, under some pressure, gave up his directorship of the Mill Hill labs because of his disability, we moved as a new small unit to the new Northwick Park Hospital. Medawar's other staff began to move elsewhere, and it fell to me to draw up a grant application for our new labs. Funding research by such grants was new, and, having done nothing like this before, I feared that the requests were deficient and that I might let him down. I looked again at the grant application and then doubled all the items of equipment and supplies requested. I took this inflated grant application to John Humphrey, then acting head at Mill Hill, and without looking at it closely, he signed it off, and sent it downtown to the Medical Research Council headquarters. Soon I was summoned by a senior administrator-scientist, no friend of Medawar I heard, and he took me over my extravagant demands line by line, including that we needed a supply of 100 mice/week (i.e. 50 multiplied by two), two magnificent microscopes (one was enough), two centrifuges and much else. I did not flinch and stared this unpleasant man out, knowing that he could not deny help for our distinguished, but disabled, Nobel Prize winner. In exasperation, he ended the discussion and said, "I think you are being too protective of Medawar." I was. It was time for loyalty. The MRC was generous in other ways, letting him stay in his lovely Hampstead home and, for getting to work, they provided a car and driver.

Our duplicate equipment and consumables came in handy. Our neighbours in the new Northwick Park research labs were another new unit called Surgical Immunology, to be headed by a noisy, talented American who had worked with Medawar earlier. After the news of Medawar's stroke, he rather disloyally hesitated to come to Britain. When he did arrive, in the confusion, he had ignored the paperwork necessary for his grant, including the essential need for many mice. He asked for our help, hearing of our lavish funding, and Medawar was sympathetic. Although I pretended to be huffy, we were well-off and could make gracious gifts until they got established.

∾

While in London, through Mitchison, I got to know his mother Naomi, who lived in Scotland at Carradale in Argyll about two hours away from Glasgow, and I kept in touch with her later. She lived to be 101, and she was a novelist, poet, Labour Party activist, Scottish nationalist sympathiser and honorary mother to the Botswana nation. With her husband Dick, they bought their Scottish house in Argyll in 1950 and it was her base throughout the year, with her family and their children and her guests gathering there in summer. I joined them when I returned to Glasgow. Her style was a curious mixture of progressive and traditional. At Carradale, she expected you to dress smartly for dinner, served at the long dining table bearing the family silver, with children and teenagers at a separate table near the window. She asked me to carve the roast under her watchful eye, slicing it thin enough to feed the assembled company. The conversation ranged from the international scientific interests of her remarkable sons to the political insights from other family members in politics and journalism. None of them played golf, although a sporty golf course was next to her small estate, and I had the honour of introducing some guests to the game. One feature of the spacious house was her collection of paintings. Apart from her early appreciation of English artists like Wyndham Lewis and Lowry, she collected new Scottish work, including works by Joan Eardley when she was little known. Mitchison bought these Scottish works economically in Glasgow by attending the Glasgow School of Art's end-of-year exhibition and the Compass Gallery's famous Christmas exhibition. Later, back in Glasgow, I tried to follow this lead in a small way.

At the end of my fellowship at Northwick Park, I was looking forward to the return to Glasgow, but I was asked to stay on as the head of the new surgical research unit, the unsettled American having left. Medawar, ever-loyal, suggested my name, but I was not ready nor attracted. There were already too many small transplant units in London and another one was not a possibility. One way to have a proper research-minded hospital was to develop surgical specialties.

Northwick Park had already appointed their NHS surgeons, and they all did general surgery. I talked with one of them, who when young had a research interest, suggesting that we took a specialty interest each, such as gastroenterology for him, or vascular surgery, and since our research work was on tumour immunology, I suggested that I could do oncology or take on all the breast cases. He explained that that was not the London way, and this surgical colleagues would resist it. He explained that I would be seen as a breast cancer expert and I would poach all the private breast cases in the area from them. In vain I said that I not only disliked private practice, but it was also unacceptable for a head of a surgical unit to add outside private work.

'Wait to you have to buy a house and educate children' he said, 'and your scruples will vanish.'

'Other people in London manage,' I said.[*]

☞

I headed back to Glasgow and the Western Infirmary. Glasgow's reputational damage came mostly from novelists, who wrongly depicted it as a squalid and dangerous city.[†] Instead, confidence was returning to Glasgow helped by a media campaign focusing on the cultural richness of the city. The magnificent Burrell Collection came out of hiding, and our new novelists' fiction was well received. Scottish Opera, based in Glasgow, was up and running and would have its own opera house from 1975. We rediscovered Charles Rennie Macintosh, our architect, and, besides the well-known Glasgow Boys, the Glasgow Girls painters were increasingly acknowledged. 'Glasgow's Miles Better' was the slogan graced on posters and lapel badges by the figure of Mr Happy. The result was that outsiders' perception of Glasgow changed significantly.

And Scotland, as a nation, also seemed to be coming to life.

---

[*] Fifty years later, specialism being accepted, the Breast Clinic and Cancer Service at Northwick Park was seeing 4,000 new cases a year.

[†] The damaging novel *No Mean City* (1935) was written by a journalist from elsewhere. The image was amplified by the Royal Ballet's 'Miracle in the Gorbals', performed from 1944 onwards, which included beggars, drunks, prostitutes, a devious minister and razor slashing.

CHAPTER 13

Western Infirmary

Research grants ... Peter Bell ... Kidney transplants
Mouse problems ... Curing cancer ... Domestic arrangements

BACK HOME in Glasgow in 1971, to continue the London research work, I had brought a supply of special mice back in my car, and they lodged overnight in my sister's warm kitchen before reaching their new home. From these mice, we would breed more, and for my bone marrow transplants I needed radiation, and a kindly radiotherapist offered to get me started, using the machines used for human treatment. Though these sessions were after 5 o'clock in the radiotherapy department, this was hardly satisfactory. Mice can be smelly.

I had put in for research grants to support my work both to the Cancer Research Campaign (CRC) and the Medical Research Council (MRC) and was surprised to get both, which included funds for a research assistant. Our genial and talented Professor Kay, to whom I owed much, was spending much time in London on committees, including the powerful Council of the Medical Research Council and, using a light administrative touch, in his absence, matters were increasingly run by his chain-smoking, elderly secretary. With difficulty, I explained the two grants to her and how to get the funds transferred from London to the Department for our use. Outside grants were rare then, and the local university funds met all salaries and running costs.

I appointed a talented young lady as my researcher, but shortly afterwards, our secretary summoned me to say that 'this was not the way we do things here'. The surgeons and technical staff were always male, she pointed out, and in the wards, the nurses were always female; that was a natural order of things. She added that the department's crusty chief technician also objected to my assistant, particularly as she was wearing slacks. This gender problem faded away, but there was more difficulty to come. After three months I got a letter from both the MRC and the CRC to say that my grant money had not been taken up. I had a word with Kay, and our secretary at last uplifted the money.

There had been no kidney transplantation on our side of Scotland until a few years before and regular dialysis for chronic kidney failure was only recently established and only a few, young, selected patients could be treated and then perhaps transplanted. Otherwise, patients with kidney failure died, and died slowly. Nor was it the death with dignity that the conservative nay-sayers, opposed to dialysis, described; it was a horrible, lingering death.

We had been slow to start kidney transplantation compared with Edinburgh, since Illingworth, the previous professor of surgery in Glasgow, for all his talents, had opposed organ transplantation, a not uncommon attitude at the time. This view was that attempts at grafting between humans were doomed since the biological barrier was too great and also that it was 'against nature' to try. There were surgeons in our hospital who still took this view.

After Illingworth retired, we could start transplanting, teaming up with Douglas Briggs, the physician, who ran our growing dialysis unit, together with a skilled and friendly nursing team. Prof Kay arranged for one of our surgeons, Peter Bell, to train in Denver, Colorado with Tom Starzl, the pioneer transplant surgeon and Peter returned and started kidney grafting a few years before I arrived, building up an enthusistic team. He was a charismatic leader whom we all admired, and a good teacher, letting you learn surgery under his watchful eye. An agreeable extra was that he held court on Friday nights in the Aragon, the hospital pub in Byres Road close by, and we juniors could join him in the far corner.

Next day there was more intra-hospital bonding on the golf course. After the morning hospital meeting, when not on call, there was Saturday afternoon golf at Glasgow Gailes golf course playing with Douglas Briggs, Roddy McSween, dermatologist Dai Roberts, and Gordon Allan the physician. Gailes, on the Ayrshire coast, courtesy of the Gulf Stream, remains playable throughout the year.

∿

Getting donor kidneys was a rather fraught procedure before the help from brain-death criteria and heart-beating donation. Donors were declared dead in the ward and removal of kidneys was hurried, unpleasant. The delay affected the kidneys it would take days or weeks for them to produce urine. In the rota for kidney donation, we had three teams, and the kidneys were exported or came in according to the national matching scheme based on tissue typing. It was hoped that tissue typing, when perfected, would avoid rejection, but the matching system has proved so complex that this has not been achieved. Early rejection was common and this, plus bleeds from the kidney or urine leaks, gave difficult surgery. Later, powerful drugs like cyclosporine overcame any remaining effect of tissue matching, and early rejection became rare. We did some children's transplants with the adult kidney going into the abdomen, attached to the aorta and vena cava behind the colon.

There was much extra surgical work for us junior surgeons related to keeping patients with chronic renal failure alive on dialysis – the 'access' surgery. This involved inserting plastic tubing 'shunts' joining arteries to veins in the leg or arm to provide blood for the dialysis machine, and since they clotted regularly, putting them in was needed- now, simple surgery for us. For permanent access, there was the tricky operation of joining a vein to an artery at the wrist and after a few weeks, the thickened vein could be needled to obtain arterial blood. If that failed or clotted, then we used the other arm and if that failed, then plastic or vein grafts were used. A fraught situation arose when all these useful arteries and veins were used up, and only transplantation would save the patient. There could also be horrific bleeding from these various access devices if they ruptured or the needle punctures became infected. Later, double lumen catheters replaced these older methods and, inserted into veins deep in the neck, the physicians nobly took on this task.

Liver and heart transplantation were still to develop in Scotland. There was a Journal Club at the Western Infirmary where we discussed interesting scientific papers and I hesitantly presented Starzl's now-classic account of his six pioneering Denver human liver transplants. Only one of six patients survived even for a short time and massive blood loss was a feature. The surgeons from our other units listened in silence, clearly thinking it was pointless, and one asked sarcastically if there would be attempts at transplantation of the pancreas next. At that, there were groans around the table, and I meekly agreed that the panceatic surgical challenge was too great.

Although I had the grants and an assistant, my attempts to continue my London research encountered a serious problem. After the complex preparation and skin grafting, when I removed the little bandages, my relocated mice now perversely chewed or scratched off their otherwise successful skin grafts. Nothing would prevent this, including putting on little collars, as you would with difficult dogs. Nobody in our little world of mouse skin grafting had experienced the problem and they had no other suggestions. Month after month, I had no successful experiments.

I had to change tack. Just before I left London, Medawar had felt that human organ transplantation was heading out of its developmental stage and moving towards becoming a routine therapy, and he had moved away from tissue transplantation looking instead at the immunology of cancer. This offered a seductive prospect, since if human cancer was foreign tissue, there might be a weak immune response to it. If we could boost this ineffective reaction, the cancer would be rejected like an organ graft. When I developed a historical sense later, I realised that this idea comes around every 30 years, as a beguiling one, too good to be false, then is discredited.

Joining the enthusiasm for rejecting cancer, I switched with relief to look at a nasty virus-induced malignant mouse tumour. Using an immune-boosting treatment with bacterial products like the BCG vaccine and the benign bug *Corynebacterium parvum*, positive results appeared rapidly. Like everyone else, I found that getting rid of mouse tumours was easy, and all over the world, the strategy was being enthusiastically applied to human cancer patients. The first human results were promising and enthusiasts promoted them noisily, but after five years use of both these agents or others in human cancer treatment, more careful studies showed that the strategy was ineffective. It disappeared from the choices available in cancer therapy and it was an embarrassing episode, made worse by sceptics pointing out that an immune response to human cancer might not even exist. Boosting the human response to cancer did indeed revive 30 years later, in a different guise.

～

I had a little home near the Western Infirmary, in a newly-built, single-level development with a small, private car park. My sister helped with settling in, and recruited her devoted home help to help me, and this prevented bachelor squalor. Somehow clean shirts and other laundry were mysteriously always at hand. My evening meal was usually obtained from Lucky's small Chinese carry-out shop close to the hospital, where you heard the noise of the metal scoop tossing the sizzling stir-fry food in the wok in the back shop. The owner and his wife did not speak English and in the front shop their earnest young son took the the orders and the money. If not on call, I liked to have a pint in the nearby Dowanside Bar first, getting some reading and writing done and then phoned Lucky's from the pub's telephone box. There, the alert boy increasingly recognised my voice and could quickly confirm my order before any money was put in. This speedy arrangement suited the surgical personality. Over the years, the son impressed me, and last I heard, he was a lecturer in mathematics at a Glasgow college downtown.

One night my food collection did not go smoothly. When I entered, I found some racist youths mocking the owners and I took out my hospital bleep, fiddled with it to make a squawking noise and pretended to be in contact with the police. This worked and the youths left. However, when they regrouped outside, they realised there was something odd about me, and were waiting for me outside to discuss the matter. They soon made the point that I had offended the accepted code in the underworld by impersonating a police officer and, with a few punches, gave me a black eye. When I reported the incident to the police the next day, they also made the point that I had offended the accepted code by impersonating an officer.

Otherwise, these personal nutritional arrangements worked well, and essential supplies notably of bread and milk were available at a little convenience store next to Lucky's. The Pakistani owners took in stray cats and one evening a young kitten made it clear that he thought that the two of us would get on well. He repeated this appeal on later visits and eventually I took young Monday (that being the day of the week) back home, although coming and going would be difficult for a cat. To deal with this, I put a cat flap into the back door, but Monday still liked some company and, waiting on a low wall beside out little car park for my evening arrival, would jump onto my shoulder and settle there as we walked to the house. Inside, I would offer him some Whiskas or dry food. This was often declined with a reproachful look, and the reproof might mean going out to get a tin of sardines.

I sometimes went to the Downside Bar on Saturdays after golf and although it was busy, the local Partick drinkers usually left me alone to read and write. But one night, one of a noisy group lurched over to me and said

'The boys want to know what you are up to.'

I was about to offer a short curriculum vitae, but he continued, pointing at the papers on my lap:

'There's nae money to be made writing that sort of stuff' he opined. I was well aware of that. And he continued …

'The way tae make money is, …'

At this point he crumpled onto the floor. His friends rescued him and apologised for disturbing me.

'Not a problem' I said. 'He was trying to tell me something.'

But I never saw him again.

CHAPTER 14:

Surgical Training

Vale of Leven ... Saving lives ... Surgeons
Changing surgery ... Smoking ... Glasgow College

Because of my laboratory work in London, I was short of conventional surgical training. Prof Kay suggested some extra general surgical experience and arranged for me to have a day of operative surgery at the Vale of Leven Hospital, near Loch Lomond, plus on call that day and night for emergencies. His surgical contact at the Vale was Andrew Jamieson, of Jamieson and Kay's *Textbook of Surgical Physiology,* a textbook written when they were lecturers in Illingworth's department. Jamieson's surgical colleague at the Vale was Ewan Cameron, and I soon worked with him. Cameron was a joy to work with, although he perhaps let you do too much on your own, and his formidable theatre sister was ready to push you through. Cameron was a splendid raconteur and wrote well. I dictated notes for the cases we operated on together, and occasionally I would see these patients again at the clinic. When I read the theatre notes, I thought my style was rather good, until I realised that Cameron had dictated all the notes for that day.

Cameron started using large doses of vitamin C to treat advanced cancer cases and felt it was of benefit. As a result, Cameron struck up a friendship with Linus Pauling, the Californian double Nobel Prize winner, who was famously treating the common cold with large doses of that vitamin. Pauling visited Scotland (risking getting a cold) to meet Cameron and after retirement, Cameron spent time in Pauling's unit, publishing his findings as a book co-authored by Pauling.* These claims

for vitamin C use were controversial and stimulated two Mayo Clinic controlled trials, which showed no effect of the vitamin in treating cancer. I'm not sure if Cameron believed in the anti-cancer effectiveness of the vitamin, but it gave him an absorbing interest and much travel.

Double Nobel Prize winner Linus Pauling visiting Vale of Leven surgeon Ewan Cameron in 1976.

Cameron had some other vivid events in his life. His nephew, a young Glasgow-trained surgeon, emigrated to America and married the daughter of Denton Cooley, the famous Houston heart surgeon. The nephew's father had died, and Cameron took on a formal role in this, the Texas wedding of the year. Cameron, a born storyteller, dined out on his experience, including describing the competition between the two symphony orchestras, one at each end of Cooley's estate. A more sinister event was that on one of his American trips, their housekeeper was murdered, leading to a High Court trial at which the accused was acquitted.

In hospitals outside the cities, like the Vale of Leven, you encounter some free spirits. At the Vale, one of their anaesthetists lived

---

* Ewan Cameron and Linus Pauling *Cancer and Vitamin C*, New York, 1979. It was reprinted in 1993 and 2015, since it chimed in with increasing enthusiasm for orthomolecular therapies. There is an interesting assessment of the events in Evelleen Richards *Vitamin C and Cancer: Medicine or Politics,* London 1991.

in a caravan which he parked in the grounds close to the end of a ward, which meant a running battle with the administration who attempted to charge him a rent. He and his rather exotic lady friend got to work through the ward, and she headed out of the hospital along this route during a visit by a minor Royal.

It could be busy at the Vale and you had to be resourceful. I digress here to reflect on 'saving lives', since I had a memorable case at the Vale.

∂

Lay inquirers or journalists sometimes asked surgeons about any lives they may have saved, but we react badly to this rather juvenile and simplistic invitation. Potential medical students at interviews are asked why they are going into medicine and they sometimes volunteer that they hope 'to save lives.' A jaded examiner can hardly resist the riposte

'Why not join the fire brigade?'

Saving lives is accomplished, in a general sense, by surgery, but usually at a slow tempo. However, surgeons, humble to a fault, often quietly congratulate themselves on one or two immediate triumphs. There was one for me which, for a while, gave me a 100% record in saving the lives of those stabbed in the heart. Law-abiding citizens are seldom thus attacked, but it is common in the drug-dealing fraternity. Such wounds are usually fatal but occasionally the tough, hollow pericardial sac, which surrounds the heart, may contain the loss of blood for a while. With prompt surgical intervention, the heart and the wound may be reached in time and dealt with.

At the Vale, a young man involved in the drug scene had been attacked but although there was a small knife entry wound in the left chest and although the x-ray showed no blood in the chest, he was unwell, with signs of heart 'tamponade'. I had some thoracic surgery training and on opening the left chest, saw the sac covering the heart bulging with blood, slit it open, and displayed the spurting hole in the heart. Not only could you see the hole but you could hear it. On these occasions, anaesthetists also recognise the fizzing noise and without further enquiry put out a call for more blood. The next move is easy if you have got there in time. Simply put a finger in the dyke, ask for any heavy stitch on any large curved needle to hand, push it through the tough wall of the heart and bring it back again (a purse-string suture), which when tied, closes the hole.

'Did you do something there?' said our anaesthetist, noting better signs of life.

'Fill him up,' I said grandly.

Next day the young man was brand-new, as they say, and soon fled from the hospital. But I had two private concerns. The first was that in the hurry in theatre, the sturdy curved needle and thread I used was catgut and this dissolves, though slowly. The second was that in my haste to get through the sac, I had cut the phrenic nerve and his left diaphragm was inactive. However, he survived and was available to help the authorities with their investigations, or rather not help the authorities with their enquiries. The police told me that the drug-dealing community were none too pleased that I had put him back on the streets. The word was that, next time, they would eliminate him with a better method.

I dined out on this success, but my hundred per cent record lasted only for five years. A similar case presented in another hospital, again far from a heart surgery unit, again originating in a drug gang feud. I displayed the hole, avoiding the phrenic nerve this time on the way in, and stitched the hole with some confidence, remembering to use nylon. But the knife had also done serious extra damage inside the heart, and the heart failed. Leaving the theatre with this sharp fall in my outcome stats for this operation and bearing the sad news of his death, outside I found a group of police officers who were rejoicing. Even his mother was pleased he was gone.

One more anecdote about 'saving a life' cannot be resisted. A lady credited me with this; nay she went further and announced that she would reward me. She was an elderly, obese smoker and very unwell when she came in. The surgery for her perforated colon diverticulum was routine and the saving of her life came in the intensive care unit afterwards. She returned to our ward, and when preparing to leave the hospital, she told me she would remember me in her will. One picks up one's ears on such an occasion, but I soon put it out of my mind. Years passed. One day, a letter from a lawyer's office arrived, and after understandable hesitation, inside the word from her lawyer was that she had passed away, and had left me half of her estate. I would hear further from them. When the expected envelope arrived, this time opened at speed, she had left £78. The lawyer took £64 in fees; I got half of what remained and the rest went to a cat and dog home.

It was a kind thought.[*]

Apart from some thoracic training, I also gained experience in other specialties. Ian McGregor, the distinguished Canniesburn plastic surgeon taught me a lot, and many of the smaller techniques were useful in general surgery later. Tattoo removal is tricky, particularly when dealing with slogans or football teams' names on the back of fingers; if serving the public these can hold you back for promotion. Using the skin creases in the face means almost invisible scars and when in public you notice a citizen with these well-developed 'crow's feet' smile-lines, you itch to get to work. McGregor left me to do a heroic procedure one night – a nose flap. A young man lost most of the soft part of his nose and we were consulted at 5 o'clock. I knew that a flap from the shaved scalp was possible and to my surprise he let me get on with. It was a more heroic undertaking than I thought but I got there. The patient thereafter had hair growing on the tip of his nose.

I always thought surgeons were born to do surgery, rather than were trained into it. This surgical DNA and resulting personality has its strengths and weaknesses. On the plus side, there is a liking for marching towards gunfire and an ability to deal decisively with trouble when you get there. Outside the hospitals a surgeon is a good man in a crisis – a burst pipe or a tyre puncture – and they will hasten to put a finger on, then in, any leak to hold the situation, then fix it. But don't ask them to do a tax return or send out Christmas cards. There was a consultant transplant surgeon we knew in London who after years of marriage reluctantly agreed to go on holiday, but only lasted three hours on the Malta beach before he went off to offer services to the local hospital. They were glad to have him.

---

* Current General Medical Council advice is to report such promises to the administration and to your Medical Defence Union.

Surgeons use their time well and dislike inactivity. I once saw our distinguished professor Kay standing near his wards on a Saturday, just after the hospital meeting. He looked unwell, pale and ill at ease. He seemed so distressed that I asked him what was wrong – perhaps he was ill. Through clenched teeth, he said 'I'm going to a wedding.' This was a man who never wasted a minute and was facing an afternoon of small talk extending into much of the evening. He then added that 'Sir Charles (Illingworth – his predecessor) disliked them too.' This was intended to lessen Kay's guilt.

When you are a young surgeon, you have surgical heroes, and avoid others. A few surgeons stand out. I was at Sick Children's Hospital one day, and looking into an adjacent theatre, I liked what I saw. It was a skilful job being done on a face by Jack Mustardé, the famous but controversial local plastic surgeon. But to us 'fast was good' – and the fastest surgeon north of the river was in the Western Infirmary. He was a solitary man, who did his work and left, not partaking of the hospital life. Our fast surgeons didn't look fast. It was their lack of hesitation, particularly in stitching which saved the time; since each stitch fell into place. They also might not waste time on small self-sealing cut blood-vessels. The fastest surgeon south of the river was used by the Glasgow scientists working on the human adrenal gland. It deteriorates quickly on removal and he was their man. We had no instrument-throwing surgeons but heard of some earlier. Their ire often arose from frustration at a lack of relaxation of the abdomen in the era before the anaesthetists used muscle relaxants.

There were some slow, indecisive surgeons around and they were painful to watch, and their talented juniors shielded them. We had no alcoholics in our hospital, but we had an occasional consultant smelling of drink in the morning, which is different. Otherwise, our surgeons had excellent health, never ill and never off for a day or two with coughs or colds. In the statistics for illness and time lost by the various staff categories, hospital consultants have the best record, being off one quarter of the time lost by the sickest group.

In Glasgow, we had an unusual surgical first in the first known HIV-positive surgeon in Britain. He missed out on the pioneering AZT treatments which meant that when he got triple therapy later, it was very effective. Patients and staff stood by him and although cautiously suspended for two years, he returned to do a limited range of surgery and he continued to do well.

Surgical practice changed steadily. Anaesthesia methods changed and assisted greatly in the increasing quality of surgical care. The growth of intensive care for the seriously-ill patient after or before surgery meant much better management and outcome in serious surgery. Better radiology had an important input and to the new ultrasound methods were added CT and MRI scans. These became so helpful that there were fewer surgical diagnostic surprises. Formerly, for unwell surgical patients, exploratory surgery was often needed to make a diagnosis, rewarded by the joy of confirming serious trouble – or the discouragement of finding nothing amiss.

The response to the arrival of such new expensive equipment reveals much about the different health care systems. In insurance-based systems, as in America, the new device is promptly purchased and creates new income from the charges to the patient/insurer which pays for the installation. But in the NHS, purchase of new expensive equipment creates no new income and indeed adds extra costs which must be found from the local budget. The NHS understandably drags its feet until there is overwhelming evidence that the need for the new method is established.

Awareness of medical ethics was increasing. Edinburgh in 1976, then Glasgow, set up 'Medical Groups' with input from theologists and philosophers. Doctors were at first uncomfortable having others appearing on their patch but local hospital ethical committees with lay members were soon in place. Moreover, the public was gaining other influence over health care. The Patients Association had pushed for influence and Community Health Councils emerged. Engagement with the public emerged in other ways and in Edinburgh the College of Surgeons Museum opened its doors to the public, with success.

Hospital life also changed slowly. In a former day, the consultants lunched in a dining room of their own, and the last separate consultant dining room in Glasgow was at the Victoria Infirmary. Soon, we all not only ate together, but from the 1970s took our dishes back to the counter. We got into the routine of this without difficulty, but it could cause problems elsewhere when lunching at traditionalist venues. Later, just after joining the Royal and Ancient Golf Club of St. Andrews, I rose after lunch and started to take my dishes back; kind hands restrained me.

Smoking within the hospital was pervasive and there were even ashtrays on the patients' bedside lockers. In the posed hospital photographs of the time, many of the men have a fag in hand. There was smoking in the operating theatre changing rooms between surgical cases, and the staff passed cigarettes round in the coffee rooms. The consultants smoked in their outpatient clinics and some chain-smoked, lighting the next cigarette from the stub of the nearly-finished one. Sir Charles Illingworth's legendary anaesthetist, who assisted the surgical unit's high output by running two theatres single-handed, was a heavy smoker and smoked in the anaesthetic room outside the theatre. When he took the anaesthetised patient into theatre, he parked his upright half-finished cigarette on top of the plastic light switch in the anaesthetic room and, leaving it there, he might not return soon enough to finish it. Decades later, to prove to sceptics that there was widespread smoking earlier in the hospital, I could point out the burn marks on the box where his forgotten cigarettes had burned down to the plastic.

Sir Andrew Kay, as noted above, was on the ruling body of the Medical Research Council, and in his room, he had a framed photograph of the group. They were all heavy smokers, but for the group photograph, they removed the cigarettes and ashtrays and put them under the table. But, as he pointed out, you could still see the edges of the ashtrays, peeking out under the cloth.

The Glasgow College of Physicians and Surgeons made a great comeback in our time. Between the wars it was a shell organisation and, still called the 'Faculty', they held one annual lecture. The Library was good and there was a Widows Fund dating from the days when doctors often died young. After World War II, Glasgow activists with political skill revived the Faculty's potential powers. Assisted by Glasgow's important new post-war strength in clinical research, they obtained the new title of 'Royal College'. The College's education program and lectures increased, and it took on a role in the newly-important postgraduate education in the West of Scotland.

The Glasgow College's postgraduate diplomas were now equivalent to those from Edinburgh and London and became popular as a result of imaginative modernisation, particularly introducing the multiple-choice questions which overseas doctors felt were fairer to them than writing discursive essays. The other British Colleges followed this lead later. The resulting influx of many candidates to Glasgow to sit the oft-failed first part of the surgical and medical diplomas revolutionised the College's finances.

The Edinburgh and London colleges had made an early start in holding their examinations abroad, and Glasgow was a late starter in this struggle for empire. When I was on one of the Glasgow College committees, we met with a delegation from Mosul in Iraq who were hoping to establish a local exam for the difficult first part of the surgical fellowship. The London College already had a foothold in Baghdad.

'How are things in Mosul?' I asked.

'The city itself is fine' the Iraqi replied, 'but we are surrounded by uncontrolled guerrillas.'

We didn't go.*

＆

* Later, in 2014, Mosul was the birthplace of the short-lived Islamic State of Iraq.

CHAPTER 15:

Local Politics

Sam ... Private Practice ... Trade Unions

WARD ROUNDS then were hierarchical processions. The middle-grade staff were keen to catch the senior's eye and show off their erudition while the juniors keep quiet. Sir Andrew did not favour this style and liked quick decisions, and on my first ward round, I witnessed a strange thing. The youngest of the team was leading the round, and at some speed. With his sharp eyes, he made contact with all involved, while giving a concise summary of the patient's case and the treatment. He took no nonsense from others if he considered they were time-wasters.

This was Sam Galbraith, later a distinguished neurosurgeon, then a member of Parliament and a minister in the Scottish Parliament. Later that week, I met up with him at the usual hospital Friday gathering in the Aragon pub and we were close friends thereafter. His usual greetings to friends started with a nickname, then a quick, cutting, personal remark adding his left-wing views and outrageous tongue-in-cheek statements. His provocative remarks could cause distress to those of a sensitive nature or lacking a sense of humour, and when his remarks were reported elsewhere out of their flippant context, they could cause hostility. But everyone who knew him understood and were deeply fond of him.

Sam's socialism and idealism came from the fundamentalist religious upbringing which he had rejected, but by then he was coming out of his Marxist-Leninist phase and becoming more pragmatic. He was also into single-issue politics, and he sought a ban on boxing, opposed smoking in public places and campaigned against private medical practice. In doing so, Sam made some distant enemies and some consultants at our Royal Infirmary, keen on private practice, were incensed and said so. One Sunday, someone delivered a packet of dog faeces through Sam's letterbox.

Sam, with Bill Murray, made a famous survey of Glasgow head injuries, linking them to alcohol intake, and the blood-alcohol levels they found, when first heard of, caused a sharp intake of breath. We had a pompous senior surgeon in the hospital (the one opposed to organ transplantation), who did not like Sam's informal style. When Sam rehearsed his famous paper, ready for the Surgical Research Society meeting, the consultant took offence at Sam's flippant style. 'The Society does not laugh' he intoned, which was true until then. He urged Sam to be more respectful and modify his remarks. Anyway, when Sam stood up to give his paper at the meeting, he reverted to his own style and we sat nervously on our hands. On showing his second slide with the blood-alcohol levels in the Glasgow head injuries, the audience started rolling in the aisles. The paper became a landmark study later, for lots of reasons. Sam was to write much and later co-authored a standard textbook on neurosurgery.

Sam never changed. Much later, one day at school, one of his daughters was heard reciting some bawdy Glasgow street doggerel. The teacher disapproved and added

'What would your father say if he heard you speaking like that?'
The response was simple: 'My father taught me it.'*

---

* For a biography of Sam Galbraith, see Graham Teasdale (ed) *Remembering Sam* Edinburgh, 2018. His lung transplant served him for 24 years, a world record, before he died in 2014.

Sam liked to move other things on, if there was an opportunity, and at one of our staff meeting he and I tried to tackle the age-old primitive arrangement we had at our surgical outpatients' clinic. Like all clinics of the day, all the patients had to turn up at 9 a.m. This Victorian plan was not as bad as it sounds; the word on the street being that if you came at 8 a.m. you would be seen first, or if arriving at 12 o'clock, the clinic was still open. It was time for a change, and we suggested at the meeting that we should give the patients appointments. I thought there was a flicker of response from Sir Andrew when he heard the idea, as he was then Chief Scientist in the Scottish NHS administration. But, aware of seniority and etiquette, he turned to a senior for his view, who, opposing the idea, supported the early or late arrival strategy used by the patients. He then added the additional pleading that giving appointments might mean that a consultant was kept waiting. It was the *zeitgeist* of the time – that the NHS was run for the staff, not the patient. Later, management would have to intervene in these modernising matters; we had handed over the control.

There wasn't much private practice in Glasgow in the post-war era. As a result, in the absence of competition for money, we had, unlike London, 'collectivism' and cooperation locally. For salaries, the sensible system was that the few consultants who wished to do private practice had to give up part of their NHS income, and these private fees made up for this lower state income. This was an important arrangement for the national NHS, since it meant that the consultants throughout Scotland had the same income and this helped staffing of the less popular specialties. It also assisted in filling consultant posts in the hospitals outside the cities, and there was also no financial loss in going to work in the Highlands.

We trainees did not admire those consultants doing private practice. But some of this 'affable and available' group had style. Hector MacLennan, the gynaecologist and obstetrician at the Victoria Infirmary, the only hospital with 'pay beds' for private patients, was an impressive figure.

'My dear,' he would say, 'cancer's not what it used to be.'

An orthopaedic surgeon told me of how Hector had once summoned him to his office. Hector explained:

'Dear Lady Lovell (the name changed). What are we going to do about her neck problem?'

The orthopod, sensing a lucrative referral to this Highland castle, rose to the suggestion that he might help.

'Would you indeed,' said Hector enthusiastically, 'could you go up to Lovell Castle ... now?'

The journey to the North agreed, Hector continued:

'Get up to Lovell Castle tomorrow. She is in a terrible state. There are 30 arriving for the weekend.'

Hector then added the vital detail:

'It's the cook you have to see. The cook. She's off sick with a bad neck.'

Hector added colour to the Glasgow medical world, but the medical school needed the work of another group to bring prestige. In the Western Infirmary, Prof Ian Donald the gynaecologist and obstetrician, though not noted for his bedside manner, was then pioneering ultrasound scanning and he had a small room on the floor above our surgical unit. It was Donald and some full-time surgeons, notably in the neurosurgical and plastic surgical units, who put the Glasgow Medical School's surgery on the map, attracting students, postgraduates and funding. A medical school needs the grants and endowments which come to those involved in research and scholarship; private practice adds nothing to this effort, and can hinder it. When, later, the Conservative government encouraged all consultants to do private practice, we lost this local advantage, and it damaged not only the Scottish academic departments, but also the specialties, and surgical practice in the Highlands.

There was another way that Sam and I could help push things forward. In Glasgow, the Health Board consulted with the staff via an NHS Staff Committee or rather, two committees. One involved the doctors in the British Medical Association and the other, composed of healthcare trade union representatives, spoke for the rest of the staff. This split perhaps made sense, but it had a feudal, officers/troops feel to it. Both Sam and I were members of the small, but influential, left-leaning Medical Practitioners Union, and through this, Sam was invited to join the local trade unions' meetings with the Health Board. But Sam had his hands full and I went along instead and joined the committee which included the Amalgamated Engineering Union's Jimmy Airlie, hero of the UCS shipyard work-in. When the BMA heard about it, they were displeased. Doctors shouldn't mix with troops; I had crossed the line.

These meetings had a pattern. The doctors came in and complained about their salaries and the misdeeds of the trade unions. They then left, and the trade union group came in and complained about their wages, unfair dismissals, and the doctors' lukewarm support for the NHS. The Health Board members were used to this dichotomy and were content to call these sessions a draw. Our committee always had a pre-meeting, and I soon suggested we might lift our ambitions from the traditional negativity and make some positive suggestions about improving the NHS service. So, we added an item on hospital waiting lists to the agenda for the meeting. At the meeting, I got surprising support from the Board's influential general practitioner, who agreed and supported looking into the differences in surgical waiting times in our area.

Thus emboldened, at a later meeting, I had a topical matter to raise. One of the flashpoints in the tense local debate on private practice was the 'borrowing' of NHS equipment by the poorly equipped private sector. As a trainee surgeon, a while back, working for our hospital's only successful private surgeon, he needed an unusual retractor for an operation at Glasgow's small, gloomy private clinic. To take this from his theatre, he used the usual cover story that he needed the instrument 'for a lecture'. The theatre sister, who understood the code, handed it over, wrapped and sterile. Because a gentleman did not carry a parcel, it was my task to take it to the clinic, and return it.

Just before one of our Board meetings, one of these borrowings had been the talk of the local medical bazaars, since a surgeon had used this mantra to borrow a new, expensive device 'for a lecture'. But the subterfuge came to grief. The gossip was that a new theatre staff member innocently provided only the outer part, and in the private clinic he embarked on a tricky operation in a remote part of the abdomen, only to find that the vital inner part was absent. This, even if only half true, provided much scope for the wits at coffee time throughout the city. This was just before our Board meeting. I raised the general problem of 'borrowing NHS equipment.' The doctor on the Board protested at the slur on the profession and claimed that such borrowing did not occur. I had tried to keep to generalities, but now had to offer details of this well-known recent incident.

To my astonishment, later that month, all the Glasgow doctors' pay envelopes included an extra slip with a warning not to take away NHS equipment for use elsewhere. My role as a minor whistle-blower was easily traced, and I was avoided in polite medical company for a while. I was, however, the toast of our corner in the pub next Friday night.

❧

CHAPTER 16:

Some Travels

Canada ... Libya ... America ... Brigham Hospital
Denton Cooley

'There's a farmer arrived with a bad tooth' said the nurse in the small Canadian hospital.

'When does the dentist come round?' I asked.

I had enjoyed doing general practice locums and now, with some surgical experience, there were wider holiday opportunities. In our time, many young Glasgow doctors faced a long wait at home for promotion, and instead had emigrated to Canada, where the new expanding health services welcomed them. One of my friends now settled in Edmonton in Alberta, told me that a general practitioner in the township of Fort Vermilion in remote Northern Alberta needed a locum. My friend explained that the Fort was not a top tourist attraction, nor could the doctors pay travel expenses, but it was a chance to see general practice in a different health care system. Added to this, they had a small hospital, and with one of the doctors trained in anaesthetics, they liked to do surgery locally. The Alberta government paid for any surgical procedures done, and this would more than pay for my travel costs. I did the locum on several occasions, as did Sam Galbraith.

To get to the Fort, you flew from Glasgow to Edmonton. These transatlantic flights to North America were expensive, but partly empty, and they looked after you well. The planes then had greater variety. As well as the Boeings 707s, there were the Lockheed Tri-Stars and Douglas DC 10s and our Vickers VC10 had four rear jet engines, which meant that the cabin was quiet. The Boeing company's dominance soon emerged and they produced rather dull cloned aircraft in different sizes, but similar shapes.

From Edmonton, you took a small, very small, plane to reach the Fort and its 26-bed Saint Theresa Hospital. Fur traders established the Fort on the Peace River in 1788, and 'Vermilion' came from the colour of the clay in the Peace River bank said to come from the blood shed by the rival Indian tribes before the armistice. The North West Company (later the Hudson Bay Company), colonised the area and purchased skins in winter from the indigenous trappers who hunted the animals with dogs and sledges. They sent the fur downriver to Montréal when the frozen river melted in spring. But after the fall in demand for fur, this winter hunting declined. Instead of dogs, they now use ski-dos for winter transport.

The town has a mixture of indigenous people, incomers from the south and some mixed-origin Metis, born to the Scottish traders of a former day and hence some locals have unexpectedly Scottish names. Nearby is a German-speaking community of Old Order Mennonites, who had moved from the south to escape the constraints and threats of modern civilisation, notably compulsory education and television.

I stayed in one of the doctor's houses, a wooden clapboard dwelling with a spartan internal ambience. But it had a record player and a single vinyl of Verdi's *Rigoletto*, so I got to know the opera well.

Our general practice clinics were at the hospital, and on my first day, I arrived and introduced myself. The cheerful nurse welcomed me and told me about the farmer with the bad tooth.

'When does the dentist come round?' I asked brightly.

'Next spring' she replied.

She had already laid out the instruments and drawn up the local anaesthetic, and the farmer had settled himself ready for relief. I had a look in his mouth and saw the decayed molar tooth, lower right, and it had a nasty abscess around it.

I knew that the dentists' general plan is to put anaesthetic near the nerve at the back of the inner jaw – but where? Excusing myself, I knew there were some textbooks in the doctors' room and I found a 1,200-page treatise *Anaesthesia for Surgery,* but it lacked the required instructions of how to freeze the lower jaw. I returned and persevered with the injections. Eventually, after most of the area became numb, there was success. The nurse showed how to grip the tooth and then rock it back and forth, and out it came – all of it.

'Well done,' said the nurse.

I became good at doing extractions. Sometimes the tooth would split, leaving a root, and I learned the manoeuvre to winkle it out with an elevator, leaning on the adjacent tooth, but being careful not to break it, too. Nor was this quick course in dentistry wasted. My frontier surgical skills were useful back home when, in the middle of the night, we summoned a patient from home for a kidney transplant but, as luck would have it, he had a dental abscess. Such infection would worsen when given immunosuppression for the transplant, but, just after we anaesthetised him for the transplant, I took the tooth out as a curtain-raiser, to much applause.

At the Fort, other surgical challenges emerged when a farmer brought in an almost life-less dog, run over while reversing his truck, and bleeding into the abdomen seemed likely. Hesitating to open up the dog, I phoned down to our nearest veterinary school, 500 miles away in Edmonton, and they accepted the spirit of the challenge. They said if the spleen was ruptured and I gave adrenaline intravenously this would shrink the spleen and might control the bleeding. This I did, and the dog picked up. It later sat up and went back home in the farmers' wagon.

Besides the general practice clinics. and with the other partner trained in anaesthetics, we did some rewarding surgical work together, well paid for by the government. He brought in some hernia and varicose veins cases to do and he also instructed me in tonsil removal. Other things cropped up. The hospital had a 'steam room' for chesty native children sent in from the reservations, and their mothers stayed in the hospital's relative's room. I noticed one young mother had an old injury near her right eye which had contracted as it healed, pulling a hood of skin almost halfway across the eye. I had plastic surgical training and every time I saw her, I felt that a plastic procedure called a Z-plasty would put the skin back where it belonged and restore the blocked vision. Plastic surgeons have a bad habit, when studying the human race, including its face, of yearning to make improvements, particularly if payment results. I mentioned this mother's deformity to our GP/anaesthetist and he said that we should go ahead. It went well. Afterwards, we looked at the Alberta government's fee schedule and found that a Z-plasty was a well-rewarded plastic surgical procedure, which paid my airfare.

I also got quite good at delivering babies, or rather joining our midwife during this always impressive event. At the Fort, the Mennonite community favoured large families and the deliveries usually meant the fast arrival of the latest addition. Only occasionally was there a long night of waiting for a first baby to appear. This obstetrical work prompted me to get some extra training back home. I took instruction on how to do a Caesarean section which might be required at the Fort if an urgent delivery was necessary, or there was bad flying weather. My 'see-one, do one' training was fortunately never called upon. Sam Galbraith, when he came out to the Fort on another occasion, had a fright – he had to deal with a breech delivery.

I did do a post mortem, however. The Mounties brought in the body of a young man who had been shot in the abdomen, and it was over to me to do the examination. Who else? There was much blood inside and some holes in the intestines, but, embarrassingly, the bullet was elusive and there were plenty places for a bullet to hide. We had no x-ray machine in the hospital, which would have helped locate the missile. I told the Mountie that, surely, we had a cause of death, but he disagreed. 'The boss says we need the bullet', he explained to me. The murderer's defence lawyer would be delighted if no bullet was found. I went back into the messy abdomen. I was about to give up when I noticed a small rough point on the ligaments in front of the lumbar spine. With a probe I found and followed a track into the bone and

it touched metal within.
With difficulty, I got
the bullet out, and the
Mountie proudly took it
away. The prosecution's
tick boxes were complete.

There were visits
to the clinics in the 'First
Nation' settlements,
flown there by an
alarmingly young pilot
in his small single-engine
plane, landing on small
grass strips cleared in the
birchwood forests. These
local settlements were still

*Bringing a sick baby to the Fort Vermillion hospital
from the reservation.*

centred on single-handed Hudson Bay stores, which still had the tradition
of recruiting a storekeeper from the North of Scotland. If they survived
the first tough, solitary year or two, they got promotion southwards into
the bigger city Bay stores. But with fur trapping gone, the settlements'
only income came from the lavish, but controversial, Canadian
Government social security cheques, a charitable policy emerging from
the government's guilt for the past intolerance shown to the indigenous
peoples. The settlements were sad places, and critics alleged that this
welfare policy had sapped local initiative and endeavour. There was a high
level of alcoholism and depression, and at one clinic, I saw, for the first
time, and the last, a case of primary syphilis.

These Canadian locums proved interesting and well-paid,
although a bit lonely. But, staying in the spartan house, and listening to
Rigoletto, I could make plans to equip my new home, and I had brought
with me the Habitat catalogue, a favourite source of furnishings for
young homemakers. With each surgical case, reimbursed generously
by the Alberta health service, I ticked off what I needed – the famous
Habitat duvets, bean bags, bench seats, corduroy cushions, Japanese
paper lampshades, plus a chicken brick, a wine rack, a garlic press and
much else.

But after two or three visits, these holiday-time Fort Vermilion adventures, like all good things, came to an end. Things tightened up in Alberta and the enjoyable can-do spirit of the frontier was out-dated. Now, before going up to Fort Vermilion, you had to present yourself at the College in Edmonton to check that you were a qualified doctor, since some dubious practitioners had got into Canada during the rapid expansion of their health services. On my way to the Fort, calling in to deal with this new paperwork, the College registrar had a hazy idea about clinical life in Fort Vermilion, and he was astonished to hear that, as well as general practice, I would do some surgery. He announced that surgery and giving of anaesthetics 'up there' would have to stop '... right now'. I explained to him I had a respectable training in surgery and exhorted him to exhibit the famous Alberta frontier spirit, though omitting that I could do with a set of Habitat's best Le Creuset cast iron saucepans.

His phone rang, and I listened to a tense exchange about a surgeon suspended from practice in the large Calgary hospital to the south. The man involved was a controversial transplant surgeon, well known to me. The registrar put the phone on hold and looked me in the eye.

'Why don't you go to Calgary and do the transplants?'

My pride was hurt and my loyalty to the Fort aroused.

'I want to do hernias in Fort Vermilion.'

'No,' he said.

Another interesting visit was to assist medical training in Libya. The country was then a closed and mysterious place, but a stable one under Gaddafi's dictatorship and he was keen to develop European contacts for his students and doctors. Our Glasgow College agreed to help, though cautiously and informally. The Glasgow doctor who organised the scheme was fond of Libya and did some Libyan paediatric practice, and this led to two-week visits by Glasgow doctors to do teaching and advisory work.

The Tripoli hotels were scruffy, and there was no street life or restaurants; much else, including alcohol, was banned. Foreign newspapers occasionally got in, but were redacted. Gaddafi had a firm grip on his nation, and his face appeared on posters together with aphorisms from his *The Green Book*. We, of course, deplored the authoritarian regime. Our view was that if he was overthrown, peaceful democratic elections would follow and a young elected leader, probably trained at Sandhurst and with an elegant Parisian wife, would take over and all would live happily ever after. Instead, later, after Gaddafi had gone, Libya descended into chaos, and we then realised that a fractious Islamic state is difficult to govern.

The main Tripoli hospital had huge, bare wards with simple beds. There was a mysterious operating theatre which never seemed at work, despite an impressive theatre list posted each day. The recovery room beds were unused, and, without patients, it was a cosy place for cats to sleep. At coffee time, we shared one or two cups with the genial local surgical staff and afterwards they washed the cups in the blocked, never-emptying sink.

The surgical wards were full of interesting patients showing the advanced disease no longer seen in developed countries. There were impressive ward rounds, done in a very Western style, with the professor attended by his staff arranged in the usual hierarchical order. On arrival, on one trip, we found a seriously-ill young man in the ward, with an advanced brain tumour showing awful physical signs no longer seen in the West. The professor's ward round, with us in tow, reached and examined the boy and we heard the professor's order for a CT brain scan. Next day, on the ward round, the same thing happened. I took one doctor aside after the round and asked about the scan, since the boy was distressed. The doctor then explained that there was no CT scanner in Libya. The chief's management plan was a theoretical one, an aspiration about what should be done. It was a virtual investigation, based on the Western-style template that a CT scan was desirable. The boy disappeared from the ward shortly afterwards. None of the doctors knew where he had gone, and he had doubtless returned to simple terminal care in his village.

The patients in the ward changed rapidly. Many showed multiple superficial skin cuts over the affected area, and local healers had made these scarifications earlier to 'let the badness out.' But trying to find any surgical action on these ward cases each day was frustrating. It turned out that most of the patients were poor people from the country, who, having arrived and got a surgical opinion, ran away after being put on the operating list. Hence they did very little surgery.

This, and other nuances of the culture, took a little while to understand. The Arab culture is to accept fate, rather than believe that man is in control of his destiny. If something isn't happening, there's a reason, and the phrase 'in sha' allah' – 'if God wills' – permeates all discourse.

The Muslim placid acceptance of shortcomings, the blurring of theory and practice, and a different sense of time, familiar to politicians and businessmen, was in evidence even when teaching the students. They were all bright and motivated, especially the female students. With the abundance of interesting cases, teaching was enjoyable. On the first day, I met with a small group of students at a bedside in the bare ward, and was about to start, when one spoke up:

'We must have screens round the bed when teaching.'

I felt embarrassed. I had earlier looked for screens in the ward for this purpose, but decided there were none.

Off the students went, and back they came.

'There are no screens' they said.

Next day we went through the same little scenario again, and the hunt failed again. In their culture, what had been decided one day – that there were no screens – does not apply to the next. Commentators have noticed this difference in Muslim thinking, and have suggested that it was our Industrial Revolution which brought a change, since accumulation of experience leads to increased productivity.

There was one surgical surprise. We heard that there was a heart surgery unit somewhere, and after many enquiries, we got transport. The unit was on the outskirts of Tripoli and when we arrived, prepared to encounter another unimpressive establishment, we were impressed to find a spotless marble building with nicely-tended gardens. The director, dressed in green scrubs, welcomed us to his American-style office where he had television screens on the walls letting him watch and communicate with his theatre and investigation rooms. Young nurses in surprisingly revealing uniforms shimmered in and out and supplied us with coffee. We found out afterwards was that he was a friend of Gaddafi and for this heart unit, he had obtained everything he wanted.

꙳

We did some local tourism and visiting Leptus Magna was the highlight. At this famous Roman settlement on the edge of the Mediterranean, there were no car parks, no enclosures, nor any entry points or fees, giving a remarkable ambience, as if the Romans had just left. This simplicity was government policy. One of Gaddafi's mantras on his city posters was that 'Tourism Demeans', meaning that a proud nation should not pander to visitors. I think of Gaddafi when in Princes Street in Edinburgh I see kilted gentleman playing the bagpipes.

On the last day, our exit was also a demeaning one. On arrival, a shifty man from the Ministry had taken away our passports in a plastic bag. At the hotel, to everyone's relief, the bagman reappeared with the passports and with our fee in cash tucked inside.

It was a relief to get to the airport. On the plane, there was a welcome apéritif available after a temperate two weeks.

꙳

Visits to the United States were obligatory because of the dominance of American medicine and surgery. American hosts were often curious about Scotland and it was easy to poke fun at their parochialism. In the 1960s they might ask

'D'yall have television in Scaatland?'

'Yes', was my answer, 'we invented it, and the telephone and ultrasound scans, by the way.'

One treat was eating out, and good steaks were in abundance. Their hamburgers were also outstanding in comparison to our Wimpy equivalent, but I got tired of being offered 20 different kinds.

'Just give me an ordinary hamburger. Plain vanilla' I said to a serious-minded waitress.

She was puzzled.

'I don't believe we do a vanilla hamburger.'

꙳

My first American visit had been using a student fellowship to visit Woods Hole Marine Biological Station where the talented Harvard neuro-scientists moved in the summer to escape the city heat. There they could use the marine creatures' simple nervous systems for their studies. One courtesy call was to sit at the feet of Otto Loewi, then age 86 and resident in the town, and hear of his Nobel Prize-winning discovery of chemical transmission by 'vagusstoff' in 1921.

Meeting Nobel Prize winner Otto Loewi (1873-1961), discoverer of chemical transmission, at Woods Hole Marine Biological Station in 1961.

Having met and made friends there with Gordon Vineyard, a fellow medical student, and his new bride Phyllis, it led to later visits to them in Boston and to the legendary Peter Bent Brigham Hospital. There the modern era of organ transplantation and renal dialysis started, and I was in awe of the hospital's achievement. Their dominating chief surgeon Francis 'Franny' D Moore had shielded his young staff from the naysayers while they slowly won the argument. I met the now-senior pioneers, including Joseph Murray and John Merrill, recipients of many honours, including Murray's Nobel Prize. Earlier, they had kept going in the 1950s in the face of bad results and professional hostility to both kidney transplantation and dialysis.

Moore's impressive scientific assistant, Margaret Ball, was from Scotland, and they had another Scottish influence at his hospital. After World War II, a Brigham surgeon came back from military service in Britain, and his new Scottish wife got the job of hospital switchboard operator. In this pre-bleep era, she used the tannoy to call the doctors, and instead of the American intonation calling for 'Daackter so-and so', she used her own version 'Dooctor' with broad Scottish 'o's. Thereafter in their discourse a generation of Brigham trainees used her version.

After a four-year training, young American surgeons immediately set up in hospital practice, whereas British training is longer and more incremental. As a result, American surgery was, and is, variable in quality with excellent practice and innovation at the top, but less success at the bottom. The Brigham staff dealt with outside surgeons' mistakes and complications, which often included kidney failure. My hosts at the Brigham, when I joined them on their rounds, might flippantly say that the next patient, sent in from St Elsewhere's, was a POGARF, i.e. suffering from Post-Operative Grief and Acute Renal Failure. A more serious acronymic diagnosis was FUBAR - F*cked Up Beyond All Recognition.*

Gordon and his wife Phyllis, my friends from Woods Hole days, came over in the 1960s when American cars were then at their maximum size, often gas-guzzlers with 25-gallon fuel tanks. Our British cars were more suited to our difficult economic times, and mine was an economical Mini. When driving from London to Glasgow, Gordon gallantly offered to fill up at the first pit stop. Needing petrol, I pulled into a station and he asked

'How much should I put in?'

'Four gallons,' I said.

'Why don't you fill it up?' he said.

'That is filling it up,' I informed him.

Back home in Boston, they dined out on the story.

❧

On my travels, American surgeons liked big talk and even in these early transplantation pioneering days, they would tell me that their kidney results had improved by 20% from last year reaching 80% one-year survival. A year later, visiting the same place, they said again that their results were up by 20%, thus improbably leaving no room for further improvement next year. Although I travelled widely, the one unit I didn't visit then was Tom Starzl's Denver transplantation department. He was an outsider, not one of the Boston-Brigham transplant dynasty, and knowing his fierce behaviour at meetings, I hesitated to visit. To my surprise, I was later to get to know him well.

One famous unit I did visit, notable for heart transplantation later, was Denton Cooley's heart surgery hospital at Houston, Texas. It was an extraordinary experience, even in this, the heroic age of

---

* These acronyms came into favour in the American military – starting with SNAFU, a genteel expansion being 'Situation Normal – All Fouled Up.'

Denton Cooley's parking lot at his Texas Heart Institute.

cardiac surgery. He had a circle of nine operating theatres opening from a central anaesthetic/recovery area and he was involved in all the cases proceeding simultaneously in all the theatres. The junior trainee surgeons opened the chest, put the patients on the pump, and Cooley went from theatre to theatre doing the crucial bit, with the trainees closing up thereafter. Relieved of doing the routine, physical parts of the operations, he could do the essential bit of up to 12 cases a day and he was doing a tenth of all the heart operations in America.[*] Famously calm, he was impressive to watch, and his speed came from his steady pace, with all stitches falling into place first time. It paid him well. At the time, a dean of an American medical school lamented that he didn't mind the heart surgeons having yachts or owning islands, but when they offered to buy the medical school, he thought things were getting out of hand.

Another feature contributing to his speedy turnover of cases was that when the patients arrived, often from afar, a cardiologist immediately saw them, did any extra tests, adjusted the medication and wrote a prompt assessment using an early form of word-processor which was passed on for the surgeons' immediate study. If all was well, they might operate next day. Seeing Cooley in action was also a lesson in efficiency, a contrast to our sluggish NHS habits, there being no financial stimulus.

On my American travels, I had some frights.

The worst was at Baltimore when going to visit the famous Johns Hopkins Hospital in the 1960s, and, arriving at the Greyhound Bus Station, I needed a taxi. When I moved towards the first cab in the line, a large African-American took my bag and moved to a nearby car not in

---

* This 'con-current' or overlapping' surgery was, and is, controversial and is barred in some American institutions.

the taxi rank. This was scary, but things got worse. When we drove off,
I realised that sitting in the back seat behind me was a large non-white
man. I presumed that I was doomed, or at least would lose my wallet
and bag. But we got there. He must have been Mr Big in the taxi world,
and the queue didn't apply.

With this fright, I didn't take a taxi again in America for about 30
years, until I was stranded at an out-of-town bus station, rather than
arriving, as planned, at the downtown terminus. A taxi with a large
fierce-looking driver eventually appeared. There was no alternative, and
I asked for an estimate of the fare to town, and in perfect English, he
quoted me $20. On the journey downtown, it turned out that he came
from Somalia having been educated at an English mission school there.
On arrival, he said that, after all, the fare was only $15, to which I was
glad to add the $5. Relieved on many counts, I took taxis in America
occasionally thereafter.

Public transport in America was in increasingly poor shape.
The Greyhound buses were now unpopular and their downtown
terminals decayed. The dominance of the car also meant that the
railways were neglected and public money went into roads, rather than
rail. Accordingly, there was minimal awareness of the existence of
rail transport, even when available. Much later, our son Alistair and
I went to the 2009 Walker Cup match at the Merion Club, outside
Philadelphia. Alistair wanted to go downtown to see the city and we
asked the unhelpful club steward for advice. Was there a railway link to
the city? He thought not. The words were hardly
out of his mouth when we heard the distinctive
wale of a train's bull horn and indeed there was a
light railway line station close by. The Merion club
had thrived in the 19th century because of this
railway link for golfers living in the city.

Another golfing visit was to the Ryder
Cup match in Boston in 1999, when I was again
hosted by the Vineyards. Also attending was a
noisy, kilted Scottish group from Perth, and I
asked them how they got accommodation in
Boston at this busy time. Not easy, they said,

since they had not planned ahead. Arriving in downtown Boston, and looking for last-minute accommodation, they were directed to the YMCA, then still favoured by gays. The residents of the Y were delighted when the 15 young kilted men turned up.

On longer flights, particularly across the Atlantic, there was always the chance of an announcement asking 'is there a doctor on board?' My two good Samaritan acts involved nothing serious and ended well. The first was a request to look at a first-class passenger who was drunk, but I successfully suggested I should move to the first class and keep an eye on him. I also got Brownie points from the crew by suggesting that, to arrive without delay, we should not be held in the early morning stack over Heathrow.

The second episode involved a young lady who had collapsed, and she had the ashen face characteristic of a ruptured ectopic pregnancy. In the crowded plane, with many onlookers, I had to ask about her love life, and was relieved to find that pregnancy was out of the question. It was a simple faint and she perked up soon after.

CHAPTER 17:

CONSULTANT

Promotion … Aragon group … Speyside

IN 1973, OUR Peter Bell was appointed to the chair of surgery in Leicester, and we were sorry to see him go. The transplant service now needed someone in charge and there were two of us of equal seniority, but we both lacked some months of the surgical training required for promotion. One of us needed to be in day-to-day charge of the nine-man (all-male then) team pending a definite appointment. My rival was talented and ambitious, but had few friends, and spoiled his chances by claiming, when speaking at our hospital clinical meeting, that his talent mirrored that of Jack Nicklaus, then putting up a picture of the golfer. I lacked such ambition, but had the confidence of the team and was put in charge *pro tem*, and I got the formal consultant job later.

Our kidney transplant service, as elswhere, was constrained by the lack of donors and we increasingly looked for more donors from the family. The results were improving, but cyclosporine was still to come. Our strengths were in immunology and ultrasound, having the stimulus from Ian Donald's pioneering work one floor above our surgical wards. Our transplant group in the hospital was well-staffed and stable and we had an active lab research group. My assistant Ginny Jackson was impressive and got her Ph.D. on the defective lymphocytes in our dialysis patients working with our visiting Greek physician Thanos Diamandoupolos who got his clinical M.D. degree on the same subject.

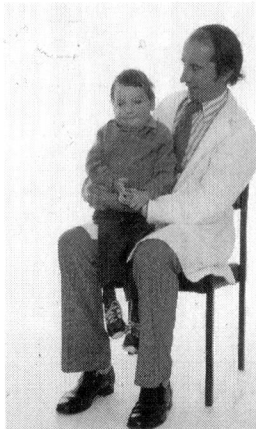

Andrew Bradley arrived from England and did a thorough job of studying the depressed immune response in intensive care patients. I was always a solitary researcher and I was glad to have Andrew's people-skills in directing our laboratory team and he later took the chair of surgery at Cambridge.

My own research in stimulating immunity in cancer had halted since there was no success with this in human cancer and indeed there was embarrassment at the false claims made in human cancer studies chasing this will-o'-the-wisp. Instead, other doors opened, with a growing interest in the history of medicine. My life was changing in other ways since added to this I was in love with one of the Western infirmary nurses.

Our youngest kidney transplant recipient, showing the effect of the necessary steroid treatment.

Beyond our group in the department, there were problems. Sir Andrew Kay had retired from our chair of surgery, leaving the department rather rundown. As we all hoped, Peter Bell in Leicester was appointed and we knew that on return he would revive the department and foster new young surgical talent. To our astonishment, the news came that Peter had pulled out of returning, the reason being that the Dean had misled him on the conditions of his post, and that lies had been told. This all seemed a bit theatrical,

The Transplant Olympic Games countered the view that the transplanted patients were chronically ill and unfit. Here our two Western Infirmary entrants are limbering up.

but later events made this explanation credible. The University in its embarrassment moved quickly to fill the post, but it was not a happy appointment.

ॐ

Our transplant team kept together at work and play. In our transplant team we had Andrew Bradley, Harry Burns, who became chief medical officer in Scotland, and Ken Calman, who had the same jobs in Scotland and England and returned as Vice Chancellor at Glasgow University. Sam Galbraith, though now in the neurosurgical unit at the Southern General across the river, kept in touch. Some of us carried on Peter Bell's tradition and met in the Aragon pub nearby on Friday nights and the regulars were Sam, Harry Burns, Andrew Bradley and Sandy Reid a Royal Infirmary pathologist. We were part of a group in the hospital, centred on Kay's department, who also took an interest in broader matters – 'Where did I go wrong?', Prof Kay asked me later, quietly proud of these extra contributions. Others in surgery in the Western Infirmary with broadening interests were Muir Gray who moved to public health work at Oxford, and had national influence. David Purdie changed to obstetrics and gynaecology and later, as an authority on Scottish literature, helped edit the *Burns Encyclopaedia*. As president of the Sir Walter Scott Society, he concluded that Scott was 'prolix in dialogue, rambling in description, meandering in plot and well, just too long'. Purdie cut *Ivanhoe* in half and republished it.

Our Aragon discourse was left-of-centre, hostile to the Tories, and deplored private medical practice. To us, the link between poverty and health was a given. Occasionally a new member of staff at the Western might arrive and join us, and, making some predictable gibe about the Labour Party, would be puzzled at the frosty reception. With Sam moving out of his doctrinaire socialist phase and tending towards pragmatism, it left Sandy alone on the far-Left. I was getting involved with Scottish nationalism, which had been a romantic lost cause up to this point but was now a serious electoral force. Sam had no time for the Scottish National Party. His mantra was still that 'the struggle of the working classes is international, not local.'

Our Friday group shared an interest in winter sport and we soon found that renting a cottage during the winter in the Spey Valley, as a

Winter climbing in the Highlands - Myself, Sam Galbraith and our future wives Jean and Nicola.

syndicate, worked well and was remarkably cheap. The weekend would begin on Friday evening in the Aragon, driving north, and regathering in Speyside. The climbers like Sam, Sandy and Andrew could climb and the skiers could ski. This was an agreeable arrangement for many years, but some of these dwellings were warmer and drier than others. One tweedy owner of one of the cottages we rented was banned from the use of the railways, even though he worked in Inverness. We were curious, but even Sam, later a minister in the Scottish government failed, to solve the mystery.

Sam was tolerant of us bourgeois skiers because Scottish skiing's early days had been ideologically sound. It started with the Glasgow shipyard apprentices in the Creagh Dhu Club, who were mountain and rock climbers in Glencoe from the 1930s. These free spirits hitched a lift on lorries, including the milk lorries going to Campbeltown via Glencoe. For shelter, they might make bivouac tents using tarpaulins from stranded lorries, and, lacking Primus stoves, instead picked up coal discarded along the West Highland Railway track. To the annoyance of the local landowners, they might poach some game. After the War, the well-off Scottish Ski Club members, who took

Alpine holidays, installed a fault-prone Poma tow, although there was still a steep walk uphill to reach it. The Creagh Dhu climbers were available for the heavy lifting and repairs, and were happy, for free skiing, to keep the weekend service going with the new erratic tow. On the mountain, the only facility was a small hut for which only the Scottish Ski Club members had keys. Despite the many adversities, including an intermittent lack of snow, dreadful weather and a lack of accommodation nearby, Glencoe offered reasonable skiing on a reasonable day, and began to attract visitors.

Soon, in the Cairngorms in the Spey Valley to the North, a new lift emerged in 1981 and a group of Creagh Dhu climbers-turned-skiers moved north and arrived. Taking the cheeky title Ski School d'Ecosse, from 1962 they offered instruction, laced with Glasgow humour.* The early days in Aviemore offered rough and ready sport with a long walk from the car park. But, for a good reason, there was, and is, an excellent après ski life, available all day. Whereas European resort villages shut down during the day, Aviemore is ready with *avant* ski facilities to entertain those discouraged by high winds, lack of snow or when too much snow blocks the road. And, in Europe, if things are bad, there is no alternative sport. Denied skiing in Aviemore, there are famous golf courses half an hour away at the coast, including Nairn (a Walker Cup venue) and their links are in excellent shape all winter.

On these weekends after the journey north on the then-quiet A9 road, we settled into the cottage for a simple dinner. Once, when we started in a new rental, the lofty lady owner explained that the table in the cottage main room was an antique. I doubted it, but to avoid complaint, I hid it away and instead brought a simple expandable wooden table for £1 from a Partick junk shop and brought it up precariously on top of my Mini on our next visit. It being my turn to cook, I put the Pyrex dishes in the oven to heat and forgot about them. When I put them out, there was a sizzling noise and a burning smell and four white rings appeared on our table. After we left, the owner snooped and sent me a nippy letter about the damage to her antique table. This was easily denied.

* For the ski school founder's autobiography, see Frith Finlayson *The Ski Teacher* (1997).

For dinner, we usually had mince and potatoes, plus some rough red wine. Despite many academic degrees and diplomas, we often forgot to bring a corkscrew and would threaten our surgical careers by trying to get the corks out with a knife and fork. If all else failed, we handed over to our brain surgeon, and Sam's nuclear option was to strike the bottle against the china sink and then decant.

After dinner, round the stove, came the dialectic. Joining us one weekend was Sir Peter Morris, professor of surgery at Oxford, and on one of the less favourable skiing days, he damaged his shoulder. We put him to bed close to the warm sitting room, and the bottle of whisky he had kindly brought helped our usual metaphysical and political discussion. Late at night, we settled the criteria for an ideal society – people would not own property but instead, hold everything in common. By the early hours, casting about for specific examples, we agreed that all toothbrushes should be shared and when you travelled around the world there should be a toothbrush always at hand. This noisy consensus meant a disturbed night for the injured professor next door. In the morning he tried to recall what was going on and asked, reasonably enough,

'What the hell was all that about toothbrushes?'*

---

* This late-night epiphany had impressive earlier advocacy. H G Wells, in his influential *A Short History of the World*, put toothbrushes high on his list of 'significant personal possessions'.

CHAPTER 18:

Politics Local and National

Devolution ... SNP Policy ... The Referendum

WITH OUR Aragon group's interest in politics, my political epiphany came one night in October 1973 when, returning late, I switched on to the BBC's *Newsnight* and saw a group of serious men discussing something to do with Scotland. It was the day of publication of the Kilbrandon Report, properly called the Royal Commission on the Constitution, set up in 1969 in response to election victories by the Scottish (and Welsh) nationalists. The Scottish victories were greatly assisted by the discovery of oil in the North Sea that year. I watched entranced. As students, we had all been sympathetic to the nationalists and their romantic dreams, but this development was serious. Kilbrandon was offering a roadmap towards some kind of Scottish self-government. Moreover, Scotland was, after all, well off. I promptly joined the Scottish National Party.

I attended local and national meetings of the SNP and met up with some like-minded doctors. Soon, I was asked to organise a committee to advise on SNP health care politics, which I did and this brought in, among others, the Glen brothers, Roy Scott the urologist and Professor Watson Buchanan the rheumatologist and formidable head of Glasgow's Baird Street Clinic. The British Medical Association people in Edinburgh were curious about our activities and asked to attend one of our meetings. Their Scottish secretary at the time was a laid-back, old-fashioned Edinburgh medical type, and he arrived unexpectedly at our next meeting. He made pleasant noises and afterwards told a friend in Edinburgh that I was an 'interesting chap'. Flattered, I requested specifics about my impact, and heard that the BMA secretary's verdict was that 'I wore brown shoes with a dark suit', almost a crime in polite Edinburgh circles.

One function of our committee was to provide the eleven new Westminster MPs with briefing on health care matters, and provide PQs – private members' questions. The plan was to build up knowledge about healthcare within Scotland, since such questions from the Scottish MPs had been unusual. One I drafted was on Scottish waiting times for surgery, which was not yet a public issue, and the detailed reply had much data of interest.

About that time, the SNP also brought out pamphlets on policy matters, and the leadership requested a health care policy statement from us. We got going, and when our policy was ready, we had a visit from Isobel Lindsay, the young, charismatic SNP's policy convener. She gently explained to us that in politics some things were politically important to the electorate and some were not. Raising doctors' salaries should not feature prominently in our document, she thought, since doctors were doing rather well. But she explained that concern for nurses' salaries was acceptable. We improved our draft and, better briefed, brought in other political issues. Watson Buchanan's big idea was to take medicine out of politics and we highlighted it as a proposal for a Health Commission. This partly came about later, when in 2013 the independent NHS Board emerged in Scotland.

Our policy document was long and still a bit technical, but it still reads well. I was interested to hear later that at a constituency selection meeting to choose a candidate, they put all these SNP policy documents in a hat. The aspiring candidates had to pick one at random and speak to it, after five minutes' study. One hopeful drew our long policy document and when I met him later, I sympathised.

In 1975, the Labour Party in Scotland started to take devolution more seriously and Gordon Brown and others produced their *Red Paper on Scotland*.* This book of essays a signal of their new interest in Scottish politics, and they offered a convoluted rationalisation that devolution to Scotland could, at least locally, pave the way to socialism.

THE PRESS AND JOURN

Doctors want NHS devolved

A GROUP of Scottish doctors are going against the British Medical Association's policy and campaigning for the devolution of health services in Scotland.

Under the name Health For Scotland (HFS) which they formed in April last year, the doctors are fighting for separate health care as they believe the NHS is "too centralised, slow, and resistant to change".

Chairman of the HFS Mr David Hamilton, a consultant surgeon at Western Infirmary, Glasgow, said: "The doctors involved in the campaign are from Glasgow, Edinburgh and Stirling, but we have many sympathisers throughout Scotland.

The chapter on health was a strange one, dwelling much on legislation unfamiliar to most voters, notably the worthy Alkali Inspectorate Act.

Gavin Kennedy on our behalf got going as the editor of a rival work offering an enthusiastic blueprint for a future Scotland.†
The title *Radical Approach* was deliberate since SNP policy sought not to lean left or right. In my chapter, I used the growing statistics on Scottish health care funding, staffing levels, public health, and the private sector, after untangling these from the usual UK national figures.

The various Scotland and Wales Bills struggled on, and during the passage through Parliament of the Scotland Act 1978, a referendum was conceded, but a mischievous and unique amendment, added to appease the Labour Party sceptics, required that 40% of the *total* registered electorate approve the Act.

Preparing for the referendum, we set up our 'Health for Scotland' pressure group to draft a manifesto making the case for the political devolution of healthcare to Scotland.

---

* The political response of the Labour government then in power was slow and the executive of the Scottish Council of the Labour Party in June 1974 voted 6 to 5 against these proposals for devolution of any political power to Scotland. Donald Dewar, later First Minister in the first Scottish Parliament, was among the five voting against.

† Hard-to-find, then and now, is Gavin Kennedy (ed) *Radical Approach: Papers on an Independent Scotland* (Palingenesis Press, Edinburgh, 1976)

We tried to make it an all-party affair, and I got one Liberal to join, but it wasn't worth searching for a pro-devolution Tory doctor since we never come across any. I had a word with Donald Dewar, but he could not help, explaining that the Labour Party would run their own pro-devolution campaign, without alliances. Sam Galbraith, rising in influence in the Labour Party, read our draft manifesto, and when he returned it to me with grudging approval, he had changed all my passive verbs to active ones.

We sent it out. It impressed me how the grateful journalists took up our HfS (Health for Scotland) press releases and they used most of our advocacy unchanged. Small groups can be influential. One interviewer, on Radio Forth, charitably let me deliver the message, then did a Paxman:

'What would you say, if I said your Health for Scotland group is just a front with four SNP activists posing as a mass movement?'

He was almost right. Then he paused and he let me off.

'Don't worry; the microphone is off.'

He then told me I was in good company. Gordon Brown, the leader of the Scottish Labour Party's pro-devolution campaign, would give out a long press release after their committee meetings, but say it was speech given at a 'meeting he had addressed recently.'

We had unexpected support from Sir John Brotherston, the recently retired Scottish Chief Medical Officer and in England from Lord Taylor of Harlech. *World Medicine* took an article from me, making it the cover story. Other doctors in England were interested in devolution, hoping to counter the London centralism,

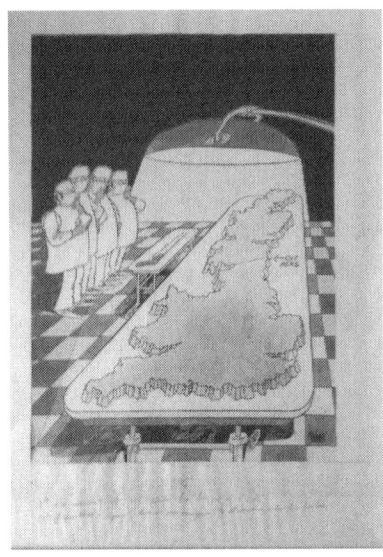

World Medicine's 1979 cover story on devolution.

and I was asked to speak at English meetings, notably at Windscale and at Hebden Bridge in Yorkshire, home of the brave little Campaign for the North.* In May 1976 the *British Medical Journal* had a one-day conference at Glasgow airport to discuss devolution as applied to health care, and in the company of the impressive editor Stephen Lock and healthcare analyst Rudolph Kline, I made our usual advocacy. James Hogarth was there for the Scottish BMA and he predictably said that there was no need for change.

I asked the College of Physicians and Surgeons in Glasgow to hold a debate on devolution and they agreed, but the audience was not supportive, with a few exceptions. Being also a fellow of the Edinburgh College of Surgeons, having, as described earlier, passed their fellowship examination with no knowledge of practical surgery, I wrote to their president suggesting a similar debate in Edinburgh. The surgeon replied and rejected the idea, telling me that the Edinburgh College was an international institution unconcerned with such parochial matters.† So, I resigned my Edinburgh surgical Fellowship.

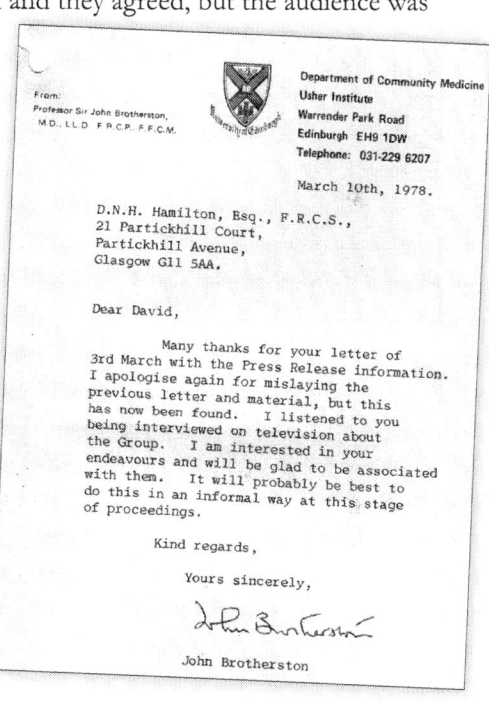

From:
Professor Sir John Brotherston,
M.D., LL.D. F.R.C.P., F.F.C.M.

Department of Community Medicine
Usher Institute
Warrender Park Road
Edinburgh EH9 1DW
Telephone: 031-229 6207

March 10th, 1978.

D.N.H. Hamilton, Esq., F.R.C.S.,
21 Partickhill Court,
Partickhill Avenue,
Glasgow G11 5AA.

Dear David,

Many thanks for your letter of 3rd March with the Press Release information. I apologise again for mislaying the previous letter and material, but this has now been found. I listened to you being interviewed on television about the Group. I am interested in your endeavours and will be glad to be associated with them. It will probably be best to do this in an informal way at this stage of proceedings.

Kind regards,

Yours sincerely,

John Brotherston

The recently-retired Scottish Chief Medical Officer, a closet nationalist, offered encouragement for our pro-devolution activity.

* Attempts to decentralise England's politics continued, but with little success until George Osborne's 'Norhtern Powerhouse' startegy.

† Much later, an Edinburgh publisher asked me to read and comment on this surgeon's memoirs, submitted for publication. They felt his text had little more than joined-up committee meeting minutes; I had to agree.

Nobody had ever resigned from the surgical fellowship of that College, and the word spread in the Glasgow medical bazaars. I thought I would be avoided in polite company, but instead, I had enquiries from other surgeons of our generation who were locked into making lifetime payments to two, or even three, of the United Kingdom surgical Colleges. They gained these fellowships from a day or two's visit to those Colleges for the examination and they often never returned to visit the distant College. The growing mood was that joining one College was enough, and that in our case the local Glasgow College now sufficed.

As the referendum neared, a Scottish parliament was increasingly likely, and the building was almost ready on Calton Hill. I went on a SNP candidates' selection course but didn't do well. Although I knew I could speak on big occasions, I didn't find it easy, or intellectually honest, to pretend to a selection committee of a dozen seasoned party activists that I understood the nuances and options of SNP policy, for instance on education. Understandably, I was shifty and got low marks for poor eye contact.

As the referendum approached, Sir Alec Douglas-Home entered the debate by promising, at the last minute, that if the electorate voted against devolution, the Tories would bring in a different, better form of devolution. With days to go, at our afternoon departmental tea gathering, our Prof Kay announced that because of Sir Alec's promise, we should vote 'no'.

'Just so, Professor' nodded his meek staff, except me.

The result was that 51.62% voted 'Yes' for devolution and 48.38% 'No'. This would normally have been decisive, establishing our Scottish parliament, but the overall vote was not enough to pass the threshold inserted in Cunningham's wrecking clause.

The day after this referendum non-defeat, I was sitting brooding in the doctors' common room in the Western Infirmary, and Harry Burns passed by and, understanding my gloom, he sympathised.

'Mark my words' I said defiantly. 'This is not the end. It will all return in another 20 years.'

I wasn't confident. But my estimate was a good one and twenty years later we got our Parliament. Shortly after, Harry became Chief Medical Officer and now an enthusiast for devolution and nationalism, he graciously recalled my prediction 20 years before.

After the referendum defeat, the SNP at Westminster felt cheated and had no option but to drop the life-support they had given to the minority Labour Government by 'confidence and supply' A vote of confidence inevitably followed and Callaghan's government fell. In the election which followed, the Tories were returned to power and would hold it for many years. The SNP, perhaps surprisingly, lost nine of the 11 members of Parliament. Scotland had lost heart.

SNP policy hardened after this failed cooperation and changed to a determination to seek 'independence, nothing less.' Many of us in the SNP disagreed with this heroic strategy and remained devolution-minded gradualists. A group within the party called the 79 Group emerged, and it included most of the authors of *Radical Approach*. We had an early meeting in Glasgow in Willie McRae's office at Levy and McRae, the solicitors, and Willie, a chain-smoking, fire-brand nationalist and veteran activist in many causes, announced theatrically that the SNP was being watched by MI5 and to 'beware of agents provocateurs'. We humbly wondered if the intelligence agencies could be bothered with surveillance of our small, demoralised, patriotic movement, now divided and shorn of most of its MPs.

We were wrong. When Willie died under mysterious circumstances in April 1985, two retired police officers testified that he had been 'of interest' to the intelligence agencies. Willie was found off the road to Oban with a bullet wound in his head and the police later found a revolver without fingerprints nearby. Suicide was the verdict, but conspiracy theorists were soon at work, and the events produced two books, three television documentaries and two plays at Edinburgh Festival's Fringe.

Although I attended one or two early meetings of the 79 group, I had lost hope of any progress with devolution in the short term, and, lacking members of Parliament, the SNP now needed no detailed advice on health care. It had been absorbing and diverting extra interest for me. It was time to try to settle back into normal life in the hospital.

❧

The Tories, now in power, caused immediate damage to health and healthcare. They favoured private medicine by allowing all hospital consultants to do unlimited private practice. The result of this was that many specialties and Highland hospital practice were now unattractive, since there was no private practice. Doing surgical research was now also unrewarding and it soon suffered. They also halted the preparation for a ban on smoking in public places.

❧

CHAPTER 19

Writings and Marriage

Book dealers … Book shops … Canongate … The Healers
Good Golf Guide … Marriage

I N OUR PRO-DEVOLUTION group we had a publisher, Peter Chiene, who ran his tiny Q Press. Peter had approved of my historical approach to Scottish medical politics and suggested that when the devolution debate was over, I should write a book on the history of Scottish medicine. After the disappointment of the referendum, I was pleased that he remembered this offer and that we could salvage something from the events. He put me to work, and he soon joined the equally small Canongate publishers who were to thrive in the revival of the publishing sector in Scotland. The devolution debate had kick-started a cultural revival.

To write about Scottish medicine, I used the local Glasgow libraries including the Mitchell Library, Glasgow's famous public library, which I had last visited as a schoolboy studying Bradley's well-thumbed and reader-annotated *Shakespearian Tragedy* (1904). Since the library had no lending rights, this meant repeated returns to consult the resources. Wondering if I could purchase these hard-to-find and useful out-of-date books, I discovered the antiquarian book dealers. There were a number who, to my delight, specialised in sending out catalogues of important used Scottish books.

When a new catalogue arrived, you looked at them quickly, and I liked one story about the great Glasgow 19th century bibliophile and bibliographer David Murray. Just as he was heading for his London train, a new catalogue arrived. On the train, to his alarm, he saw listed a book he had long been hunting. Leaping from his carriage at Carlisle, and using the platform telephone, he obtained the book and regained his seat on the train, a happy man.

In my book purchases, I did not seek good condition or elegance, but was happy to get a working copy as a source. You develop a relationship with these booksellers and one of the earliest was a Mr Stansfield who had retired to the north of Scotland. He issued lists of Scottish books duplicated on large A3 sheets and he liked to start each page with a new item. To fill up the white space remaining at the bottom of the previous page, he added some conservative Thoughts, usually about socialism and its perils. The little homilies disappeared when his wife developed an unpleasant disability and required long-term NHS treatment and care. With his help, and that of others, I built up a good working library.

One of the most exotic of the book dealers, even by international standards, was, and is, found a mile away from the University and Western Infirmary and I bought books steadily from him. Later, with his quirky help, I also built up a respectable library on the history of golf. Though using the romantic name of Voltaire and Rosseau, the owner, Joe McGonigal is a Glasgow man, and he dislikes paperwork and declines to send away interesting items to auction.* When Glasgow houses are cleared, he takes in entire libraries, and buying low and selling low, cash is best. Like all great bookshops, he usually has a contented, sleeping cat, who must also go out, because kittens appear and have a risky upbringing endangered by the landslides of books from the overcrowded shelves. Joe's stacks of conventional shelving reach to the roof and on each shelf, the front row of books conceals a further row behind. There are extra piles on the floors which conceal much of the lower shelving. There is a rough classification within the

---

* At the time of writing, V&R characteristically has no email or website, but nevertheless is awarded enthusiastic five-star reports by impressed visitors.

shop, but these boundaries overflow into each other, and you are on your own. Behind Joe's head is his reserve bookshelf which holds recent arrivals, but if he does not like the customer, he may deny they are for sale.

There was, at the back, a store within a store, a secret Aladdin's cave, which he might open up, if he liked you. There he piled the books up in volcano-like circular chimneys, and on reaching a certain height, he then filled the middle cavity inside with more volumes. But there was a disastrous fire in this part of the shop and he did not replenish it. Of his various helpers, at least two moved on to open their own, less quirky, bookshops nearby.

❧

My book on Scottish medicine matured, and the always-essential readers were my father and, later, Dr John McConachie, still a friend from my GP locum days in Lossiemouth. Their work was essential to deal with my terrible spelling; later, the word-processors were a blessing. There were other traps. Father prevented my claim that 'John Knox dealt with the Church, education, and Parliament and then turned his attention to adultery' and noticed my description of 'the close relationship Highland general practitioners had with their local telephone exchange operators.' For a title, the main thing was to get to away from dry academic wordage. Famous guidance came much earlier from the book destined to have the stuffy title *History of Europe A.D. 100 to 1400* but was instead inspirationally called the *Decline and Fall of the Roman Empire*.

It was time to submit the text to Canongate. Started in Edinburgh in 1973 by Angus Wolfe Murray with a £2,500 float from his wife Stephanie, in his absence she carried on alone at Canongate in Jeffrey Street, successfully finding Scottish themes and new authors. In 1975 she published Antonia Fraser's *Scottish Love Poems* and then handled Jimmy Boyle's *Sense of Freedom,* a controversial bestseller in 1977. In 1981 came Alasdair Gray's *Lanark* and the surprising bestseller William Lorimer's *The New Testament in Scots* of 1983. Alexander McCall Smith was on the editorial board and metaphorically held her hand during the many difficulties.

I liked to call in at Canongate's small two-roomed office, and in the back shop I reported progress to Stephanie and Robin Hodge, who soon after, set up his successful and enduring events magazine

The List. I enjoyed hearing their news and one day they told me about the launch of Lorimer's now-famous Bible and that it had not gone well. Even the Church of Scotland bookshop had turned Robin away without any orders, because 'it was not the sort of book they would take.' Canongate put out a press release, suggesting the bookshop had banned the book, and media interest aroused, orders started coming in, and have never ceased.

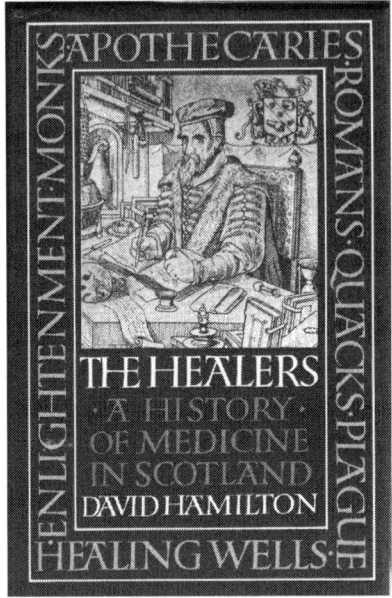

It was easy for me to enjoy the romance of publishing, but their obvious struggle to earn a living was less romantic, even during these now-famous publishing events. Stephanie was an astute publisher, but a poor businesswoman, and the perpetual crises prevented her from paying out regular royalties. Hence you also got no sales figures. After my *Healers* book came out in 1981, I found a way. Sales were the responsibility of a cheerful staffer in their front office. He had the monthly sales figures in a ledger on his desk and I could look over his shoulder while we talked. Also on the desk were irate letters from less tolerant authors threatening, sometimes in capitals, to take legal action to get their royalty payments.

Although I was rarely paid, I was pleased when they asked me to write another book, a wee guide to Scottish golf courses, and I rattled this off in 1983, two years after my *The Healers*. I learned later that it had sold well, but again, other than the reward of being in print, there were no royalties, until, I think, the second edition in 1995 when Canongate was in new hands. I was glad my sporting work had contributed a little to supporting Canongate and Stephanie's serious literary output until her final crisis.

❧

All my life I had collected golf courses, and I called on this awareness for my golf course book. While others were collecting stamps, on summer holidays, I was off looking for hidden courses. Most guide books then assumed that Scottish golf comprised only Open Championship courses, ignoring the strength in the little 'hidden-gems' distant courses. While doing the study, I was asked to leave the greatest and humblest courses in Scotland. While checking something about Muirfield quietly in semi-darkness, to my surprise the legendary fierce secretary appeared and enquired where I came from.

'Glasgow,' I mumbled.

'Out,' he said.

In Glasgow, at Knightswood's small municipal course ('Royal Knightswood' as Sam Galbraith called his home course), a small queue forms to hire clubs, but if you have your own, you can go to the front and play-off. They have a notice saying 'Clubs Must Not Be Thrown About' and I thought I would take pictures of this colourful scene, but the starter appeared and asked if I had written permission from the Council to photograph.

'No' I said

'Out' he said.

❧

To illustrate my golf book, Canongate favoured a talented Edinburgh artist and a jazz musician with the stage name of Harry Horse, and the preliminary sketches he offered ranged from the inspired to bizarre scenes involving grotesque animals. We had a frosty meeting at Canongate and though complimenting him on his excellent little golfing vignettes, we said that the menacing animals had to go. He walked out, complaining about having to work with a right-wing doctor, which I thought was a bit hard. He had a troubled life and moved to Shetland later, and, after killing his disabled wife, he killed himself.

Years later, when I was looking at the 1920s golf-related work of a *Punch* cartoonist, I recognised the origins of Horse's attractive artwork. He had copied them shamelessly from *Punch*. Posthumously, he got away with it; no-one else has noticed the plagiarism.

For the book's layout, Canongate did things well, and brought

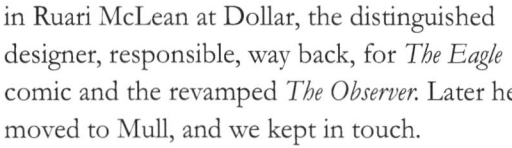

in Ruari McLean at Dollar, the distinguished designer, responsible, way back, for *The Eagle* comic and the revamped *The Observer*. Later he moved to Mull, and we kept in touch.

It's not often you get Brownie points from your children but my little *Good Golf Guide to Scotland* earned some later. Stephanie had used her charm to get an Introduction for the book by Sean Connery. By the third edition, Connery had a knighthood and the publishers asked me to ask him, if, despite being a democrat and a nationalist, he wanted his gong added to the title page. I wrote to him, and soon after, our son came to find me in the house with the breathless news that

'Dad, Sean Connery is on the phone for you.'

I was inclined to say 'Tell him I'm watching television.'

He wanted the 'Sir' added.

❧

We were first acquainted on the back stairs of Phase One of the Western Infirmary on a Bank Holiday Monday in 1980. As we passed, Jean noticed that I had my typewriter (yes, a typewriter), under my arm and she thought this was odd behaviour for a bank holiday. I, on my part, noted this new very attractive nursing sister and was told she had just arrived from the Royal Infirmary across the city. I next saw her in the Aragon pub, but she was always accompanied, although occasionally the two of them joined our free-thinking group. One day, after a family funeral, made more melancholy by her relationship ending, she returned to Glasgow and feeling low, and the day being Friday, she thought she would call in to the Aragon. By her account later, she saw our group, and getting closer, hid behind a pillar. I then spotted her, noting her lack of a male escort, and was glad to make her welcome. Later, the others drifted off and she agreed she had not had her tea and accepted my bold invitation to adjourn to a local Italian restaurant. The rest is history. Jean was warned that I never would marry, but she nobly took me on.

My plan for our engagement might have been problematic. I was to meet her at our group's Sunday post-ski haunt, the Overflow Pub. I had worked all day alone in the lab in the hospital and had not realised it was the change of hour day; my watch and the clock on the wall were both an hour behind. Although I was an hour late, she was in good company until I arrived. Matters being explained, Jean was, as ever, non-judgemental and unruffled and I popped the question in that night.

With the launch of my book, the *Good Golf Guide to Scotland* coming up, the publishers suggested a launch and photo-opportunity at my golf club. But I was less certain and nervous, since my club was the conservative, all-male Glasgow Golf Club, but I went ahead. The *Glasgow Evening News* arranged for a photographer to attend, and we waited for him in the club, Jean rightly feeling conspicuous. Their sports photographer emerged from a taxi, just back from the Olympics, and he had a three-day growth of beard and was tie- and jacket-less. A few members were around and they noticed. With relief, he suggested that the three of us move to the second, distant, green for the required pictures. But on discovering that we were getting married, he was more interested in Jean and the romance than the golf book. The photographer then suggested that Jean should climb on my back for an affectionate piggy-back photograph. Members passing on the drive were getting ruffled. He repeatedly asked if we had met in the operating theatre – perhaps with knowing glances exchanged over the masks? Regrettably, we could not assist him with this Mills and Boon trope, since we worked in different departments. However, back at the newspaper office, the sub-editor felt otherwise. Too good a story to be false, the item went out with the subheading – 'Theatre Romance'.

The other males in our group – Sam, Harry, Andrew – took note and the mood was that the time had come to settle down. One by one, the bachelor dominoes fell, a metaphor much used then in the

Wedding group – (back row) my father, mother, best man Roddy MacSween, Allan and Ailsa (Jean's brother and mother). Bridesmaids were nieces Sarah (left) and Susan.

debate on the Vietnam War. Only our Leftist Sandy Reid remained unmarried. Jean and I were married in September 1982, my father officiating, at her home town of Castle Douglas. My mother, by this time, had advancing dementia, an uncommon affliction then, and would die soon after. Jean's mother was the family's matriarch and I gained a valued brother-in-law and I shared interests with Jean's sister Hazel, an increasingly successful artist.

I sensed that Jean, a good bit younger than I, was, like myself, not keen to settle in suburbia, content to wait for bigger confidential merit awards. Also, being a bit older, if a family came along, we might not manage to travel later in life. My research experimental work had stalled, although the others in the lab were doing well and were self-sufficient. There were difficulties at the top of our Department. Looking inwardly, I seemed more interested in broader matters, notably in the history of medicine. If I was to expand on to this, perhaps writing a history of organ transplantation, I would need exposure to professional historians.

About this time, an Australian surgeon friend re-appeared and I remarked that it was good to see him back so quickly. He replied that it was seven years since he had last visited, this being a further sabbatical visit allowed in Oz. In the NHS, we had no such chance for any mid-life refreshment. This was the legacy from the bad old days of private practice, since if you took a year out to travel, your practice would be lost. Added to this, for the trainees, surgical training was becoming standardised with no provision for experience in other centres. The BTA degree (Been to America) was no longer encouraged, nor sought.

I felt strongly about this increasing parochialism, always a danger in Glasgow, and attempted to get a sabbatical year off. This failed. Meanwhile, at Oxford, the best history of medicine department in Britain, the distinguished director offered to take me in for a year, but of course, could offer only a room, but no money.

❧

CHAPTER 20:

Oxford

*The visitor ... History of Medicine Unit ... Oxford
University Press ... Early word processing
Letterpress printing ... Litigation*

H E WAS short of stature and had a twinkle in his eye.
A distinguished physician and a past editor of the *Irish Medical
Journal*, he was now in charge of the Irish government's specialist
hospital in Baghdad, capital of Saddam Hussein's Iraq. Doctors are a
gossipy lot, and when looking for a transplant surgeon for his hospital,
he was told that I was seeking to take time out in middle life. Hence his
mysterious visit, and he wondered if I would like to work for a while in
Iraq. I did not, but I had an idea.

Our plan for a sabbatical year off to develop my interest in the
history of medicine had got a certain distance, but foundered, and we
were still welcome to go to Oxford. Although we could survive without
income for a year, having sold one of our flats when we married, there
was another problem. It was my old one. After three weeks of full-
time study in a quiet room in the dreaming spires in Oxford, crippling
depression would set it. Hoping that 'this time it will be different' was
risky. This weakness, I knew, was easily prevented by having some
clinical work. Here in front of me was a man with the answer, perhaps.

He confirmed that the Irish hospital's Baghdad kidney transplants would use only family donors, since Middle Eastern society did not accept organ donation after death. I enquired how many transplants would be likely each month and the figure was low. I suggested that they would not need a surgeon all the time, and that if they grouped the grafts from relatives together, I could come out, perhaps two weeks out of six, to do them. After surgery, I suggested, the unit's capable renal physician, already in post, could look after these transplanted patients.

After he returned to Dublin, he agreed to this plan, mentioning a good fee for the short visits, and our visit to Oxford was now possible. The stars were aligned. I would get my 'sabbatical', avoid my black dog problem, and we would have some income and some travel. The stars shone a little brighter when he added that Jean could also come out for these two-week stints, both of us, he added, travelling first class to and from Iraq. We decided to go; a door was opening, though the longer-term risks were obvious, and I might be unemployed.

We would stay in Oxford for two years.

Off we went, plus Monday, our cat. We stayed first in Wheatley, a small village outside Oxford, renting an ancient, low-ceilinged house with a pub adjacent, and Bob the Log kept us supplied with wood for our open fire. On one trip back to Scotland we loaded up with a sack of peat and, putting some on when we got back, the village filled with a North Uist perfume. Jean enjoyed village life and with her gardening interests there was the famous Waterperry Gardens nearby.

I enquired about golf. Yes, there was the Oxford University staff golf club which met at 11.00 a.m. on Wednesdays, which said something about these leisured academics. I didn't go; I was there to write.

Charles Webster, our Unit's director, was finishing his official history of the NHS, and he told me of the founders' hopes that the doctors and the rest of the staff would pull together in one national endeavour.* He had almost abandoned hope, but was cheered to see a Glasgow brain surgeon addressing the workers during the Upper Clyde Shipyard work-in. He asked if I knew who it was. It was Sam, and I told him about Sam Galbraith. He was impressed.

---

* Webster was known for his *The Great Instauration* (1975) proposing that science flourishes in revolutionary times.

We settled in. The image of Oxford as a snooty place was wrong, at least in the staff level, and instead the place seemed to belong to anyone visiting with a serious purpose. I joined Green College, recommended as a pleasant place for lunch, but making my first visit, I had an odd encounter. The custom was to sit down together at the long tables and, introducing myself to a thoughtful-looking man across the table, we exchanged pleasantries. But when he heard I came from Glasgow, he stiffened and launched into an attack on our Glasgow dean of medicine, calling him a liar, as alleged in the Peter Bell affair. I remained silent but knew the difficulties the dean was still causing back home and fresh stories had come through.

It was a pleasure to mix with the young historians and join the seminars in our Department. We had some retired doctors, including the author of a standard work on the history of plastic surgery, and he would be helpful in my studies.[*] Historical studies – 'historiography' – was changing. Kings and battles, the mother-lode of academic history earlier, were now being side-lined and social history, including healthcare, instead flourished. The type of medical history favoured by doctors, mainly biographies and hospital histories, no longer sufficed in academia. Instead, public health, medical education, medical ethics were attractive topics, plus women in medicine and nursing history.

I only reluctantly admitted my interest in golf history. To my surprise, this was applauded. Even the history of sport was now respectable, as part of the history of leisure. You are in good company, they told me, Sir Raymond Carr, Oxford's star historian, was now publishing on fox hunting.

The Oxford Unit was excellent, and there was also much talent in London at the large medical history department of the Wellcome Institute. There, the tension between the rival approaches to the study of medical history could emerge at seminars and lectures. Some Harley Street men might slip in to the meetings and were dismayed. The situation was fraught. The doctors reasonably felt that medical history was their preserve and moreover the young academics, who were

---

[*] TJS Patterson translated and reprinted Zeiss' 1863 history of plastic surgery and in 1978 added his partial update as the *Patterson Index of Plastic Surgery, 1864-1920.*

hijacking the subject, did not know one end of a stethoscope from the other.

Academic study of the history of medicine in Britain was well supported by funds coming from a fixed proportion of Sir Henry Wellcome's huge bequest and the grants were increasing. Dispersing these generous funds was largely in the hands of a medical man at the Wellcome Trust. His distaste for the non-medically qualified historians who he had to support was well known. He deplored their casual clothes and left-wing sympathies and was not pleased when on an inspection tour of his Wellcome History of Medicine Unit in London, he saw some posters speaking highly of Che Guevara. I would encounter the man and his views later.

As planned, with a room of my own, I got started on my history of organ transplantation and needed to look no further than around the corner for a publisher. To my surprise, the prestigious Oxford University Press accepted the proposal. Then there was another surprise. They explained that my manuscript need not be a typed text, but could use a new strategy. With a computer and a word processing programme, I was to prepare the text as a file on a disk ready for typesetting. OUP's view was that this new strategy justified the gift of the computer to the author. All of this was new and impressed the others at our Department.

OUP gave me a Sirius computer, the first successful personal word-processing computer. It had just come out in 1982, and the IBM's famous PC did not arrive until a year or two later. The Sirius was selling well, although costing about £2,500. It had green text displayed on the heavy, bulky cathode ray screens used until the mid-1990s. OUP generously added in a dot-matrix printer, the standard printer until the end of the decade, using printer ribbons and a long fan of paper held in position by sprockets. To write, you first loaded the operating system and then the WordStar program from brown 5½ inch floppy disks into the left-hand port and then loaded a data disk into the other port.[*]

---

[*] WordStar was the dominant word processing program until about 1985 when, failing to evolve, WordPerfect became favoured, only to be overtaken shortly afterwards by Word for Windows.

WordStar was first to display WYSIWYG (What You See Is What You Get), i.e. showing on-screen what the printed page would look like, rather than the usual lines of dense text. To show italic or bold, you marked the word before and after with the codes ^PI or ^PB. This was a tedious business, since the mouse had not arrived yet, but we managed. It was a new exciting world.

I also decided that I might print and publish by myself during the Oxford stay. In my golf history studies, I had come across an interesting item which seemed suitable for publication, but costs

---

OXFORD RULES FOR THE PREPARATION OF TEXT ON MICROCOMPUTERS

APPENDIX A

Compatible Microcomputers

Oxford University Press can accept floppy disks from microcomputers of the following types:

Act 1 Sirius
Superbrain
Apple II
Xerox 850
Cifer
Osborne

Text Category Commands are inserted at the start and end of a piece of text which you intend to have a particular prominence or quality. Text Category Commands must always appear in pairs. They each consist of a circumflex (but see page 5, note 1) followed by one or two letters.

The portion of text sandwiched by a pair of Text Category Commands will be given the desired quality or weight by the typesetting system. The Rules permit you to nest one pair of Text Category Commands within another, so you can nest a portion of Greek text within a displayed quotation. Text which does not appear within a pair of Text Category Commands will be treated as main text and be set in upper- and lower-case roman type.

List of Text Category Commands

^B ...... ^B	Bold text
^D ...... ^D	Semi-bold text
^S ...... ^S	Italic text
^T ...... ^T	Superscript
^V ...... ^V	Subscript
^QA ...... ^QA	Heading level 1
^QB ...... ^QB	Heading level 2
^QC ...... ^QC	Heading level 3
^QD ...... ^QD	Heading level 4
^QE ...... ^QE	Heading level 5
^QF ...... ^QF	Footnote reference
^QG ...... ^QG	Transliterate to Greek

---

were high. It was a forgotten poem describing golf in Glasgow in 1715. With modern publishing and printing methods moving fast into electronic typesetting, something was being lost. With the old-fashioned metal type used on good paper, you get a pleasing three-dimensional effect. I decided to learn to print, or rather return to the black arts I encountered at school.

Looking around, I found just what I needed. The Oxford Printmakers Co-operative's workshop, largely devoted to screen printing and engraving, also had an Arab letterpress printing machine, surviving from the days when it was much in use for printing tickets, letterheads and much else. The Co-operative also had metal type, masses of it. Oxford University Press had recently made their momentous decision to give up their traditional 'hot metal' printing methods, and they gifted many of these trays of type to the Cooperative. To set the text, you fished out individual letters from these mahogany trays. But setting type is a tedious business.

My companions were engravers who used dangerous-looking baths of corrosive liquids, and stern notices on the walls described the acid's dangers. I shared the Arab machine with a poet who was printing his own work, and told him how I proposed to print and sell a slim book on golf, and get my money back. The poet took the view that life was not that easy. These were the early days of a boom in collecting golfiana, including books, and the limited number of classic books, when offered, were showing sharply increasing prices. The hunt was on for rarer items. Hence if I could produce my own *Early Golf in Glasgow,* it might sell a few copies and help pay for the project.

I needed two kinds of help. The first was with the mechanics of letterpress printing and I found the local Oxford Guild of Printers and, after attending one of their meetings, I asked a young man, Jonathan Stevenson, at his Rocket Press, to give me hands-on instruction and he agreed. He was much admired for his letterpress work and when Macmillan, the publishers, that year discovered the original woodblocks for the illustrations in the 1865 publication of *Alice in Wonderland,* they looked for a printer with traditional skills. Jonathan had just landed the contract, and they entrusted him to produce a limited edition from these precious boxwood engravings.

My second need was to get help with setting the type. I could set small projects, like a Christmas card, using our OUP type trays, but I would never develop enough speed to set long passages. Nor was I up to the tedious task of putting the type, once used, back in the pockets in the composing trays.

For his books, Jonathan used the legendary Bill Hughes based in Upton-on-Severn to the north, who set type from a Monotype type caster. These famous machines, now suddenly out-of-date, create single letters from molten lead, but there were few of these now in use.

I sent my text off to Bill and he not only set my text but provided tuition in the ancient skills and language of typography, including avoiding 'widows' and 'orphans.' * Bill showed me how to use 'drop' capitals to start a chapter, and he helped with the headers – the title at the top of each page – pointing out the need for small capitals and generous spacing of the letters – not EARLY GOLF but E A R L Y G O L F.

When my long galleys of metal type were ready, I drove up and, being a distance away, stayed overnight after correcting the proofs in a delightful pub by the river. Back home, I split the type into pages, added the headers, and at the end, as usual, Bill had provided extra type with a full alphabet plus numbers, to allow you to correct the proof yourself.

I took the pages with my early attempts back to Jonathan for his expert advice and suggestions – fine tuning the choices in ink, pressure and paper. I decided that a limited edition of 150 copies might attract collectors, and also, after printing this number of sheets,

boredom sets in. The pages needed separation by tissue paper and the ink was dry by the next day. Jean helped my printing projects as a proof reader and collator of the pages and she joined the visits to Jonathan and the Cooperative.

I now needed The Fine Bindery near Northampton, a legend in the little world of private presses. It was a joy to visit and look at their work in progress, getting ideas from the many expensive projects on hand. My project was tiny, but they warmed to it. For the endpapers, hand-marbled paper has a freshness, and I used Anne Muir as a supplier.

Early Golf in Glasgow was ready. I now christened my venture as The Partick Press, from my home and hospital district in Partick in Glasgow. Nae more, it was the Partick Press, *Oxford*, there being nothing to stop me claiming this distinguished locale. Marketing of a limited edition, normally difficult, was as easy as I hoped. I used our

---

* These melancholy terms describe unsightly single words left alone at the end of a paragraph or page.

British Golf Collectors Society and put flyers out to the 700 members, and a heady six orders arrived on the second day after posting, and they kept coming in. At £4.50 *Early Golf in Glasgow* was a snip and all 150 copies sold eventually. They occasionally appear in the specialist golf book antiquarian catalogues listing them at 25 times this price. I kept a few; no pension fund could ask for more.

Before leaving Glasgow there had been local concern, not restricted to the Aragon Friday night reformers, about a medical mishap. One of the notoriously fast Glasgow surgeons, during a removal of a benign neck lump, shut off the carotid artery to the brain and the young schoolteacher was paralysed down one side. The sympathies of the doctors in Glasgow were with the patient, and unusually, he took legal action, borrowing heavily on his house. But when the case went to court, the professor of surgery at the Royal Infirmary agreed to defend the surgeon, while making it known in private to the Glasgow medical world that he was only doing so to maintain the standing of the profession and discourage any such future claims. The disabled patient lost the case.

One way forward was to have a different system to replace the vagaries of our adversarial, expensive, litigation. A no-blame system of arbitration, as in New Zealand, was preferable. I wondered if I might contribute, in a small way, and in Parliament there was a Liberal peer who was attempting to bring in this no-blame legislation. I visited him in his elegant Hampstead house, staffed by Filipino servants, and he explained the difficulties ahead. In the short term, he had a suggestion. Doctors were opposed to speaking critically of their colleagues. Could I do some medical reports on claims for negligence, since these were almost impossible to obtain? I would not have done so in Glasgow, but here in Oxford, and unknown, it was possible. He put me in touch with a young, newly qualified lawyer called Martyn Day whose firm Leigh Day would later become famous, and then controversial, when involved in large international class actions. I met him and he was pleased to get help, and passed on some cases for me to look at.

My first report was an easy one about an unacceptable surgical blunder, and I said so, in only two pages. I charged no fee, being more interested in the principal involved. Martyn came back to me and said that the clinical details were too brief and in such matters, it was customary to add extras and suggested extending it to perhaps six pages. Also, he said, unless I charged, I would not be believed.

All the subsequent cases I reviewed could not be defended, and in the one or two which went to court, the defence failed. Among these cases was the work of a surgeon on the south coast who trusted to his own judgement when diagnosing breast cancer, proceeding without a biopsy at any stage, and attempting to conceal occasional tragic mistakes. I did these reports for a while, and the requests increased, but the work was rather distasteful, and I declined further cases. Soon after, in the mid-1980s, the mood changed, and with claimants now getting a balanced medical report, this aided justice and also helped improve standards in surgical care. The downside was a reasonable concern that this rise in litigation encouraged over-defensive medical care. A no-fault compensation system would have been, and still would be, better.

Every six weeks or so, our life in Oxford was enlivened, and funded, by the visits to Baghdad.

᷍

CHAPTER 21:

Baghdad

Baghdad politics ... The hospital ... Al Rashid hotel ...
Duncan born ... Wellcome Trust Unit

OIL-RICH IRAQ was the wealthiest country in the Middle East.
Despite the smouldering war with Iran, starting in 1980, the
economy was healthy. The oil money was finding its way to the citizens,
and most goods were available and subsidised. Petrol was cheap,
electricity installed throughout the land and provided free, and every
family had food allocations, education, and healthcare. These social
services were unprecedented in the Middle East; Women's rights and
education were also advancing.

It was a secular regime but there was an underlying political
tension between Saddam's dominant minority Sunni Muslims and
the majority Shi'ites. It was like pre-Reformation Scotland, or the
Highlands with their clan rivalries. In Scotland, these passions burnt out
and the Enlightenment followed; the Middle East has a long way to go.
Iraq had the classic weakness of dictatorship – there was no graceful
exit possible for the leader.

Saddam's gated compound had villas, government buildings, shops
and a hospital for use by his inner circle. He occasionally consulted our
visiting hospital doctors on his health problems, but I did not have that

pleasure. We heard about these strange consultations from others, and a visiting surgeon told me of interviewing Saddam about his haemorrhoids. The stilted question-and-answer session with Saddam had to pass awkwardly through interpreters, with the doctor kept 20 yards away in case of an assassination attempt. Saddam rewarded these medical consultations with a kitsch gift – a gold watch bearing his portrait.

First-class travel back and forth to Baghdad sounds attractive, even romantic, but the Iraqi Airways' first-class cabins were usually full of well-off Iraqis, with their well-behaved children. Meanwhile back in the 200-seat economy part there were only a few humble Iraqis, and on the flight back, getting a sleep, fully stretched out, was always possible by retreating to economy.

The Iraqis set up the Ibn al-Bitar Hospital to provide specialist surgery not available locally, such as kidney transplantation, heart surgery, plastic surgery and complex orthopaedic operations. Our patients were ordinary citizens of Iraq and some were fast-tracked by an impressive presidential voucher from Saddam's home district of Tikrit. Previously, the government sent Iraqi patients needing specialised care to Paris, but now it was more economical for the government to bring the surgical expertise to Iraq. The patients were not too pleased, since they and their families enjoyed the paid-for visit to France, one attraction being shopping there at Marks & Spencer's.

Our hospital largely kept out of trouble but we knew of the underlying unpleasantness in Iraqi politics. Weeks before the hospital opened, the advance staff were told to expect a high-level visit, and the Minister of Health appeared, surrounded by minders and armed guards, and he unexpectedly called for a cup of tea. The hospital stores had just arrived and the head nurse went off and with difficulty located what looked like the necessary items. She returned with a cup of tea plus a sugar bowl and the minister added three or four spoonfuls. Drinking it, he immediately stood up and spat it out. His armed escorts cocked their weapons and looked menacing. He had been given salt, not sugar. He later disappeared when he fell foul of Saddam.

More unpleasant was the hospital's involvement in the Bazoft affair a few years later. He was an Iranian-born journalist working for *The Observer* and after hearing of an explosion south of Baghdad, he asked one of the senior nurses to take him there in the hospital Land Rover. At the sensitive area, suspecting a radiation leak, he scooped up samples of soil for analysis. At the airport, they found the samples, and arrested and executed him as a spy. She was imprisoned but released after a few months.

We heeded the obvious advice to keep any opinions on local or international events to ourselves. We also knew that the well-groomed girls who interpreted for us in the hospital were the daughters of party members, and through this hospital work they were privy to our attitudes.

Our hospital had a simple modular construction and had the latest equipment. Next to our operating theatre there were visiting surgeons hard at work doing cardiac, vascular, plastic and orthopaedic procedures.* Our kidney transplants went well and one particularly rewarding case was when a young doctor received a kidney from his brother. When I returned for the next visit, on the first day, he was waiting on the walkway to the hospital to embrace me. The junior doctors were on rotation out from Ireland, and not only did they enjoy the adventure, they were looked on favourably for promotion back home if they had helped in Baghdad. Later, all remembered their

---

* *Ibn Al Bitar Hospital Baghdad 1983-1988,* Dublin 1988 is a proud record of these times; there are some extra personal accounts listed on Google.

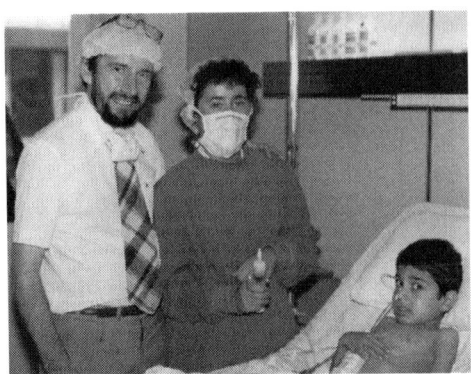

secondment with pleasure. The nursing staff were Irish girls, and since many of them came out from hospitals run by nuns, they enjoyed working in the more relaxed atmosphere of the hospital and they had the night life of the Hospital's riverside staff club.

The war with Iran was a person-to-person conflict like WWI and the wounded had a pattern of injuries not seen in the West since then. One unpleasant surgical challenge (for the vascular surgeons) arose when shrapnel fragments from the small bombs and mortars used in the trench warfare remained in the body and slowly eroded into arteries and the adjacent veins joining them as an arterio-venous fistula. These could be nasty, particularly in the neck, giving a pulsating mass involving the large vessels to the brain.

In Iraq we stayed at the legendary 428-room Al Rashid Hotel, run by the Indian Oberoi group, one of the best-equipped hotels in the world. The rooms had the finest fittings, including silk sheets and cashmere blankets. This lavish expenditure had prepared the hotel for an international conference of non-aligned nations which never took place. The hotel was never dull, since it hosted all the city's visitors, including politicians and foreign businessmen seeking the Iraqi government's many infrastructure contracts. Saddam also entertained Iraqi warlords arriving from distant areas, known to the hotel staff as the 'flying sheikhs' who, never having seen hotel lifts before, would delight in the novelty, accompanied by their armed bodyguards.

In the early 1990s, after Iraqi's retreat from Kuwait, the hotel inserted a famous mosaic image of George Bush into the floor of the hall entrance and when visitors walked over it, this delivered a traditional Islamic insult. There was excellent room service, particularly the curries, but times could be hard. They might have gin but no tonic, or plenty tonic and no gin. Ahead of our visits, we received messages about current shortages, in the Hospital, and brought out supplies of the missing items. Bacon was understandably not available, and a pack or two were well received in our the renal ward kitchen for a staff fry-up. The government-run television was dull and the single government daily newspaper carried the thoughts of the leader and pictures of him with his many visitors. The first pages were dreary but the back page's reports on the English Premier Division football was a surprise. The emphasis was on the manager, rather than the players, in accord with the local *zeitgeist*.

Jean could move about safely, and the route down into the city went past the cheerful armed guards at the hotel and the soldiers of the anti-aircraft station guarding the important military communications centre next door. Downtown Baghdad was noisy and smelly, without the glamour of Sinbad the Sailor's city or the romance of Omar Khayyam's *Rubaiyat*, and it had plenty portraits of Saddam. Jean could walk about in a normal dress and she enjoyed visiting the famous National Museum of Iraq close to the hospital,

The hotel had an elegant dining room, but an even better place to dine in an evening was in the outside restaurant. It had skilled chefs and Tandoori ovens, and on a warm evening the calls to prayer from the muezzin in the nearby minarets gave a unique ambience. On Fridays, the local holiday, there was a gathering of hospital staff at the hotel pool, and the British ambassador, John Moberly, an Arabic speaker who had worked in many Middle Eastern countries, might join us. He was holding down one of the trickier foreign office posts, since Britain (but not Ireland) was out of favour. Later, in retirement, Moberly had prominence by considering that the Bush invasion of Iraq in 2003 was a mistake. He believed Iraq posed 'no grave or imminent threat to Western democracy' and predicted that Western military intervention would not bring stability to the region.

During the invasion, the hotel had fame when the journalists staying there witnessed the 'shock and awe' bombing of Baghdad. John Simpson of the BBC, had affection for the old Baghdad's 'fish restaurants on the Tigris banks, alleyways, calls to prayer and teahouses' and when looking out his window he claimed he saw a Tomahawk missile 'head down the road and turn left at the traffic lights'. The bombing destroyed the military building close to our hospital and with the hospital now empty, looters took away all the equipment. Soon after, in the chaos following the invasion, despite warnings by historians and promises by the American army, Jean's Iraqi Museum was unprotected and was also looted. The thieves were well-informed and selective, even skilfully removing large objects, and they returned twice for more, without opposition. Later, the international antiquarian community acted to identify the precious missing objects and returned some stolen items. The Museum reopened in 2015, as had the Hospital earlier.

Getting in and out of Iraq was always a nerve-racking business. Coming in, you might be in the queue behind a long line of sad North Korean construction workers, just off a jumbo jet. When leaving, the hotel regularly presented you with a huge personal bill for the stay, for which we had no local money to pay; a hospital manager arrived and sorted it out. Then, having escaped, there were more hurdles, including airport security, where they searched our luggage carefully. Only after the welcoming thump of the stamp on the thin desktop did we feel safe. Jean got out more easily. When they searched ladies luggage and found perfume, the female security officials would suggest that an exit could be speeded up if the bottle was handed over. Jean didn't argue.

After our first year in Oxford, we moved into the city, around the corner from the History of Medicine Department, renting a house in a small street off Banbury Road close to the centre of Oxford. It had some small shops and restaurants plus the Rose and Crown pub and a launderette used by Ruth Laurence, a local academic celebrity, and her father. As a child prodigy in mathematics, she had reached Oxford University age 12.

The good news was that Jean was pregnant. It was prudent for her to avoid alcohol and our pub instead offered her St Christopher's non-alcoholic lager. Although the saint traditionally protects travellers from harm, we thought it best that Jean did not risk any more Iraqi visits, and I did the last trips alone.

Jean sailed through a shortish labour confounding my suggestion in the middle of the night that there was no need to rush in. Our Duncan James Hamish Hamilton arrived safely and with an English passport, he can play the English card when necessary. Our best man, Roddy MacSween, was pleased at the news, but as a gaelic speaker, tut-tutted at the James/Hamish tautology.

Young Duncan behaved well and fed well. One of Jean's friends had a difficult baby and Jean took her to consult Sheila Kitzinger, the natural childbirth advocate, who lived nearby. Jean stayed outside the room and breast-fed Duncan during the consultation. Sheila noticed and afterwards quietly complimented Jean – 'someone can get it right.'

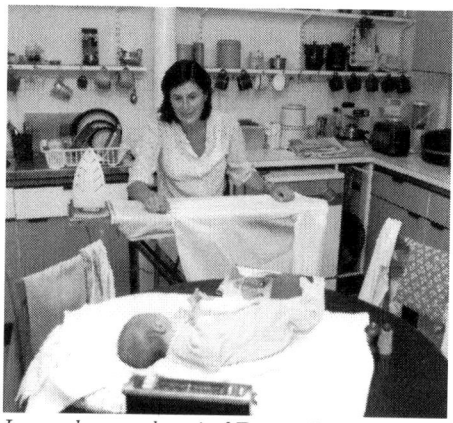

Jean and our newly arrived Duncan James Hamish Hamilton.

We had enjoyed our time in Oxford, and it had gone quickly. It had been productive and enlivened by the intermittent surgical work in a distant land. I had given little thought for the future. Although I had surgical training, getting back into the NHS was notoriously difficult. I knew there was a shortage of transplant surgeons coming up, since with the pioneering days over, the nocturnal work was now unattractive. I could have gone into administration, but I feared the bouts of depression. I thought that something might turn up, and it did.

The head of the Oxford department told me I was in favour with the Wellcome Trust organisation and I would get a phone call. I did and a meeting followed with the senior, powerful Director of the Wellcome Trust, unloved in our niche part of the Wellcome's growing empire. Knowing his dislike of scruffy historians, I put on a jacket and tie for the meeting and he noticed this with approval. He then gave me an opportunity to criticise the Oxford unit, hinting that a doctor would not approve of it, which I did not care to do. He then came to the point, and said he wanted me to head a history of medicine unit in Scotland, I was expecting something like this, though not so big. I was not flattered, knowing what was going on. By supporting me as a doctor, one unknown in academia, he was giving a signal to the professional medical historians that he was not pleased, and that he wanted to tip the balance back to control by doctors.

This murky politics didn't please me, but it was a door was opening, indeed the only door opening. But I knew I could not risk taking a full-time academic post, because of my problem with solitude-induced depression. I had no option but to tell him I would need some surgical sessions in my contract. To my surprise, he agreed, doubtless seeing this as another signal to the full-time academics that he wanted to return the history of medicine to hospital-linked staff, and he agreed that one third of my salary would come from this clinical work. My Unit would have a staff of three plus a secretary and generous support funding. One other condition, a reasonable one, was that I was to start medical student teaching. Less welcoming was that he added that, of course, the unit should be in Edinburgh, because of its place in medical history. I pointed out that Glasgow had recent strength in this area, but he was unimpressed. He told me to wait for an invitation which would come shortly from the Principal at Edinburgh University, and we agreed that I should also go and see one of the professors of surgery in Edinburgh regarding surgical work.

There was no immediate news from Edinburgh, but I made an appointment to see the professor in Edinburgh. When I got there, his secretary told me he had gone to London and she suggested that, 'since I came from Glasgow', I could come back another day. I returned empty-handed to Oxford. A planned meeting at the Wellcome Trust followed in London soon after. When I started by reporting that I had not heard from Edinburgh's Principal, Williams became annoyed. On hearing of the additional snub from the Edinburgh surgeon, Williams drummed his fists on his desk, saying that since the Trust, for once, were trying to give money away, this was unacceptable. He would, he announced, instead move the unit to Glasgow. I was pleased but this was unpleasant power politics, and I was a pawn in the game.

For my surgical work, Professor Kay, our previous politically-savvy professor would have fixed it with a couple of phone calls, but local leadership was lacking and our increasingly-discredited Dean of the medical faculty was involved. Time passed with no news from him. The interviews for the two lecturers' jobs came up, and in Glasgow, on the day, I told the committee, chaired by the Dean, that I was unhappy to proceed without having my own appointment settled. The Dean then told the committee that surgical work had been agreed and there was a letter to me already in the post. I was prepared to believe him but when I got back to Oxford there was no letter. He had lied.

I met with Williams at the Wellcome Trust soon after and with the lack of progress, he asked me if I wanted to continue, since they were minded to pull out of Scotland completely. This was alarming. All I could say was that, once I was back in Glasgow, surely things would sort themselves out. I had a quick meeting with the lofty Principal at Glasgow University seeking help, but the Dean had told him that my hospital sessions and contract were all arranged.

My surgical sessions never appeared. Two years later, the University would take action and remove the Dean from the post.

We shut our eyes, and we, the three of us, went back.

ح

CHAPTER 22:

Return

Blues … Printing … Hillhead politics … End of the Dean

Back in Glasgow and with a sense of foreboding, I saw the unpleasant Dean again. Blaming the 'timid local surgeons', he had still not organised the surgical part of my job, nor the medical student teaching, as requested by the Wellcome Trust. Neither ever appeared.

I was heading for predictable depression and it kicked in on time, as before, after about four weeks of solitary scholarship. I knew the pattern, the cause and the solution, though when you're in it, there seems no escape. Dragging myself into work I just looked at the wall all day, unable to write. The book on the history of transplantation ground to a halt despite having all the time in the world to write. The staff in my unit did not know me from earlier and hence were unaware of my problem, or if they suspected, tactfully did not care to probe. Socially, I had to hide, as a likely drag on others. Old friends were puzzled that I was not back at weekend golf, but I excused myself saying that with a family now, weekends were for them.

Resigning was a possibility, but that was running away and in the past when a director of a Wellcome unit left, the unit also closed. I couldn't risk destroying the jobs of my two talented lecturers. I could have taken legal action, but my problem would then have come out and the Dean would have got rid of me and his problem by putting me off as sick. The medical world does not like litigious, mentally ill doctors, and I might not have worked again. The best hope was that a grown-up in the University might emerge and take charge or that something would turn up. Which it did, but too late.

Eventually Jean and I decided I needed help. Our general practitioner, a wise friend, was surprised to see me. Knowing me well, he was concerned at my mental state and knowing something of the university's troubles, my explanation made sense. We tried anti-depressants, waiting hopefully for the three weeks build-up, but had they had no effect. After a while, he had to suggest that the time had come for me to see a psychiatrist, but I declined. The fewer people involved the better.

I found one beneficial strategy. Exercise is well known to help in depression, and my printing with a foot-operated treadle machine had the same effect and the typesetting involved problem-solving. At the weekend, it eased my mood a little. I needed equipment to continue the Oxford work, and I discovered Harry Brooke, a Paisley printing engineer who also sold old equipment. From him, I got a sturdy Arab machine which went into the garage at our new home in the West End,

Duncan and my new Arab press.

plus much other equipment from the now-dying world of letterpress printing. He was to be a good friend thereafter and was full of stories about Glasgow printing. There was a Glasgow convent which printed theological works and, being a closed-order of nuns, they did not allow men through the doors, except Harry who serviced their printing presses. Harry also told me many a tale about the printing underworld. There was the Patrick Printing Company which, after purchasing a modern machine from him, went on to print a nice Danish kroner. It took four policemen to move it out, and after their arrest, Harry was a suspect when he claimed to have installed their machine single-handed.

There were occasional weekend meetings, which also helped. I was no longer an SNP member, being out of sympathy with their new 'Independence, Nothing Less' policy. The Labour Party, though out of power, was still committed to devolution, and I joined the Hillhead constituency local branch. In the 1987 election, George Galloway, our Labour Party candidate, had unexpectedly beaten Roy Jenkins, but there was trouble brewing.

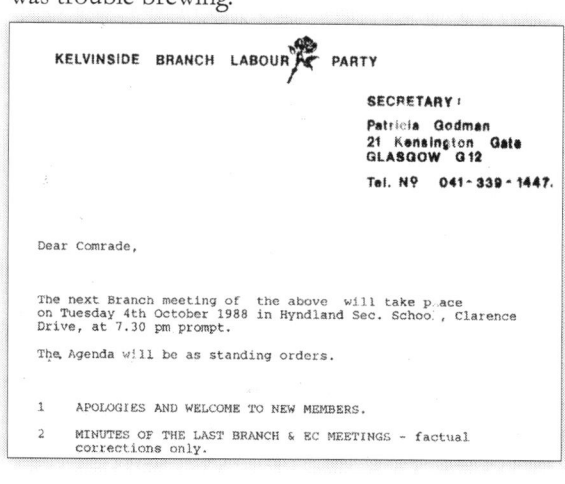

At Labour Party meetings, before the Blair era, we still used the salutation 'comrade'.

Our committee possessed a simple litho printing press which we used to make election leaflets for ourselves, and we offered economical printing for other local constituencies. I helped with this, and one day, during our local government elections, our local Labour Party councillor, a pal of George Galloway, arrived with his minders, while I was labouring on his leaflet for the election. With 5,000 sheets already printed, they studied my work, conferred and took me aside; the Boss is not pleased, they told me. He was unhappy with the quality of his picture on the leaflet and they told me that I should pulp the work and start again. It was like Chicago, but without the guns.

The misgivings about George grew. One year after his election, our executive committee passed a vote of no confidence in him and mounted a de-selection challenge, but he survived, winning Glasgow Kelvin in 1997 and 2001. Expelled from the Labour Party in 2003, he continued to survive in England as an MP representing his own Respect Party.

On another occasion, my printing came in useful when Sam Galbraith successfully stood in the 1987 General Election campaign. One weekend his activists gathered to distribute their election leaflet when it had arrived from their printer. But it was an A4 sheet with the message printed twice to be divided to give two smaller A5 handouts. There were 65,000 sheets, and Sam's committee started on the task with scissors. Then Sam remembered that I had a guillotine and, bringing them over to our house, it took me 15 minutes' work to get the now 130,000 leaflets ready to go.

At the University, serious complaints about the Dean continued to reach the Principal, who simply passed the complaint back to the Dean, who then got his revenge. The Dean could shrink a complainant's budget and one smear he used was to claim he had heard of financial irregularities in the complainant's Department. Incidents continued, including alienating local Jewish support of the Medical School. Some Glasgow medical graduates in Canada invited him to a celebratory occasion, but there were angry phone calls back to Glasgow. At the formal dinner he said that although there had been emigration from Glasgow to Canada, the best graduates had remained at home.

This all added to the damage done over years, and the Faculty decided, at last, to act against their oppressor. They asked a senior clinical professor to investigate whether the Dean should continue in office. Submissions were invited and I wrote a short memorandum highlighting his deceptions when dealing with the Wellcome Trust. But if the Dean survived, and others did not back me, I was a marked man.

With my short memorandum in my hand, I went over to the hospital to hand it in, and suggested to his secretary that I might have a quiet word with the professor.

She sized up the situation.

'It'll be about the Dean' she said. 'Don't worry, the professor is a very discreet man.'

I was reassured.

She opened a lever-arch file, adding my contribution to an impressive number of documents already inside. It was good to know I was not alone, and below mine, I saw a copy of a brave and unique event – our medical student's magazine attack on their oppressive Dean.

The report went to the Faculty. It listed the Dean's grave failings and damage done, without any balacing achievements, and the recommendation was that the Dean should not continue. When the Faculty debated it, all, except for one, agreed with relief, that he had to go.

It took a while to get him out. When the next Dean arrived, I thought it was worth one last attempt to set up the clinically-orientated history of medicine unit and get the student teaching started. I met him in mid-afternoon and he offered me a whisky, and after this unpromising start, it was clear he was reluctant to get involved with such an old, forgotten problem.

It was all over.

I said I would not continue beyond the end of the first period of the Wellcome grant. When I left, the Unit survived, as a successful Arts Faculty academic unit, but without the clinical links. For a second time I had brought back money and new thinking to Glasgow, this time adding some colour and support for the humanities to the Medical Faculty. I had been defeated by a malign Dean and his timid surgeons.

I was heading back towards hospital work, with all the difficulties, but crucially I had evaded the gossip about mental illness which would have been fatal. After I decided to leave, my phone rang. The local surgeons were, after all, watching and needed short-term surgical help.

For some time, I was to see a lot of the NHS in the West of Scotland, and this included some of its unlovely parts. Later, I returned to transplant surgery in the Western Infirmary.

ॐ

CHAPTER 23:

Wanderings

Kilmacolm ... Golf and schools ... More printing ... Golf Collectors ... Hospital work

THOUGH I WAS not in conventional employment, the main thing was that the long period of blues had left no damage, and I restarted reading and writing with relief. With the growing family, it was also time for family life, rather than long hours in the laboratories and hospitals. The home was now my base; it was a new way of living, even adding a sense of freedom. I would survive for some years as a surgical odd-job man, a useful man in the West. When there was a gap after a consultant retired, or an alcoholic was sent away to dry out, or if a hospital suspended a surgeon, or a remote hospital could not get a surgeon, I could help. Further North, my friend the Oban surgeon also needed locums. Money didn't usually concern me, but at the University, the missing hospital work had not been paid. Now back into the NHS, my income doubled, a welcome uplift with a growing family and a new house.

We needed a new home for our growing family and sought the country, heading out to Kilmacolm to the south-west of Glasgow. There we bought a large neglected house above the village with a big garden for the children, recreating the ambience of the manse of my childhood, and Kilmacolm's golf course and its family-friendly club meant that Jean and the children started to play.

We moved in. Village life meant that newspapers were delivered and the two rival Kilmacolm milkmen also called in to seek our patronage. One of the two local Church of Scotland ministers appeared at the door just after we arrived and sat with us among the removal boxes in a room warmed by a paraffin heater. My minister father had told us of how when he arrived unexpectedly during his parish home visits, the owners concealed any drinks. Since we were enjoying a can of lager, I did not hesitate to offer one to our clerical visitor, which he accepted. Rev Bernard Lodge was clearly a thoughtful and tolerant man and we soon joined his church. Later, Jean was keen to have our youngest baptized, but I hesitated and told Bernard about my religious doubts. He made the helpful suggestion that we go ahead with a Sunday baptism, and he would not grill me on my faith, but turn to Jean and question her alone at that point. This choreographed, modified baptism went well. Months later, at the golf club, a proud new father told me of his similar dilemma. I sent him to Bernard, who again agreed to the Sunday baptism strategy. The day of the christening came, but to the father's dismay, Bernard was away and a locum was in charge. There was no escape for father from the vows.

We attended Bernard's church, and when he retired eventually, he was a loss to the village. Nationally, the Churches were loosing membership and money, and responded by local mergers, retrenching to use the church with the best fabric or hinterland. Kilmacolm had two notably robust churches and loyal congregations and the situation became fraught when both ministers encountered criticism from their congregations. Things were getting difficult for all professionals, even ministers. Society was now less deferential,

In Kilmacolm, we now reconnected with some old academic friends, and even the professors of the surgery and anaesthesia at Edinburgh University (Carter and Spence) lived there and commuted to the east for a while. A report in 2000 claimed that Kilmacolm had the highest concentration of millionaires in any postal code area in Scotland. We didn't know any, nor did others, and the search was on. At the golf club, there were demands that the suspects should identify themselves and buy all the drinks from now on. Wives accused their husbands of concealing income and houses of reclusive residents were studied from outside. Catching up with our non-millionaire friends, we soon had the Masons round to dinner, Sir David Mason, being then the head of the Glasgow Dental Hospital and School and an old golfing friend.* Our children lined up at the door as he came in, and piped up, 'Have you brought as any sweeties?' not the most tactful remark to the President of the General Dental Council. Sir Graham Teasdale the brain surgeon of Glasgow Coma Scale fame, also lived near, and we had a pint together occasionally.

❧

The family were growing. With Jean just making it to hospital, young Alistair had been born at speed in 1988, unharmed by having the cord around his neck for a while. Hazel was born in January 1991, and in case we were snowed in, we planned ahead with a home pack, and an obstetrician friend in the village was ready to help. Jean was to cope well with the young family, and also looked after me.

In our rambling house, we had a cosy west-facing conservatory, full of plants, to which I added a vine, putting the roots outside, and it spread nicely inside. Weekend evenings in the conservatory when the children were off to bed were a particular pleasure, somehow recalling Omar Khayyam, or something of our Baghdad days.

> *Here with a Loaf of Bread beneath the Bough,*
> *A Flask of Wine, a Book of Verse—and Thou*
> *Beside me singing in the Wilderness—*
> *And Wilderness is Paradise now.*

In Kilmacolm, there was, and is, an excellent state primary school in the village, a short walk away from our home, and our children did well there. One daily highlight at the end of the school day at the time was arrival of a 4x4 with smoked glass windows which collected the children of 'Gazza', Paul Gascoigne, the footballer, who played for Glasgow Rangers

Alistair's first day at school.

---

* Sir David Mason, in addition to his many academic works, not only co-authored the Kilmacolm golf club centenary history *A Very Pleasant Golfing Place* (1991), but later produced a useful 25-year follow-up.

and lived nearby. Soon after, neither his career nor his marriage prospered.

For the children there was plenty to do. We had a large rambling garden, the golf course, the Scouts and football in the park on Saturdays. A favourite family Sunday outing was to the cycle track running through the village created by the Sustrans charity which used the old railway line to the neighbouring Bridge of Weir village. Going the other way, there was a little-used track reaching Port Glasgow and Greenock. Our Alistair, always adventurous, one Sunday decided to explore and went off towards Greenock on his bike. Later there was no sign of him, but, after some concern, he returned, still with his bike, which had been in danger when passing through Port Glasgow.

Jean with Hazel and Duncan on the Kilmacolm cycle track. [Across] Alistair's school report recording our Saturday outings.

To give Jean a rest at the weekends, there were plenty other diversions including local parks with adventure swings, the cinema at Clydebank or back to visit Glasgow's museums. At weekends there was golf for all and our children and Jean learned the game. A rite of passage for the children was when they played off the first tee alone on their first medal competition, an agony for father watching from a discreet distance. All played well, particularly Duncan who became junior captain and junior champion twice.

❧

In my surgical work, I helped at several hospitals, mostly in the West nearby, but also in Oban. I was getting older and out-of-date. I had grown up using hand stitching in surgery – we knew nothing else – and now the stapling devices were coming in which cleverly joined up tissues. Us old-timers thought at first that these methods were expensive, unnecessary, gimmicky and demeaning and would cause loss of the traditional surgical skills, but by the 1990s the young surgeons were stapling everything. The various fibre-optic diagnostic devices had started life in the hands of a few specialists, but now all the trainees had training in endoscopy of the upper or lower abdomen and the various endoscopes, formerly scarce, were now widely available.

To add to this, minimally invasive surgery appeared, using special tools passed through small incisions rather than using the usual large incisions and direct vision. They were first used in the West of Scotland by Graham Bell at Greenock, near us, and I was helping at Greenock at the time after the Health Board suspended one of their hospital consultant surgeons. The town of Greenock feels strongly about its hospital and they took an interest in the affair. The surgeon had friends inside the hospital who leaked information to the local newspaper about the progress of the various inquiries, and in the town some cars carried stickers supporting him. There were even threats against the hospital administration and that the surgeon's room – temporarily my room – would be bombed. The room, full of my books and files, as usual resembled a bomb site and when the police arrived, they were not clear if a bomb had gone off or not.

My anaesthetist was a cheerful and resourceful man, still loyal to the absent surgeon. I explained that on future travels I might end up doing challenging surgical work, and he taught me how to do spinal anaesthetics. I also helped in their Accident and Emergency Department, but I was again struggling, since this specialty had become more professional. But I picked up some useful skills. Also, saving lives can happen in A&E. After one spectacular, almost biblical, revival of a moribund, cyanosed, hardly-breathing, overdosed Greenock heroin addict, using Narcan, he sat up and wished to go home. His grannie outside was not pleased. He had lost money. She said we had spoiled his fix.

એ

Our large house had a little-used commodious East wing, perfect for expanding my printing ventures and I moved in my Arab press and added new trays of type and racks for paper. I bought a superb Vandercook proofing press, the Rolls-Royce machine in our little letterpress world. Too big to come in the front door, we took a side door off its hinges and got it in, delivered by my ever-helpful printing engineer Harry Brooke. I added a magnificent composing 'stone'. It was a mahogany table six-foot square with multiple drawers on all sides and a flat cast-iron top which allowed accurate typesetting. I got these extras easily at the auction sales since many traditional printers were closing or when moving on to more modern machines, discarded the old equipment. I got the formidable stone at auction in Perth after the demise of the large printer who made the elegant and colourful labels for the bottles of whisky produced by the local John Dewar company. The stone, a splendid relic from an earlier era, weighed a ton, and when the auctioneer got to this item, not expecting an answer, he started by saying 'who will give me £5?' To his surprise, I raised my hand. If I had hesitated, he would have gone lower and I would have got it for £1. At Perth there were unwanted heaps of expensive laminated paper used for printing the whisky bottle labels. I could not resist taking some and they also went to me for a small sum. I was glad to see that Harry Brooke was there with his lifting devices and van and he got these items back to Kilmacolm for me. The luxury paper came in useful for making paper hats at the church fete and I printed the child's name on them.

After my unproductve time at the University, I restarted writing with enthusiasm, but being out of transplant surgery, it seemed pointless to revive and finish my Oxford University Press transplant history book. Instead, I concentrated on my growing interest in the history of golf in Scotland. While looking for new golf heritage material, some scraps on the history of curling also turned up, and

I got to know Scotland's curling historian, Sheriff David Smith, and he passed on any golfing history scraps to me.* He was a formidable bearded figure on and off the bench, or on the ice, and he dispensed justice in the Kilmarnock Sheriff Court where he had crammed his office, like his house, with curling memorabilia. As a determined

collector, he showed the way to the rest of us by using the possibilities when eBay emerged on the Internet in 1995 offering items for auction from all parts of the world. Curling items, including long-forgotten trophies and medals, turned up for him to snap up. Equivalent golfiana also appeared, but was more costly.

Before the era of digitised newspapers, historical research involved tedious page-turning, here searching bound volumes of the Dundee Evening Telegraph, *looking for forgotten golf reports.*

We had the Smiths to dinner in our house and, because he liked a drink, we insisted that he did not drive from his home in Troon, but take the train to Johnston near Kilmacolm. On the train, hooligans he had banned from the pubs in Ayr were on their way to drink in Glasgow instead and they recognised him and took pleasure in bumping into him, spilling their cans of lager.

'Whoops ... Sorry, Sheriff.'

Helping elsewhere, at the Island of Arran's Lamlash Hospital, the consultant surgeon had retired. The parsimonious attitudes towards the small Scottish hospitals meant that he had been paid a reduced salary, and understandably no-one applied for his job. I worked there a few days each week for a while, while they sorted it out, sharing the surgical work with the local GP Alistair Grassie, trained in surgery. I got to know him and his wife Libby well. They had an ideal general practice

* David B Smith *Curling: An Illustrated History*, Edinburgh 1981. Died 2015

Waiting for the new small air ambulance using the Arran football pitch c1998.

on the west side of the island and it was a delight to join them in the evening and hear his well-told stories of rural practice. Libby's father had been the Principal at Glasgow University and when newly married, they lived in the Principal's house for a while. At dinner, their baby vomited over Lord Reith, the University's stern Chancellor.

One day, we heard that a committee of inquiry was coming from the mainland. They arrived for dinner and stayed overnight and heard evidence the next day. They returned home and reported. The complaint investigated came from a local claiming that the hospital was being run as a brothel, and they rejected this. The only evidence offered from this reclusive citizen was that there was a red light seen in the building. Their report started with the mantra that 'we take all complaints seriously.'

In Arran, I had one of my great musical experiences. The nurses offered me a ticket for an opera performance in Lamlash Town Hall which I dutifully accepted, secretly hoping that there might be something surgical to detain me. All was quiet. Arriving at the Hall there were an assortment of old chairs and an upright piano. On came a young man with his music, he sat down, and soon gave a thrilling rendering of the overture to the *Marriage of Figaro*. Young singers then appeared and gave us the opera with elan. It was the Scottish Opera on tour.

Arran had survived a tourism crisis. The island's accommodation had declined in quantity and quality, and the stone-built hotels on the Brodick seafront had seen better days, with many closed over the winter months. Even in summer it was difficult to get a meal after 6 p.m. But Iain and Linda Johnston stepped in in 1988 using the improbable strategy – 'build it and they will come' – and they converted the Auchrannie mansion and grounds behind the village. They put in first-class accommodation and a restaurant with fine dining, plus a bistro and swimming pool. And Lo, the people came, including us Hamiltons, for weekends and at New Year holiday time.

à

At Oxford, I had produced my first slim, limited-edition book *Early Golf in Glasgow* and I now could work on more in the same genre and a small series followed.* I needed typesetting and would have gone back to Upton on Severn for it but I discovered that Edinburgh had a Monotype setter. Harry McIntosh was the last of his kind in Scotland meeting this niche market and would supply me with type for many years. He was a genius since he had linked the clunking Monotype machine, with its pot of molten lead, to a computer and could typeset from a file. If hot metal composition had survived as the industry standard, he would have been rich and famous, but the new photographic litho methods were taking over.

PARTICK PRESS

Fine Printing since 1984

With our Compliments

Enclosed is your copy of
The Thorn Tree Clique

'Dalliefour'
Barclaven Road
Kilmacolm PA13 4DQ

PRINTER to the Press *David Hamilton*: Assistant
to the Printer *Jean Hamilton*: Correctors of
the Press *John MacConachie* and
David B. Smith.

For letterpress printing, wood engravings match the text well, but wood engravings require damp paper to show the best effect. It is not possible to feed in damp paper into modern printing machines and you need letterpress machines to get the best effect. John O'Connor, famous in the illustrator's world, but now in retirement, was much in demand for wood engravings, including providing regular items for Ingram's *The Oldie*. He had moved to live near Jean's home town, and when we visited, he enthused about my golfing needs and did illustrations for two of my books, for a low fee.

---

* These hand-printed works were *Game at Golf* (1987), *Early Golf at Edinburgh and Leith* (1988), *The Sporting Padre* (1991), *The South Sea Brithers* (1992), *The Thorn Tree Clique* (2002) and *Precious Gum* (2004). My *Early Aberdeen Golf* (1986) was printed by Tom Rae in Greenock and *Early Golf at St Andrews* (1987) was printed by letterpress at an Oban print shop.

He died in 2003, and thereafter I worked with another wood engraver, Kathleen Lindesley in the Isle of Skye, who had moved there from London with her husband.

My hand-printed books were now appearing in the antiquarian book catalogues, and it was pleasing to have a place in this wider world. On one occasion, Pacific Book Auctions listed the Oxford hand-printed book of mine, and they noted that it lacked the label from the spine. My early choice of glue had been poor, and I sent them a replacement label to add to the item before the auction. They were astonished to receive it, thinking I was from an earlier era, and perhaps long dead.

I didn't enjoy taking on any outside projects because I disliked being constrained by a timetable, but some interesting requests came along. Our distinguished Scottish man of letters, the Glasgow poet Edward Morgan, had noted my book on early Glasgow golf, ordered it, and continued to support my letterpress efforts. I enjoyed delivering them to him and I got one of his essays to print. Golfing poetry is the worst kind of poetry in the world and I tentatively suggested that he give me a really bad golfing poem for one of my little books, and he nobly rose (or fell) to the occasion. He also suggested to the Glasgow novelist A.L. Kennedy that I might print a collection of her poems, which I did.

David Smith's standard work on the history of curling now encouraged me to do the same for golf. For my conventionally-printed history of golf in Scotland, I found a talented Edinburgh designer, George Bowie, who would be a friend thereafter, and with his help completed a scholarly, large format, well-illustrated book *Golf – Scotland's Game* (1998) which is now the standard work. One way of trying to get the costs back, even with the conventional publications for sale in bookshops, is to have an additional limited edition with quarter-leather binding and a slipcase. For this edition, I added a rear pocket with a map of Scotland and a slim leather bookmark stamped with the old clubmakers' marks and icons. Marbled end-paper was traditional for such books but didn't look right for this one; I needed handmade paper with a golfing connection. I favoured using paper incorporating grass from Edinburgh's Leith Links, home of the first golf club. Cautiously, I asked the District Council's permission to cut some grass, and, entering

The special limited edition of my Golf
– Scotland's Game *was useful when a
gift was needed for Colin Montgomerie at a
charity event.*

into the spirit of it, they replied saying I was welcome to cut the entire Links, if I was so minded. I went through to Edinburgh with my shears, but when I started, I felt a hand on my shoulder. I presumed it was an official and reached for my permission letter. Instead, it was a local citizen who pointed out that they were mowing the grass at the other end, and this would save me some time.

At the launch of the book at our house, we had a sociable gathering of my golfing friends and my reader Dr John MacConachie from Lossiemouth attended. The group included my oldest golfing companion from school days, Donald Dewar, now Secretary of State for Scotland after the Blair victory in 1997. He came along, leaving his chauffeur outside, but we invited the man in.

Along with writing, I increased my collection of old golf clubs and books. Nostalgia for golf seemed to be increasing, perhaps as a reaction to the wealth available in the professional game and the complexity and cost of modern equipment. There were many old hickory golf clubs available at auction and my friend Joe at Voltaire and Rousseau, who had provided so many medical history books, also put aside any interesting old golf books, adding an occasional old club or two which he scooped up when he helped empty a house. The value of old golf clubs and golf books was not yet realised, even by Joe, and I did well.

On our travels, we also left requests for any old golf clubs at any antique shops we visited and a man in Elgin phoned us to say he had just cleared a house and there were some clubs which, according to his description, sounded interesting. Jean went back north and got them for a modest sum and beauties they were – a bagful of well-preserved

Dalgleish woods and many Willie Park smooth-faced irons from the 1890s, still with the elegant original grips. Returning on the train, the man opposite Jean said that 'your husband should get you better clubs for Christmas.'

Going to one of the American golf collectors' meetings, I took a few of the Willie Park clubs in an old bag to sell. Entering at New York Customs the ever-hostile officer knew I was up to something, but he, like everyone else, lacked awareness of the value of smooth-faced Park cleeks. His interrogation having failed to uncover my plan, he asked what I did for a living. I said I was a doctor, and light dawned. He concluded that under socialised medicine I couldn't afford to play with better golf clubs, and he let us through. The sale of the clubs paid for the trip.

Many of us now had collections of hickory clubs which we bought in quantity seeking only the one or two rarities in the bundle. The rest, the 'good ordinary' clubs, lay about the house and to do something with them, our thoughts turned to playing with them. We soon found that these older clubs were playable, with surprisingly good performance, and they had interesting qualities. Being a natural product, all hickory shafts are different. It is said that Bobby Jones while on his travels always called in at local professional shops, testing the clubs on sale while seeking the perfect shaft. This variety contrasts with the one-size-fits-all modern golf clubs. Titanium-headed drivers do outperform the older hickory woods by driving the ball further, but woods from the hickory era can give topspin and a long roll of the ball on running links courses. But we deplored the distance gained by these metal drivers since it had destroyed the layout of the well-established courses. The ruling authorities lost control of the traditional game and were too late to catch up. Well-off golf clubs with space could afford to make back tees to lengthen the courses, but most Scottish golf courses with limited space and tight budgets could not. Playing with the old clubs was a protest and support for the older layouts. Eventually our enthusiasts coaxed some golf clubs to award 'hickory' handicaps.[*]

---

[*] At first, seven shots were added to the usual (steel) handicap, but this reduced to five as hickory play improved.

What started as fun 'hickory-hacking' outings changed to serious play.[*] This habit gained momentum and hickory-only competitions emerged with our Scottish Hickory Championship, first organised by John Rigg. Starting in 1985, as the first freestanding hickory competition in the world (since the days of old), it attracts a growing entry, including players from Europe.

One memorable event was a hickory event at Dunaverty, the club near Machrihanish, and its yardage (4,700 yards) which suits hickory play. To play it with titanium drivers is inappropriate and even sacrilegious. It still has sheep and cattle on the course with electric fences around some greens. The small clubhouse has a close view of the action on the 18th hole, and being warned that the Club had no licence, the attendees, notably the Swedes, had brought ample supplies. The conviviality was complete when none other than Belle Robertson, the Curtis Cup player and Captain, Dunaverty's most famous member, presented the prizes.

Related to the rediscovery of the hickory-shafted golf clubs, I became interested in the gutta ball. I wondered if this rubber, from Malaysia, was still available. One day, when my dentist was getting on with my root canal filling, I asked him about the materials he was using. He replied that he used fine posts of gutta percha, and I nearly fell off his drill.

After that, getting the gum was easy. A single source in Switzerland supplied the dentists in Europe and they got a surprise order from me for un-purified lumps of dark gutta straight from the jungle. To make the balls, I got an original gutta mould from Archie Baird in Gullane, and warming up lumps of the rubber in hottish water, compressed them in the mould. The balls I turned out were not replicas, there *were* gutta-percha golf balls. Playing with them made you sympathetic to the early players. It seemed like hitting a stone; they also broke easily.

---

[*] To our delight, the scientific testing of the performance of 1930s hickory irons, when compared with modern clubs, showed only a 10% difference in distance of flight, equating to a 0.1% gain per year, despite the ecstatic claims by the manufacturers for annual progress. The greater torque in the hickory shaft means that the clubface can open during the down-swing, enabling creative shots.

My friend, Robin Clark, the Oban surgeon, needed help. His post was single-handed and when he started there, he was on call at all times for emergencies. Thereafter, the Board softened slightly and said that he could take alternate weekends off, but only if he could arrange for a surgeon to do the weekend work. They could not pay anything, but would give 'generous expenses', and provide a spartan room for the visitor in the hospital, but not a hotel. I helped, and they did pay my petrol. This mean-spirited attitude by the Lowland administrators to the Highlands, as seen in their slow, grudging acceptance of helicopter evacuation or resisting installing telemedicine clinics, would reap its rewards later. The obvious reforms came a bit late.

At Oban, the speed of the surgical service could be impressive; you could get things done quickly, and much faster than in the city. When a local bank manager visited his G.P. reporting recent short, sharp, upper abdominal pains, the G.P. phoned me at the afternoon clinic. I suggested he came up at the end of the clinic and our radiographer helped by doing a plain abdominal x-ray. This film showed multiple tiny stones in the gallbladder region.

I knew we had space on the theatre list next day, and he went back home to collect his pyjamas and toothbrush, and we operated next day. No one, including the great and good, or a celebrity, could have had faster treatment. Moreover, treatment had been economical. If the Oban hospital did not exist, arranging for tests and surgery in Glasgow would have meant many letters back and forth, a wait for x-rays and treatment, and about four or five journeys, a hazardous one in winter, for the patient and relatives. There were suggestions at that time that the Health Board would shut the hospital, and I helped the locals who fought to keep it open. They won the argument.

It survived.

The Great and Good can be a bit of a nuisance in a small hospital. The Oban staff told me about a minor Royal admitted with a fracture after a winter fall at a local estate. She insisted first on having a private room, there being none, but to appease her, they gave her the one single room. There were boiled eggs for tea, but she sent them back to the kitchen claiming they were too hard. She then summoned a Harley Street surgeon to give a second opinion, and he headed for the overnight sleeper to Glasgow, having ordered Elastoplast strapping of the limb. Snow held up his train, and he eventually made it to Oban two days after the injury. The strapping being removed, there were now allergic skin blisters revealed beneath. The pair headed back to London, to the relief of all, but with any open surgery prevented by the skin reaction.

Oban was never dull. One Saturday, a biker with a serious compound fracture of the leg appeared, brought in by ambulance. The bones were sticking out through the skin and since it was not one for us, he had to go to Glasgow. However, there was a problem. It was midday on Saturday and the radiographer had just left the hospital, giving me the strict, cheery instructions that, since she was representing the hospital at this important annual town parade and Highland Games, she was to be undisturbed. I told the ambulance to wait, and with the engine still turning, I did a simple patch-up, and they were soon on their way. I then phoned the Western and got through to a pompous junior surgeon who wished to make some lofty points. He gave me a tedious tutorial on the early management of compound fractures, and I knew what the final question would be:

'What did the x-rays show?'

'Listen, sonny', I said, 'the situation is that this patient is on his way to you and already half-way down Loch Lomond.'

We had a visit from the local Procurator Fiscal. Straight out of central casting, he had a suitably hairy face with a touch of a boarding-school accent overlying his Highland upbringing. He was wearing plus-fours and his tweed hat displayed salmon fishing flies. He had a question for me about a body in the hospital morgue, to help his preliminary report.

The Fiscal told me the story in detached legal discourse. Beginning with 'It would appear' he explained, 'that the deceased, a local man, had gone to Glasgow for an evening of heavy drinking, being denied similar facilities in Oban because of earlier local misdemeanours. Falling asleep in the carriage during the return journey and slumping to the floor, when the train returned to the Oban terminus, the station staff, checking for any remaining passengers by using the simple method of looking through the windows for any heads, declared the train to be empty'. The Fiscal continued that 'it appeared that the train then started to move a short distance out of the station to reverse the coaches back into the station ready for the morning journey to Glasgow. At this point', the fiscal opined, 'the man awoke, and fearing he was heading back to Glasgow, left the coach but, having partaken heavily, collapsed once more across the line, sadly the line also used by the returning train.'

He described the body, in three parts. Was this tripartite condition consistent with being run over by railway engine? I agreed.

In Oban, the chef at the excellent Indian restaurant was troubled with haemorrhoids and I operated. Such surgery is tricky and unpleasant, but both he and I were pleased at the outcome. I knew that there were clever Indian cooking methods used in the restaurants and thought this was my chance for a tutorial. Emboldened, I said I wished to learn some cooking skills and I arranged to attend at 11 o'clock on the Saturday morning. But cooking was not in progress and he showed me how to marinate only, not what I had in mind. The secrets remain.

Perhaps the most famous incident at the Oban hospital came later, when in 2007 they appointed a new, senior male nurse. He soon courted the hospital's theatre sister, who had her own yacht and a large house. The two became engaged, but the police contacted her with information about him which they could not withhold. They gave her an 'Osman' letter which described not only her fiancé's other wife and son, but added that her life might be in danger. Their concern came from their investigation of the mysterious death of his heavily-insured first wife, and other incidents. The Oban nurse then discovered punctures in the life jackets on her boat. Malcolm Webster was convicted of the earlier murder in 1991. The necessary evidence from many women and scattered police forces meant it was the longest-ever Scottish criminal trial involving a single accused.[*]

Our golf history societies prospered at this time, notably the British Golf Collectors Society, which closely followed the foundation of the similar American venture. Apart from the big annual meetings,

* The ITV programme *The Widower* (2014), describes this famous case and several books also resulted.

local groups emerged, often playing with hickory clubs and dressing traditionally. Those of us who produced books on golf history met together as the 'Literati of the Links'. With this sharing of information and assisting with reading each other's work, standards of golf history writing improved and our journal *Through the Green* became a respected peer-reviewed magazine. We were proud to hear that it was the 'most-stolen magazine' at the older golf clubs.

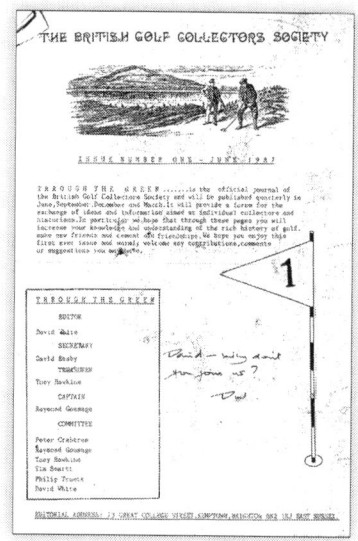

Thanks to Sir David Mason, I became a member at the Royal and Ancient Golf Club of St Andrews. You need a substantial number of letters in support and David had to do the hard work. When I got my letter telling me I had gained membership, my first thought was to drive through in the evening to join in the activity at the club. I arrived at 7 p.m. and introduced myself to the hall porter, later a friend, and enquired if the club was busy. 'Only one person in', he said and hinted that I should not disturb him. I heard later that, because of under-use, there was a threat to the evening opening, and to prevent this, he was sitting-in, enjoying a whisky and catching up with the day's papers.

I liked to visit St Andrews and the R&A, and my routine was to study in the library, then stay overnight at a Bed and Breakfast establishment nearby in Murray Park, better known as 'Guesthouse Gully'. Over the years, I got to know the owner well and I had the same room. This led to a problem on one occasion when visiting during a busy tournament and after a convivial evening, on reaching 'my room', there seemed to be a problem with the key. Instead, I was in another room, as the lady inside pointed out forcibly.

~

At Kilmacolm, Jean was soon on the ladies golf committee. Following the Equality Act 2010, in a mixed club, all members had to be equal. and the debate was a cause célèbre in the suburban clubs.

Many had 'Ladies Sections' with much of the clubhouse restricted to men.* There was concern at many clubs and at a special general meeting at Kilmacolm, the club's traditionalists blocked full membership for the ladies. When the significance was realised, the members reluctantly accepted the reform at a second meeting.

Thereafter all the public rooms were open to the ladies at the Club, but at Kilmacolm there had always been a sacred place for men – the 'dirty bar' or 'spike bar' – used after coming off the course. There, the men put their feet up, told stories and drank. A few days after the ladies gained full membership at Kilmacolm, the Ryder Cup was to be shown on big television screens throughout the clubhouse. Jean was keen to watch the event, but, held up in the house, I went ahead, but found that only one large-screen was available, and it was in the Dirty Bar. I phoned Jean back at the house, explaining that this was a sensitive problem, coming up so soon after the local revolution. Perhaps she might not care to make a determined stand on her equal rights, so quickly. Perhaps after a year or two?

'Not at all' said Jean. I'm coming up.'

In the Dirty Bar, I sat on my hands quietly, studying the floor.

The door opened. The golfers looked up.

'Hi Jean,' they said, 'can we buy you a drink?'

The traditional golf clubs were changing. Apart from the Equality Act, smoking was no longer permitted in the clubhouse, and the drink-driving regulations had tightened up. Risks were no longer taken.† The private clubs had always had long waiting lists, but these were now shrinking. Income from the gaming machines, a reliable cash-cow, mysteriously dropped. The clubs put up their fees for visiting societies and these golf outings decreased. The clubs' response was to be entrepreneurial with initiatives such as weekday-only membership,

---

* Western Gailes GC had a painted white line on the shared clubhouse balcony marking the territories of the two sexes. At many clubs the 'ladies section', with reduced fees and limited starting times, was a strategy often preferred by the women members.

† A story, probably an urban myth, told of the captain of a local golf club who was breathalysed on the road after consuming a few whiskies at his club. The breath test was negative. Next day, he returned and found that the club barman had been watering the whisky.

two-for-one visitors' fees, open days and trial memberships. But it was too late. Some long-standing Scottish suburban clubs did not survive.

એ

For my writing, I was keeping up with the world of personal computers, having had a flying start in Oxford. Cheaper and more powerful rivals had now bypassed the expensive IBM PC. I bought my first light-weight portable – there were 'luggable' machines before – the famous Toshiba 1000 – which came out in 1987, and, at a reasonable price, and powered from a battery, it offered word-processing while on any travels. For the house, we bought a succession of Dells which came with a heavy laser printer in the package. Michael Dell became rich by pioneering this direct sale of computers, cutting out the usual intermediaries. The cathode ray screens heavy were still heavy, but they had colour now, and the mouse, pioneered on the Apple machines, arrived about 1987 and smaller stiff 'floppy' discs appeared.* Our children queued up to use the machine, though Duncan monopolised it, and I had to insist on the others 'getting a shot.' Duncan later would work in the world of computers, and hence he was perhaps not wasting his time. The first computer games arrived and *Monkey Island* was at least a testing, humorous game. Jean wisely limited the children's time and rationed the Internet when it arrived later.

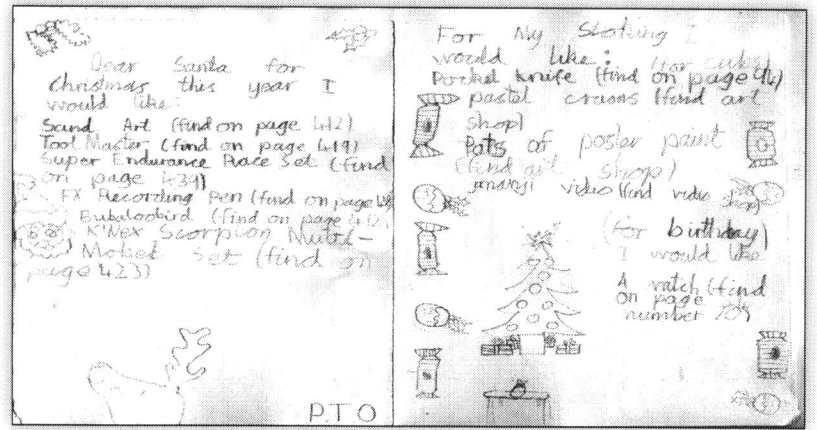

Alistair's requests to Santa Claus, directing him to the Argos catalogue details.

* In 1990, the famous first version of Word linked to Windows came on 12 discs and needed hours of loading.

Robin Clark meanwhile was restive in Oban, and took the surgeon's post in Gibraltar, a town not dissimilar to Oban, though the climate is better. I continued to do his locums there, in holiday time, with the family joining me.

∂

CHAPTER 24:

Gibraltar

The Border ... Foreign bodies ... Eating out ... AIDS
Surgery on the Rock

ROBIN CLARK, the Oban surgeon moved to Gibraltar. There, the administration had the bad old Scottish NHS idea that they would pay for only one surgeon, with no time off, but later Robin got some relief when he and the Naval Hospital surgeon arranged to cover each other on alternate weekends. The Crown Colony is a bit like Oban – a community of 34,000 perched on a rocky area with narrow streets.

The Gibraltarians are fiercely patriotic and are hostile to joining Spain. Britain gained Gibraltar 'in perpetuity' through the Treaty of Utrecht (1713) and the inhabitants can quote you the chapter and verse from it. Spain's desire to annexe Gibraltar is equally fierce, deploring having a British colony attached to their landmass, although the Spanish case is weakened by having their own enclaves in North Africa – Ceuta and Melilla. When the Gibraltarians have voted on proposals to join Spain, the verdicts are decisive – in 1967, 99.64% voted against joining Spain with only 44 in favour, and in 2002 this 'No' vote was slightly down at 98.97%. These votes have a finality not seen outside North Korea or East Germany of old.[*]

Spain's annoyance comes from the low-tax environment in Gib, notably on cigarettes, alcohol and electronic goods. Anyone can visit, purchase items in bulk and take them back over the border, hoping not to be stopped for one of the rare passport and car checks. 'Smuggling' the Spaniards called it; 'exporting' is the Gibraltarians' term, and 14,000 Spaniards cross the border each day to work in Gib. But the political tension is lower than in Franco's era when he completely shut the border. Only occasionally does the Spanish side check up on all those crossing the busy border, leading to long hold-ups and traffic queues. One day I took our children over to a well-known market in La Linea across the border with the border open on our way out. It was closed when we returned, and although I had my passport, the children were on their mother's passport back at the hotel. Would I get the children out of Spain? Fortunately, the Spanish police like a quiet life.

Arriving in Gibraltar can be fraught. The airport is ranked as the most dangerous in Europe, the hazard being the Mediterranean wind from the east which hits the vertical face of the Rock and spills upwards and sideways over the adjacent runway, causing nasty gusts across the runway. Nervous about landing, the pilots will circle hoping for the winds to drop or will divert to Malaga, not far away up the coast.

When you look up from the airport, the Rock dominates the scene. Looking more closely at the Rock's cliff face, there are little openings high up, which the defenders used to fire on the Spaniards who have tried to get Gibraltar back since the first attempt in the siege of 1779-83. When Hitler threatened to take the Rock in 1940, the British Black Watch regiment added anti-tank defences at the bottom of the rock, to which they gave Scottish names – the ditch is the Caledonian Canal and they called the three pillboxes Fort William, Fort George and Fort Augustus. You pass these when travelling into the town.

---

* In the Brexit referendum, Gibraltar again felt strongly and by huge margin (96%) wished to stay in Europe. Britain's absence from Brussels would, it was argued, made Gibraltar vulnerable to pressure from Spain.

On one visit, after a flight delay, I arrived late in the evening, ready for work next day, and, glad to have arrived, had a lovely meal in the warm piazza outside the Holiday Inn hotel, and then slept well.

Early in the morning at the hotel, my room phone rang.

'I am the Procurator Fiscal of Gibraltar and I'm in the hall downstairs, and I would like to speak to you.'

What had I done? Maybe last year's taxes?

I hurried downstairs.

He was distraught.

'My father is ill at the hospital. I need your opinion.'

The Rock in summer has a good side and a bad side since an east wind from the Mediterranean (the Levanter) can blow high humidity air against the Rock's vertical east face, and the resulting condensation hangs over the town on the other side, excluding the sunshine. If all the family made the trip, we usually stayed at the Caleta Palace Hotel on the good side. Our small beach at the hotel was perfect for a young family with suitable food during the day at the small cafes. They and Jean enjoyed the beach, while I healed the sick, and although Gibraltar is not a gourmet paradise, in the evening the little cafes had lots of dishes to suit all tastes – chips, fish, burgers, swordfish steaks, prawns pils pil (in a hot garlic sauce), spicy meatballs and salads shared by all. We could also barbecue on the hotel suite veranda, or visit a delightful North African restaurant overlooking the beach. The smuggler/exporters enlivened the view in the evening by appearing in their inflatable boats with powerful outboard engines. Faster than police vessels, they collected cigarettes from the beach and then left for Spain.

T8 OUT

The Seawave

Catalan Bay – Gibraltar   Tel: 78739

	£	p
1 Food crisps		
Bread (3		30
1 olives	1	20
1 Gambs Pil Pil		50
1 Grilled prawn	3	50
1 Carne salsa	3	50
1 chicken finchitas	3	50
1 chips	1	50
1 ice 1 x Big BAR		80
1 ICE TUB		
Sub Total	16	20
Drinks 1 x P. LAGER 1 x P 1/SH.	1	50
1 Pint lager	1	50
1 Pint chandy	1	50
2 Tango orange	1	20
1 Limon		60
1 TANGO/ORANGE		60
TOTAL	24	60

Thank you for your visit
Please call again

9C 42aI

№ `2268

Gib has a marina, with some large exotic vessels and it was said then that to predict the next British financial scandal, you should note the newest big boats in the marina and source the owners. Barlow Clowes in 1988 had his ostentatious yacht here, paid for by those he duped, as did Robert Maxwell, who left from Gib to commit suicide in the Atlantic in 1991. The marina was not only a haven for the rich, but, close to the sheik's private yachts and financiers gin palaces, were cheaper berths, including the boats of hippies, with their free-ranging children, chickens, old bicycles and a clothesline.

Like Oban, Gibraltar hospital life was never dull. From one of the many humble hippie boats in the Marina came a case of HIV/AIDS, just when the disease was emerging worldwide. The girl, dying of pneumocystis lung infection, the well-known complication, was doomed since there was no HIV treatment then, but it was worth treating the pneumonia in the short term. She needed a tracheostomy and ventilation to tide her over while the antibiotics took effect. There was fear then, dispelled by later experience, that, like hepatitis, small needle punctures could transfer the disease. Usually, when surgeons cause 'needle stick injuries', they puncture their assistants, not themselves, and to do the tracheostomy, I kept other staff at a distance, safe from injury during my backswing. Double-gloved, I took my time.

When you are a locum for a short time, it is prudent not to do any heroic surgery, since you don't do the follow-up. In Gibraltar, Robin left straightforward cases for me, such as hernias, but some of these short cases could be challenging. There were groin hernias in young boys which pop in and out and you must check them again for yourself, and, crucially, check the side – left or right. At surgery, the little hernia sac is so thin and transparent that it may be elusive. Am I on the wrong side?

And there were circumcisions. Not for religious reasons but for narrowing of the foreskin in older boys which causes ballooning and retained secretions. This is a tricky operation, and judging how much foreskin to take off is challenging, and being the locum, you never saw the final result. I still have a fantasy that I could assemble all these now grown-up patients on the beach and, at a word of command, inspect the results.

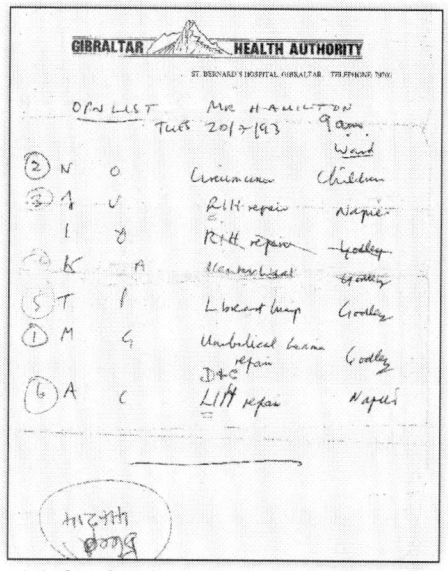

A (redacted) Gibraltar hospital theatre list.

An unusual arrangement enlivened the routine lists. There were two anaesthetists, and instead of working on alternate days, they helped each other. When one case finished and the anaesthetist took the patient out, the other anaesthetist wheeled in the next case, anaesthetised and ready to go. One day, they phoned me from Casualty about an abscess needing opened, and as the last case was wheeled out, the patient with the abscess was wheeled in, already anaesthetised, with the abscess marked for me. Their cooperation gave an agreeable pace to the day.

'It lets us all get to the beach a bit sooner' the anaesthetist explained.

👁️

With the long-standing political problem, no cross-border co-operation on medical care existed, even when specialist medical help was needed. For such surgery, the patient needed to go to London, not Spain. There was an ever-present prospect of doing emergency surgery on the British politicians and senior army personnel who were always coming and going. The worst fear was if a British VIP came in with a leaking aortic abdominal aneurysm.

This didn't happen to me and the only drama I had was when

a young lad appeared with a blocked throat. Any food he had eaten, even saliva, came up immediately. The x-ray showed a Gibraltar penny coin stuck halfway down his oesophagus, and it had been there for two days. Because of the politics, the nearest available ear nose and throat surgeon was in London, and there was nothing for it but to try to get it out. Looking down an adult bronchoscope (this was the pre-fibreoptic era) the saliva was usefully bubbling up showing the way down to the brown coin and I gripped it with biopsy forceps. Out it came, and I had a few anxious moments fearing serious bleeding from the ulcerated oesophagus. All was well.

When the boy woke up, he wanted the penny back.

When I retired to the small theatre changing room, I found a well-dressed stranger. He introduced himself and said he was the visiting ENT surgeon from London, having arrived early to do his monthly clinic next day. He thought he would pop into theatre.

'I would have been glad to see you an hour ago', I said.

I had another success with a 'foreign body.' It was the bulbous wooden end of a curtain rail in a man's rectum and the rail had broken off, leaving it inside. To remove it needed a general anaesthetic and even then, on inspection, the situation was fraught. The sharp, splintered wooden edges of the broken pole pointed out towards me and they dug into the lining of the bowel when attempting to pull it out. I called for obstetric forceps. Someone showed me how the two blades fitted together, and placing them confidently, out it came, to cheers in theatre.

Helping with other challenges was Gibraltar's resourceful bacteriologist-haematologist-pathologist who had travelled the world and had seen much and was always available to help with any mysteries. A young girl appeared with a red lump on her face beside her eye which looked like an infected sebaceous cyst, but something held me back from removing it. The pathologist had a look and said it was instead a sand-fly bite, namely leishmaniasis. Yes, the family had been in Africa recently. The treatment is tricky and is medical, not surgical. If I had operated, the problem would have spread further on her face.

An unusual extra was an occasional patient from one of the increasing number of cruise ships visiting Gibraltar. From one came a farmer from the Carnoustie district and his appendix was badly diseased by the time he arrived, and I took it out. I got to know him in the ward and he mentioned that he was up for membership of the Royal and Ancient Golf Club. On hearing that I was a member, he asked if I would write one of the necessary letters of support. I did so, mentioning that I knew him inside and out.

These travels in the wider world of surgery ended when there was an exodus of surgeons from the Western Infirmary academic unit, and I was glad to return to the hospital.

CHAPTER 25:

Western Infirmary Again

Living donors ... Assistants ... Egypt ... Surgical change
Internet arrives ... Tom Starzl ... Devolution achieved

ARRIVING BACK, I had a different operating theatre, one with a balcony reachable from our store cupboard. On my first day back, and glad to see everybody, about mid-morning, I had a surprise visitor, in his surgical scrubs. It was one of the nay-sayer surgeons who had not supported my history of medicine unit. He offered some pleasantries and seemed to hang about. When he left, I said to my anaesthetist, who knew something of the earlier messy politics, that I thought this was perhaps a gesture of reconciliation from this otherwise reclusive man. The anaesthetist made no response.

At the same time during next week's list, the same scenario unfolded and I said to the theatre sister, who was also well-informed, that I was pleased with this rapprochement. She rolled her eyes, the anaesthetist smiled and they took me aside and briefed me. The surgeon, working in the adjacent theatre, was, as I knew, a heavy smoker. He had to break from his work and use my balcony.

It was good to be back to kidney transplantation. We had one kidney donation between twins, and when putting in the kidney, I felt we were re-enacting the first successful kidney transplant in 1955 in Boston using a twin as a donor. The local staff in Boston tried to discourage the surgeons from going ahead, as had some of our local surgeons years before, but now organ transplantation was incorporated into the routine work of the surgical world. Some serious medical ethical problems can have a short life. But it was still a fraught operation and the others in our team disliked doing living donor kidney transplants and this fell to me again.

Results of all kinds of organ transplants were improving notably after cyclosporine arrived, but donor numbers lagged well behind the need.

MEMORANDUM

FROM: MR D HAMILTON, CONSULTANT TRANSPLANT SURGEON

TO: DR M WATSON, RENAL UNIT, WIG
MRS S MACPHERSON, SENIOR LECTURER IN SURGERY
MR K KYLE, UROLOGY DEPT, GGH
DR BRIGGS, RENAL UNIT
DR JUNOR, RENAL UNIT
DR RODGER, RENAL UNIT
DR McMILLAN, RENAL UNIT
SISTER IN CHARGE, LEVEL 7 EAST
SISTER IN CHARGE, LEVEL 7 WEST
MADGE, RECEPTIONIST LEVEL 7
DR N PACE, CONSULTANT ANAESTHETIST, WIG
MISS NANCY HENDERSON, TISSUE TYPING, ROYAL INFIRMARY
MR IAN GALBRAITH, TISSUE TYPING, ROYAL INFIRMARY
TRANSPLANT CO-ORDINATORS
LINDA McMULLEN, THEATRE MANAGER, LEVEL 5
SISTER McKENZIE, LEVEL 5
SECRETARY FROM DEPT. OF ANAESTHESIA
MISS C SCOTT, RENAL NURSE MANAGER, LEVEL 7
DR A McLELLAN, E3/4, WIG
SISTER G CARLIN, LIVE DONOR NURSE PRACTITIONER

DATE: 5 May 1998

REF: DH/CB/LD

A live donor transplant has been arranged to take place from Ann P   to her son James
P   on Wednesday 20 May 1998.

Living-related kidney donation needs a big team.

The public were sympathetic to organ donation but in practice getting permission when needed was difficult. National schemes involving opting-in or opting-out were attractive, but in day-to-day practice, potential donors always had family in attendance and the family views would always be respected, irrespective of any permissive legislation. To increase donor numbers, donation after deaths which occurred outside of intensive care slowly came in, or rather, came back. In view of the shortage of donor organs, there was new pressure to use 'marginal' kidneys, which were unsatisfactory in some way. With use of more living donors, the possibilities broadened, including grafts from husband to wife or vice versa. Some of these cases were memorable and more taxing than usual, such as transplanting from a lawyer to her lawyer husband. In another, we used an early 'emotionally bonded' kidney donation with the kidney coming from a lifelong friend rather than a relative. Meeting the pair, it was clear that this gift was acceptable. This strategy expanded and has worked well.

In our living donor operations, a skilled urologists took out the donor's kidney, and in the choice between the two kidneys, the left is best. A glance at Gray's *Anatomy* shows that the right kidney vein is very short, hardly two inches in length. Both surgeons need as much of it as possible. One needs enough for inserting the vein in the recipient and the other surgeon, dealing with the stump of the vessel in the donor, needs to have enough length to close it safely since the menacing inferior vena cava vein is nearby. These rival priorities lead to some good-natured banter as kidney removal nears. The main operation of kidney transplant insertion was quickly standardised from the early days, but word had arrived of 'keyhole' transplant surgery being achieved. Us seniors accepted that we were old 'cut and stitch' surgeons but, no stopping progress, we were glad to leave this revolutionary approach, and the stressful learning curve, to others.

Those accepted for kidney transplantation were changing. In the early days, you had to be young and fit to be transplanted, but these criteria were steadily relaxed as management and results improved. Earlier, dialysis patients were thin, which helped the operation but dialysis treatment became so good that obesity was now a regular problem. Faced with this added challenge, to clear a way into the pelvis, I began taking out a large segment of skin and fat on the operative side, like a plastic surgeon. For these patients, I offered to do the same 'tummy tuck' on the other side six months' later, mentioning, with my tongue in my cheek, a large fee, in guineas. But this balancing operation was never requested. Second or third or more kidney grafts in the same patient were now common. Second transplants go in on the opposite side of the pelvis, but finding a place for a third could be difficult.

We accepted more unusual cases. Children with spina bifida and renal failure have small legs and their vessels in the pelvis are also small. Otherwise, the human body is usually of standard layout. But when a Tibetan monk from a Scottish monastery needed a transplant, we wondered if his anatomy inside might differ from the familiar Glasgow design. It wasn't; it was a testimony to the brotherhood of mankind.

The upper age limit for receiving a kidney, formerly 45 years

With our Dr Mary Watson and Sir Roy Calne at a transplant meeting.

of age, moved upwards after pioneers like Roy Calne and Tom Starzl passed this birthday. The age limit would almost disappear later, with each case instead judged individually.

శ

Surgeons like their work in theatre. Apart from enjoying operating, there are other plusses. The theatre is a peaceful cocoon, and disturbances from the outside world, notably phone calls, are discouraged. In the staff room, between cases, there is the limitless supply of the coffee needed by surgeons and anaesthetists to keep their brains alert, and to mark a life event, someone may pass round buns or cake. During these breaks there is a sharing of the latest hospital news and gossip and if all else fails, tabloid newspapers are lying around. Although you wouldn't buy them, it is worth turning their pages with disapproval.

The older surgeon has some benefits. The younger surgeons who assist you have less experience but have sharper eyes and quicker brains and may do the operative work as well or better. One of the great pleasures is to assist a talented experienced trainee doing something within his power and much of our theatre time involved the routine access surgery for various forms of dialysis. Or, letting another junior assist, you can perch on a stool nearby, keeping an eye on things.

We once had a particularly talented and charming Indian junior surgeon. I noticed that he was not only good at his own work but somehow his presence, as an assistant, meant things went well. Every little help is welcome when doing the living kidney donor transplants and I liked to put him on the rota for theatre that day. With his serene assistance, the many stitches neatly fell into place. He lacked ambition and was short of paper qualifications; despite my enthusiastic references, he did not progress in the tough world of surgery.

After he left, during a living-related donor operation, I had a less helpful, fidgety assistant. After I had united the artery and vein and blood flowed nicely into the kidney, all that remained was to connect the ureter. I paused for a while, as one does, to catch up with our anaesthetist's news, notably the prospects for his favoured Glasgow football team in that evening's European match. When I returned to the surgical matter at hand, I was distressed to see that the kidney looked blue and the stitching of both the artery and vein seemed awkward and twisted. I was sure I had not left it thus. Then, light dawned. The ureter, which I had left pointing towards the patient's feet, was instead angled towards the chest. While I was diverted, my hapless assistant had lifted up the kidney, fiddled with it, rotating it through 180° thus twisting the artery and vein, and let it settle back. Re-lifting the kidney and turning it back through half a circle, meant all was well.

One silly mistake on another occasion was my fault. I put in a kidney upside down; I can explain all. I was jet-lagged after a long flight, and while I was away, the theatre staff, thinking we needed some variety in our life, had turned the operating table round through 180°. When I placed the kidney in the pelvis, I used the old orientation of the theatre rather than the patient's anatomy and I only realised the mistake after connecting the blood vessels. The kidney was working well and there was no way back. The urine had to go uphill at first, then descend, but all was well. We informed the patient, but he took the view that, if we were happy, he was happy. The kidney continued to be happy, but I left careful notes for future surgeons that if the kidney ever had to come out, the ureter would prove elusive and would be found first to the north rather than the south of the organ.

I was sorry not to get back to experimental research. But a verdict from my historical studies was that progress in clinical transplantation had come from surgical improvisation and serendipity and not from basic immunology alone. Added to that, kidney survival results could hardly be better. I would have liked to get back to hamster-to-mouse skin grafting (or growing chicken feathers) but my xenografting methods were not the way forward and that would have been a selfish pleasure at the expense of the world of mice. The answer to providing

With David Cooper (centre) the xenograft expert and historian and Charles Bryant at an American Osler Society history of medicine meeting.

organ transplants for all would certainly come from using animals but by changing their organs, not treating the recipient, and the geneticists were hard at work modifying pigs for human use. Although monkeys are a closer genetic fit for human grafting, they breed with difficulty in captivity and their use in research is restricted. Pigs, by contrast are fertile and, being used for food, do not attract animal rights defenders. Hopes for their use in human transplantation lie in the capable hands of David Cooper in Alabama.*

I was burdened with the administration while the hospital looked for a new young director of our unit. After a long delay, we appointed one and he arrived from America, but did not last long. Everybody wondered why he was here and it had escaped notice that he was embroiled in some legal difficulties there. He soon complained, with some justification, that the Medical Faculty had broken their promises to him, and he left.

We had helped train an Egyptian junior surgeon, and this led to a visit to Cairo to assist the work of their transplant unit. For religious reasons, organ donation after death is excluded in Muslim countries and they used only living kidney donors. Before our arrival, the hospital had advertised in a Cairo newspaper, urging possible recipients and their donors to appear in the hospital at the time of our visit. On arrival, we met to study these pairs and were on our guard since the donor might not be a relative and instead had been offered money to donate. This

---

* Cooper was also attracted to writing surgical history, and his *Open Heart* (2010), a history of heart surgery, was followed by his definitive biography of Christiaan Barnard, the heart transplanter.

practice was not unknown in the Middle East. The first pair we assessed were a senior army officer and his allegedly willing donor. There was no eye contact between the two, and when we started with some elementary questions, the donor, undoubtedly a lowly soldier coerced into offering a kidney, fled from the room. Later, some pairs were convincingly related and we proceeded to the next stage of blood grouping and tissue matching, followed by the transplant operation.

Cairo newspaper invitation to potential transplant donors and recipients.

We had some time on our hands in Cairo and our hosts provided tours of the impressive local antiquities and museums. This involved terrifying car journeys driven by government chauffeurs keen to show off the aggressive driving skills needed to evade trouble in the unstable city. Weaving in and out of traffic on the broad city highways *sans* traffic lanes, the additional hazards encountered included donkeys sitting down on the road and men on scooters with their wives sittings sideways on the back holding a delivery of vegetables.

We had a trip south by air to the Valley of the Kings and set off from our hotel on a guided tour. But in the hot afternoon, after the tenth tomb visit and with the sun setting, when the guide yet again intoned that 'now we go to the temple of … ', Jean, having no cardigan, spoke up saying 'No, now we go to the hotel for a cool drink'. The others returned later, shivering.

Fortunately, our hosts did not offer a hot-air balloon trip, although these were available. My view is that anything run by human beings is only about 98% safe. Not long after, Roddie McSween, our best man, having retired from the Western Infirmary and, touring the world with his wife, was in Egypt and took a flight in one of these balloons with a local teenager in charge. It crashed. Roddie sustained a badly broken ankle and had a difficult journey home.

General surgery was still changing. Some surgical conditions and operations were disappearing. Appendix removal, either as an emergency or for alleged 'chronic appendicitis' was declining, as was childhood removal of tonsils and adenoids. I was a sceptic earlier about surgery for alleged appendicitis and I liked 'cooking up the appendix' in the ward, watching and waiting, and usually, the pain would go. If not, the patient was in the right place.

Accordingly, when, one Friday, I developed lower right abdominal pain, age 60, I kept going, hoping it would go away, but even an aperitif or two would not shift it and by midnight on Sunday, I was suffering and tender on the right side of the abdomen. I phoned myself into the Western Infirmary and the journey, starting with the bumps on our drive, didn't help. The on-call trainees got a drip up and gave me morphine. I picked up and told the on-call consultant that whatever was wrong, it could wait till the morning and we could all have a sleep. Also, at my age, I thought appendicitis was unlikely and that it was something nastier which needed daytime assessment. Paul Rogers, the consultant was also expecting trouble, and sensibly opened me up with a midline incision (a wound still holding strong to this day) and, after all, it was a only ruptured appendix. All went well, except the necessary morphine drip produced the hallucinations often described by those receiving morphine, notably in intensive care units. My stay was, as ever, a humbling education in seeing things from the patient's point of view. It's a long day in hospital as a patient, particularly in a single room, and being a doctor, they leave you alone. Four-bedded wards give companionship. Also, if you collapse, somebody will notice.

Most changes in surgery occur slowly, so slowly that the shift can only be detected in hindsight. But the same cannot be said for the arrival of 'laparoscopic' or 'minimally invasive surgery'. News came from Europe in the early 1980s that surgeons were using such instruments to carry out the appendix removal. The understandably Luddite reaction was to ridicule this costly alternative to traditional hands-on surgery, but when the news came that it was also possible to remove the gall-bladder, the technique merited consideration.

The first in the West of Scotland to get the instrumentation for abdominal minimally invasive surgery was Graham Bell, a surgeon at Greenock's district general hospital. In a personal initiative, he went to Lyon in about 1988 to watch the new methods, and when he returned, he successfully ordered the expensive equipment from an inattentive administrator. There was a learning curve, with incidents. The technique impressed the trainees rotating through Greenock and they came back to the city with the news and experience of the technique. The method was spreading in a manner not seen since the rapid acceptance of ether anaesthesia in the 19th century.

This was no mere technical triumph. The speed of acceptance of laparoscopic methods was because the usual post-operative pain and chest complications after abdominal surgery, which needed a stay in hospital, came, it was realised, from the skin incision and muscle wound, not the surgery inside. Now the pain and suffering were absent; the patient could go home next day.

As these and other changes bedded in, there was a new emphasis on surgical results and outcome. The first stirrings of quality control in Scotland was The Lothian Surgical Audit, which started in 1982 as a weekly review of all cases treated in that health board area. It helped raise standards and changed practice, even showing that specialism gave better results. Trends in surgery, notably for duodenal ulcers, emerged using the pooled data and any innovations were heeded.

The first national assessment of quality within a specialty emerged in our British transplantation community who cooperated in looking at kidney transplant results in each unit in 1985, using visits and audit by a small team from other centres. The data showed a 'centre effect' with variation in results ranging from good to moderate, with 3-month first kidney graft survival ranging from 82% to 54%. Even the existence of the study seemed to improve results, since a later audit showed that the results were now bunched together with no statistical difference. Following this, similar studies of cardiac surgery followed, and eventually, reporting results nationally by individual surgeons was accepted.

The end of the millennium saw a change in mood. The results

of transplantation were now excellent and all forms of cardiac surgery had matured to be a routine. Medical treatment had also achieved much from mid-century, but new pharmaceutical agents were few. No new antibiotics appeared, and resistance to the old ones increased. There was an unusual reaction. The public, accustomed to the earlier continuous progress, seemed unhappy that some afflictions remained untreatable. For help, the public turned to other healers, and alternative medicine soon flourished in the high street.

Now back in a transplant world, I returned with pleasure to work on my neglected history book, and this received an unexpected boost. I had met all the pioneer transplant surgeons and knew some of them well, except one. I had always avoided Tom Starzl at scientific meetings, although he was, with Roy Calne, the crucial innovators of the era. In the 1960s, Starzl not only brought in the vital combination of immune suppression by steroids and azathioprine which made routine transplantation possible, but he also met and solved the formidable challenge of liver transplantation. He was one of the intense American surgeons of that growth era in surgery starting in the 1960s to whom surgery was a calling, and they led a monastic hospital lifestyle which justified sacrifice of much else. These men never went home and locked their trainees in the hospital. I was in awe of Starzl's clinical contributions and now also noted and admired his perceptive historical writings which were appearing during his retirement.

I was surprised when one day my secretary said there was somebody with a name like Starzl on the phone. It was indeed Tom Starzl, and after introducing himself he explained that he had read some historical things I'd written and wanted to say he agreed with a point or two I had made. We had a long talk, and when I slipped in that I had a book in preparation, he offered to assist and suggested that I spend some time with him in Pittsburgh.

Not long after I took up this offer. Pittsburgh, like Glasgow, had thrived as a city based on heavy industry, then declined, and in helping the revival of the city's fortunes, Starzl had put Pittsburgh on the medical map. As an esteemed citizen, he had the honour one year of throwing the first baseball pitch at the opening match. Now retired, he worked in a small flat over a fast food outlet across the road from the hospital's transplant institute, which they had named after him. There, he had his office, his archives, his secretary and a dog. I listened at length to his reminiscences, prompting him with questions. Before

With Tom Starzl in Pittsburgh in 2000.

visiting, I had a dark thought he might try to influence my narrative and emphasise his own contributions, but he did not, and indeed his massive contributions needed no further polishing. I had two long visits to Pittsburgh and in between, we had a fruitful correspondence. He read the manuscript of my book, chapter by chapter, and was a kindly and perceptive reader. Moreover, he added that he would do an Introduction.

I finished the book and went back with the good news to Oxford University Press, many years late with the text. Although accustomed to dreamy academics failing for years or decades to submit their book, they had lost my contract, and with their financial problems, they were

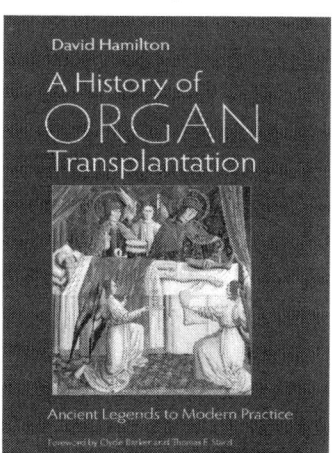

reluctant to start again. Starzl now took charge. He walked over to the University of Pittsburgh Press close by and, telling them loyally that my book was 'a page-turner' and that it had to be published, they agreed to proceed. In Pittsburgh you didn't say 'no' to Tom Starzl.

Thereafter, this encounter with American publishing did not always go smoothly. It soon involved a brush with a 'which hunter', the pedantic text editors who change 'which' to 'that' (or indeed 'that' to 'which'). My fussy editor went well beyond this, adding vivid tabloid phrases notably her flourish at the end that 'transplantation goes fast forward into the future with confidence.' Of her many other infelicities, most of which I resisted, her most bizarre objection concerned my description of the miraculous leg transplant carried out in mediaeval times in Rome by courtesy of the saints Cosmas and Damian. The donor leg came from a recently-deceased black African gladiator and it was used to replace the cancerous limb of a white church official. My witch hunter ruled that it was politically incorrect to refer to the blackness of the leg and she removed all references in the text to its colour. I responded that we should not ignore the facts in the mediaeval text, particularly as the cover for the book, already chosen, was one of the many colourful paintings of this miracle, showing the black leg nicely in place postoperatively.

Writing methods were changing, and the computers were getting smaller, more powerful and cheaper. The heavy cathode ray tube screens were gone, replaced by the elegant thin, flat screens. The cheaper inkjet printers appeared towards 1990 and soon they could print in colour. Windows 95 appeared in 1995 and now offered a coloured, attractive starting page plus click control by a mouse. The launch was a huge international event featuring celebrity endorsement, music by the Rolling Stones and there were queues for its midnight release. Other changes came rapidly. Feeding programs in over hours using many floppy disks was thankfully gone when CD ROM discs appeared and soon programmes, now known as apps, could be downloaded from the Net. USB memory sticks (i.e. flash drives, thumb drives) soon with huge storage, emerged about 2000. The first computer viruses appeared in 1986, and caused serious damage before protection started to appear. Scanning of images, formerly expensive, was now available using economical printers, and with the Internet, these images could be easily shared.

Computer manufacturing firms rose and fell quickly in this tough world and Atari, Amstrad, Acorn and Amiga had much support but disappeared. The expensive Apple computer, with its own operating system, lost ground by 1970 to the cheaper PCs and nearly disappeared. But, with the devoted support of its anti-PC admirers, the company revived when the elegant, dependable iMac emerged in 1998. The company then triumphed with the iPod in 2001, then the iPhone and iPad.

The new information highway was broad and easy to use, but there was some resistance. The libraries disliked computers being brought in but relented and soon provided rows of power points. The NHS also initially discouraged the use of personal machines within the hospitals. In the world of publishing, those producing large reference works hesitated. Although massive information could be compressed onto readable disks, for lexicographers and encyclopaedists, publishing multiple volumes was an ancient, hallowed tradition. Microsoft made the first move with their Encarta encyclopaedia in 1993 and offered it on a multimedia disc costing £250. When the multi-volume Oxford English Dictionary made history and became available on a single disc in 1992 it was priced at £581.63 to protect sales of the print version. The *Encyclopaedia Britannica* continued to plan for a new 30 volume 15th edition to appear in 2010, written as usual by many distinguished experts and then further edited and fact-checked by a large editorial team. But in January 2001, the *Britannica* received a fatal blow from Jimmy Wales who launched his online Wikipedia. Inviting unpaid contributions from outside, he accepted all of the avalanche of articles, starting with 1,000 in the first month. Within a year, his encyclopaedia exceeded the *Britannica*, and he met criticism of inaccuracies by recruiting unpaid volunteer as text reviewers. The one-millionth English article was posted in 2006 and was 'Jordanhill [Glasgow] Railway Station.' After 10 years, Wikipedia had 20 million pages, all topical and up-to-date, with good references.

A neighbour who worked for British Petroleum gave me, in the late 1980s, the first hint of the Internet to come. I asked him about his day's routine, and he said that on arrival at work he opened his mail. 'Letters?' I said. 'No,' he said, 'messages on his computer.' I didn't understand. He explained that it was the BP 'intranet'.

Soon, all the intranets in the world used the same language, and the challenge was to link these intranets up as a 'world wide web'. This done, it became the Internet, arriving in 1990 and in its scratchy early days it was exciting to hook up to your expensive local provider, and wait for the grinding 'dial-up'. To quote Dr Johnson, it was 'not so much that it was done, it was that it was done at all.'

I started emailing about 1995, a bit late, when I noticed that the young surgeons were using it for messaging. Older computer users like myself learned a lot from our children during this rapid time of change.

Our Duncan helped me create a website, and Alistair showed me how he kept in touch with medicine via the latest apps, and he impressed the family while on holiday with an iPad translation of the menu in an Italian restaurant. In a Polish ski resort, I failed to obtain a *Daily Telegraph* and, at the top of a lift in the High Tatras, mentioned this deprivation to our Hazel. She got out her Blackberry and I caught up with news from home.

Hazel on the slopes.

'Dad, do you want the *Dundee Courier* as well?'

Joining the Net involved new skills and some of my generation procrastinated, feeling that they could manage with conventional communication by pen, ink and post. By about 2015 most societies and clubs accepted the inevitable and moved over to contacting members by email only. Some organisations with senior membership knew that these members had not mastered computers and the Net, and understood and were prepared to delay during this transition. In hospital life, new patients had paperless clinical notes, but return patients with long case histories still had the older folder.

The Net led to the rise of online commerce, and it featured Amazon's speedy ordering and delivery. In the cities, there was Uber's new way of hiring a taxi.* These changes brought in impressive quality control and feedback, empowering the consumer. TripAdvisor and Booking.com became a powerful force for bookings, and hotels and restaurants dreaded and heeded any poor reviews.

The Net and Web brought joy to historians since the now-digitised old newspapers, magazines and books could be consulted from afar, saving visits to archives and the tedious task of turning dusty pages. You could search any digitised item for any word, and our golf historians found new hidden valuable golf material in this way.

Mobile phones intruded at first, and some places needed stringent rules, but the rise of silent texting mitigated this. The phones soon had tiny cameras of remarkable power and quality. With a closer focus than ever, the 'selfie' picture was possible, and their improved performance in poor light needed no flash. This made the phone cameras acceptable at sporting events and particularly in museums and art galleries.†

The digital revolution changed lecturing methods. Slides and projectors disappeared with the advent of PowerPoint, difficult though the complex projectors were in use. The *British Medical Journal* of December 2007 described the PPSD (the PowerPoint Stress Disorder) affecting the speaker when appearing in an unfamiliar place. I had a related fright. I was booked for a local history society meeting and I asked ahead if they had PowerPoint. They replied that they did. I arrived early and enquired again about the promised PowerPoint.

'Yes', they confirmed, 'we have PowerPoint – it's over at the wall' They pointed to a 13 amp plug.

Towards the end of the century, Scottish nationalism was getting electoral support again. The Labour Party brought in a referendum for a second time and as this 1997 devolution referendum neared, a few of us, some veterans from the 1979 defeat, got together again to make the case for devolution of healthcare, twenty years after we first did so. This time we were included in an umbrella organisation run by

---

* Amazon became popular about 2008, and we used Uber first in 2018 when our family ordered a taxi for us after a Glasgow gathering.

† The 'selfie' and PowerPoint presentations came into routine use about 2010.

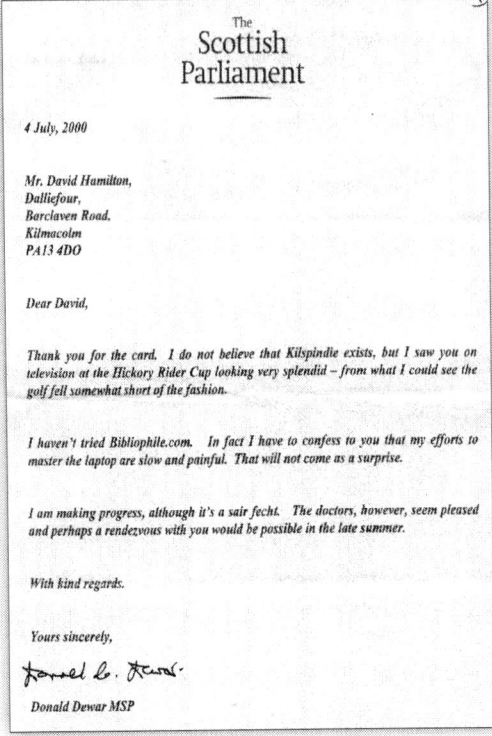

The
Scottish
Parliament

4 July, 2000

Mr. David Hamilton,
Dalliefour,
Barclaven Road,
Kilmacolm
PA13 4DO

Dear David,

Thank you for the card. I do not believe that Kilspindie exists, but I saw you on television at the Hickory Rider Cup looking very splendid – from what I could see the golf fell somewhat short of the fashion.

I haven't tried Bibliophile.com. In fact I have to confess to you that my efforts to master the laptop are slow and painful. That will not come as a surprise.

I am making progress, although it's a sair fecht. The doctors, however, seem pleased and perhaps a rendezvous with you would be possible in the late summer.

With kind regards,

Yours sincerely,

Donald Dewar MSP

A letter from Donald Dewar shortly before his death.

Henry McLeish called 'Scotland Forward' but there were fewer meetings and less debate. Our document went over familiar advocacy but with stronger popular support, it was almost an open door. Even the Scottish British Medical Association was less hostile and the Colleges in Glasgow and Edinburgh took more interest.

The referendum of 1997 gave a 74% vote in favour of devolution and the Scottish parliament was established in 1999. It had been a long and difficult haul, not least for the Labour Party.

Donald Dewar was made First Minister. He required heart surgery soon after but, after a 'sair fecht' died in October 2000.

For retirement to avoid my old problem, I had to make sure I was busy. Surgical locums no longer appealed but one opportunity appeared and this was to do medical tribunals for the benefits agencies. It sounds like routine, dull work. It wasn't. The 'sore back circuit' was full of interest.

CHAPTER 26

The Sore Back Circuit

Appeals Tribunals … Dundee … Glasgow … Aberdeen
Orkney … Ayr … Kilmarnock … Kirkaldy … Shetland
Edinburgh … Elgin … Greenock … Oban … Inverness

OVERWEIGHT and smelling of tobacco, she appears before our three-person tribunal, and she is anxious to make a point. She tells us she is not guilty of housing benefit fraud. Her words and body language are clear: *Moi? A fraud?*

We explain that the tribunal today will instead hear about her claim for a bad back, turned down by the Department of Work and Pensions. The fraud hearing must be on another day, at another place.

We start.

But her teenage daughter has moved forward close to the tribunal bench, near me, and she instead flicks through a girlie magazine. I suggest to her she might pay attention to her mother's case.

She stops but starts texting on her phone. The lawyer in our panel asks her to 'respect the Court, or leave'.

Starting to leave, she turns and tells us that

'It doesn't look like a f*cking court to me.'

It is a court, of sorts. I applied for this Appeals Service tribunal work as a necessary interest in retirement. To be considered, I needed a reference and Sam Galbraith, then retired from the Scottish Parliament, loyal as ever, obliged saying 'I was a friend and supporter of the working class from the earliest times.' That was a bit theatrical, and class warriors were not what was wanted, but I was appointed.

In the early days of the welfare state, disability matters were simple. If you could not walk, then you were entitled to a mobility benefit to help you get about. If you were unable to use your hands and hence unable to cook, a care payment would get help to prevent starvation. The family doctors used to have a role, signing people off 'on the sick' and assisting with other benefits, but this was unsatisfactory and the government took over, bringing in a national scheme, adding a medical assessment. Since then it has got much more complicated, and despite better national health, the bill for these incapacities and disabilities has risen to remarkable levels.[*]

If they turn down your application for benefit, you can appeal, and this is where our tribunals come in. Apparently a dull, worthy matter, the appeals work turned out instead to be full of interest. It is also a sensitive political issue, and even gives insight into disease missing from routine clinical work.

Over the years, I kept notes on our work, which took me to many venues throughout Scotland. In what follows, I have joined up some cases in the form of a diary, and although the locations of the tribunal venues are correct, and the hearings described here are open to the public, I have omitted the names and transferred the location of the cases from one venue to another.

Today I am 'sitting' at our Dundee venue.

To travel from St Andrews, I use my Scottish senior bus pass and the bus delivers me close to our meeting place. We gather and will consider about four cases in the morning and the same in the afternoon, if they all turn up. Three of us sit – a lawyer, a doctor plus a care member, someone who works in social services or related agencies.

* The UK's Disability, Sickness and Incapacity payments are £45 billion annually at the time of writing.

The 'appellants' who have been turned down for benefit payments, appear in front of us at our table. The lawyer explains the procedure and then hands over to me to ask about the medical conditions. Usually, instead of one problem, they describe several ailments.[*]

My next task is to find out about the appellant's disability, starting with their walking and then their use of their hands. Simplifying the scoring system, if you can walk only 50 yards before stopping, it entitles you to the benefit. If you can manage one hundred yards and then stop (actually 100 *metres*, to please Europe) you are half-way, 6 points, towards getting an award.[†] We have to trust what we are being told. Unlike a court, we don't cross-examine.

Our first appellant is a tiny elderly lady crippled with Parkinson's Disease and her daughter is with her. She shuffles into the hearing at a slow speed. I had seen her arriving outside the venue, hardly moving, and this is an easy, deserving case. There is no fraud involved, nor 'over-egging' of her problem to get the benefit money. It is a puzzle they have denied her the benefit; the reason soon becomes clear.

All she has to do is tell us she cannot walk. They train us to ask 'open' questions – such as 'Tell us about your walking?' but a leading question is instead more appropriate here.

I put it to her – 'You can hardly walk.'

'Not at all' she says, 'I can get there if I take my time. 'We are off to Marks & Spencer after this.'

We have a stoic in front of us.

I switch to the problem with her hands. If she tells me she can't pick up a pound coin, then she gets points towards an award. She replies that the shopkeepers always put change into her hand. I try to help further; the ability to use a mobile phone is the ultimate test of dexterity.

'Can you dial on an iPhone?' I ask.

---

* The most frequent physical ailments claimed are COPD (chronic bronchitis), fibromyalgia, irritable bowel syndrome, arthritis and back pain. The main mental health complaint is depression.

† The details of the arcane scoring system in the different forms of benefit have been omitted, and indeed these are constantly changing.

'I don't have one.'

We turn to her daughter, who confirms the obvious inability to walk, and that she has no power in her hands and cannot cook. We give her the money.

This response of different people to illness is known as the bio-psychosocial model of disease. Individuals with the same level of affliction show responses varying from stoicism to invalidism. When applying for benefits, stoicism is a handicap, and the Department's medical examiner may not have seen her walking and accepted her denial of difficulty.

Next to appear should be an alcoholic who has been denied benefit. His representative (see later) has attended to speak for him but there is no sign of the man himself. We put alcoholics early on our list, hoping they have not started drinking that day. In his absence, the procedure is that we wait 10 minutes before moving on and we decide, after looking at the paperwork on his case, not to allow the appeal.

Half an hour later, the alcoholic turns up outside and is incoherent and incapable of giving his case. Technically the case is over, but the next appellant has not turned up. Shall we start again? It turns out that his representative has now left the building. The case is over. He will doubtless be listed to return another day when he offers an excuse. Some legal and ethical problems are involved here. Alcoholism is deemed to be a disease rather than a lifestyle choice, and hence disability payments are available.

In the afternoon we hear from a train driver who hit and killed a man on the track who was intent on suicide. For the first time in 20 years, he has been off work, with flashbacks and he needs counselling for post-traumatic stress disorder (PTSD). But the Department has turned him down. He is in bad shape, withdrawn and miserable. His doctor has sent a supportive letter We give him an award.

Over the day, we allow four appeals and turndown four. This agrees with the national figures which show that 40% of appeals are successful.[*]

---

[*] The cases mentioned here, being appeals, probably do not reflect the pattern of disability seen in successful applicants. However, good national data is not available on the medical diagnosis given in disability claims.

Back to St Andrews by bus. A St Andrews University lecturer has noticed one of his students in a seat across the aisle and he is loudly explaining the subtleties of Kant's philosophy to her, with hand signals.

☙

To Glasgow ...

I take the St Andrews bus to Dundee and then catch the south-running Aberdeen train. Taking the train or bus is preferable to driving to Glasgow, particularly in winter, and parking there is difficult. You can read and write on the train, and in today's paper, ITV's CEO says that he uses public transport to get some work done. Agreed.

They allow us first-class travel, but it is pointless to take it on this route, since Aberdeen's prosperity means that the tiny first-class area is full of people using mobile phones and talking to headquarters.

In Glasgow, I meet up with the lawyer chairman and our care member for today. Our experienced clerk has the paperwork ready and will guide us through our day.

We start.

The first appellant has a sore back and he has had hospital investigations. He has claimed that 100 yards is his walking limit and I ask how he measured that. He can't help; he didn't measure it. So, as ever, I help, and I suggest a comparison with the length of a cricket or football pitch. For those not interested in sport, we suggest the distance between lampposts or ask about their most familiar walk. If all else fails, and we have windows, we can look outside and suggest a virtual walk.

Malingering and fraudulent claims are rare. Instead, 'over-egging' is common, given the very human desire to impress and gain money. When doctors ask how much people drink and get the answer 'one unit a day' the doctor mentally doubles this to give a realistic estimate; doctors themselves, asked the same question, may also embellish the truth. It's human nature.

Credibility is important. The lawyers are good at assessing this and those who do criminal work are particularly alert. If the lawyer concludes that the appellant is not telling the truth, then the case is over. We doctors are more credulous; we trust people.

The next appellant claims three medical problems – chronic

bronchitis, the irritable bowel syndrome (IBS) and pernicious anaemia. She has quite a thick file from other tangled dealings with the Department. The medical side, though alarming, can be simplified since she is not anaemic. Her many blood tests done have shown a small fall of no significance in blood vitamin B12 levels. Her bad chest is a smoker's cough.

Her abdominal complaint is being investigated, but all the tests are negative, hence gaining the always-unsatisfactory label of IBS. She is aggressive and claims that she therefore requires benefit for supervision and assistance and it will come from her daughter. We ask if her daughter keeps good health and it turns out she does not. We are curious. The daughter also has abdominal problems and has her own benefits for the supervision and assistance given by her mother.

I ask for clarification, and she agrees.

'We look after each other.'

We are unimpressed, but adjourn to ask for up-to-date medical evidence about the mother's condition.

⁓

Today, to Aberdeen ...

The train north to Aberdeen offers a busy seascape with much off- and on-shore oil developments, and we stop at Carnoustie, Arbroath and Stonehaven, the home of deep-fried Mars Bar. It's a short walk from the Aberdeen station to our venue, and I pass the famous Station Hotel, which has seen better days. A scruffy notice on the door says 'Drug Dealers Will Be Asked To Leave.'

A young female heroin addict attends to make her appeal and there is a strange 'friend' sitting on the seats at the back. Soon, he interrupts, trying to coach her replies, and we ask him to stop. When they leave at the end, we hear that her friend is a local drug dealer, perhaps adding other roles in her life, and was attending to help maintain his income stream.

The appellants can make their appeal themselves or get help from organisations like the Citizen's Advice Bureau, or a trade union or even use a lawyer, and our next case is a man discovered in middle life to have Huntington's Disease, an ultimately fatal ailment which after a slow start gives disturbed behaviour, dementia and eventual paralysis.

He has the initial mental symptoms of mood swings, bad temper and occasional memory loss, but even so, this was not enough to impress the Department. Before he comes in, we are sympathetic; if he tells us of the difficulty concentrating (6 points towards the 12 needed) and we add 6 more for memory loss, we will wave through the appeal. As usual, his representative speaks first for him, but unexpectedly also claims he has difficulties walking, bending and holding things with his hands. I must get these new issues out of the way, before hearing about the sinister mental problem.

Since the paperwork say he is a golfer, I ask about his golf, and he tells me he plays 18 holes twice a week and, yes, he can bend and pick his ball out of the hole. At this point, he rises and says my questioning on golf was unfair, and he leaves the room. The representative has over-egged a good case and lost it; the representative is now contrite. However, we decide that even though the appellant has technically given up his appeal, we will call him back another day.

Following on, our next claimant has a diagnosis of PTSD. He lost a half-inch disc of skin from the tip of a finger in an accident at work, and a small skin graft was placed. He was then off sick with post-traumatic stress for three months and his firm paid for private counselling. I ask about the cause of the stress. No, he says, it was not the injury but the delay and uncertainty in the wait for surgery. The plastic surgeon, he recalls, must have taken at least four hours to arrive and operate that evening.

We are not impressed.

PTSD started life with a clear formulation. It was diagnosed after the patient had endured a life-threatening event. But now the label has been greatly extended and benefit is regularly claimed for the effect of less harrowing events.

࿐

Back to Glasgow ...

We sympathise with a multiple sclerosis sufferer who needs to self-catheterise her bladder and has walking difficulties. In this disease, these problems are variable, and she must have been in a good phase when the medical examiner for the Department was unimpressed. Instead, we make an award, aware that she will get worse in years to come, although this should not influence us.

Next, a young man comes in on crutches, with a bent knee holding his foot well off the ground. He had fractured his lower leg in an accident and was in a plaster for the usual period, plus a crutch, but when the plaster was removed, he declined thereafter to put his foot back on the ground. Physiotherapists spoke firmly to him to start weight-bearing, but he was determined not to do so. His orthopaedic surgeon, in his reports, uncharitably concluded that the appellant was deliberately avoiding walking to get a better cash award from the accident. This 'compensationitis' is a familiar situation in orthopaedics, and the disability disappears when the claim for injuries is over and a cheque has arrived.

We are also unimpressed, but our situation is different. If he continues to avoid using his leg, he is disabled, even though it is self-inflicted. What to do? We compromise, and make a short award; things may be different on the next visit.

The next appellant has phoned in to say that since she has managed to get an appointment for her doctor that morning, she wants to come to the tribunal another time. We are interested in her priorities, but go ahead and consider the case on the papers submitted to us.

Mental health cases are booked for this afternoon. Poor mental health is our biggest area of disability and within it, the commonest diagnosis is depression. Within this, there is a spectrum ranging from unhappiness resulting from personal situations to the profound, unbidden depression requiring psychiatric or even inpatient care.

To the Islands ...

To get to Orkney, I need to stay the night in Aberdeen for next morning's flight, and staying and eating in Aberdeen is expensive. The offshore workers coming and going to the rigs are young and fit, and after the monastic life of the rigs, they enjoy a drink. In the morning, there is the struggle through Aberdeen's notorious traffic congestion, but I get there, and Aberdeen's airport is busy but in an unusual way. There are flights to Norway, even one to the oil-rich Middle East, and there must be as many helicopters as planes.

Our small plane has old-fashioned propellers and the young pilots make cheerful announcements from their seats close to us. I prefer old pilots, since they are Darwinian survivors of life in the air. These young men will doubtless progress and when they eventually fly Dreamliners using computers they will reminisce about hands-on flying to the Islands.

But back in the cabin, it is not a happy place. We have a tough lady stewardess, perhaps demoted from Dreamliners, and she is keen to make us suffer. I am travelling with my ancient shoulder bag, survivor of many journeys around the world. It is open at the top, letting you lift your papers in and out vertically, and the zip needed to close it broke years ago. Our tight-lipped stewardess now informs me I am sitting in the emergency row. All five rows look alike to me, but that's the rule and there is a problem – I'm not allowed a bag under the seat in front.

She says my old bag will have to go in to the overhead rack. But the rack is full, she announces with pleasure. Turning on the angst, she adds that the bag will have to go to the hold. I offer my beloved zip-less-open-at-the-top bag to her.

'Zip it up,' she, and.

'There is no zip,' I say.

She ostentatiously fetches some broad brown tape and after cocooning my bag, removes it with distaste. I'll be glad when we get to the Isles.

Flying north from Aberdeen on a good day can be thrilling, especially if you have an interest in golf, and Donald Trump's controversial links and the Moray Firth courses look good from the air. This time I'm not staying in the capital Kirkwall, where we have our hearings, since to see more of Orkney, I've booked in for bed and breakfast in Stromness to the west. Walking along the famous paved, twisting alleys sheltered from the wind and weather, I pass the Museum which tells of the Arctic explorers who loaded their supplies here and the sunken WWI battleships in Scapa Flo.

I am thirsty and hungry. At a side street, there is a signpost to a wee restaurant and, gosh, it has a Michelin star. But it is early in the evening and, having good reading material with me, I study this first at a local bar. Then I phone the restaurant and, yes, they have a table. On arrival, it is an impressive place with an open fire and a blackboard menu, and the owner-chef and his wife greet me. This place feels good.

I confidently ask for a glass of cold sauvignon blanc with olives and I enquire about the dish of the day.

They study me carefully.

They think I am a Michelin inspector.

Things go well.

After a sound sleep I take the bus back to Kirkwall to dispense justice, and we hold our hearings in the Community Centre. The first case has cancelled and this gives a chance to hear about Orkney from the local lawyer. He tells us about a national Quality of Life Survey recently which put Orkney top of the list. Their criteria included employment, education, crime, and school class sizes.

After our first day's sessions, at night I find a pleasant place in Kirkwall for an aperitif before a curry. But a lady and her pals out for the night disturb my reading in the pub. I gather they are from a remoter area, and she is in charge and is back-and-forth to the bar with the orders. They are enjoying themselves.

Next day, who should appear as our first case but the group leader from the pub, claiming both inability to walk and a social phobia. The procedure is that if you have any personal observation to add to the case, you must give the appellant a chance to comment. When I describe how we had met before and that she seemed then to be in good form physically and mentally, she is taken aback. Otherwise, the papers show that her case is weak. and we make no award.

We fly back. The security staff are not stretched by only six daily outgoing flights, but make up for it by fastidious attention to detail. Our clerk makes this journey regularly with her large bag of legal papers, but although they know her well, their view is that she may have turned to drug running and they always take a humourless interest in her bags of Appeals documents.

It's getting late when I near home and reach Leuchars Railway station. The last bus to St Andrews may not be along for a while and it's been a long day in the North. Taking a taxi, as we are allowed, seems justified. I hail the single taxi and explain to the other man waiting for the bus he had better join me if he is to survive the night. He understands his plight, jumps in quickly and his cognitive skill is soon explained. It turns out that he is the Professor of Linguistics at Oxford, giving a lecture at St Andrews in the morning.

❧

Dundee again ...

Word comes that the first case has phoned in to say that she can't get a babysitter. She has known about this hearing for many weeks, and we should be firm and proceed without her, but we roll over. It seems from the papers she is a young, single mother and has not cancelled or caused difficulty before. We agree to give another date, with a warning that no further adjournments or postponements will be granted. Perhaps one thousand pounds would be a reasonable figure for the cost of each appeal.

ADHD (Attention Deficit Hyperactivity Disorder) cases today, a condition unknown some years back. The number of ADHD appeals vary from venue to venue throughout Scotland, depending on the altitude of the local hospital doctors. Some paediatricians say it hardly exists, while others say instead that it is a much under-diagnosed problem.

Today, one ADHD case is an easy one, since it involves a restless child who is never still, never sleeps and is disruptive at school, leading to truancy and exclusion. Award given.

The second case is also straightforward. ADHD has been suggested by the family doctor, but the child's adverse behaviour is rather ordinary, mostly sitting down obstinately in the street, and the challenging behaviour in the home is refusing to go to bed. The school report is crucial in these cases, and this child behaves well at school, joins school outings, has never been excluded, nor have the parents been summoned for any incidents.

No award.

During any lulls we tell each other our life stories or talk about holidays and the latest family life-events. Cautiously, the lawyers often ask us doctors about some medical mysteries, the most common being the appellants who claim to be in pain or are exhausted yet there is no obvious disease and all investigations and tests are negative. Can there be pain or prostration with no organic cause?

'Yes', we say.

This is not malingering; the appellant's experience is real, and we see many cases. We assess disability, not pathology.

Hand cases this afternoon. With hand cases, the best question to ask is about car driving. Way back, when I starting appeals work, I thought I had a good, probing question.

'Can you brush your teeth?' I said cleverly.

'I don't have any teeth' said the man.

I didn't use that one again.

To Ayr ...

For this, one of my favourite venues, the train takes you down the Ayrshire coast, and there are golf links and golfers everywhere. Today, in the summer, the links fairways are brown, but the grass has long roots into the sand and will revive when apparently dead. From the train we see the spectacular mountains of the Island of Arran, but Robert Burns never noticed them, nor visited; other things were on his mind.

Ayr's great Station Hotel flourished in earlier times as an elegant stopping-place for travellers and as a centre for local events, but it is now crumbling. The main street has seen better days, and Ayr's famous Free Church was a casualty. Now taken over by Wetherspoon, the conversion inside was interesting, including imaginative use of the pulpit.

The benefits system and its regulations are steadily changing and there is a new award for former coal miners, called 'miner's knee' and hence some appeals are already coming through from those turned down. After a few sessions, you get a little jaded looking at these senior citizens' knees and trying to discount any effect of ageing, i.e. how would these knees have looked at their age if they had not been miners. With the monotony of this knee work and since our Ayr lawyer is such good company, I regularly forget to ask if these senior appellants have any work. If you are at work, it reduces the benefit.

For once, I remember to question a spry eighty-year-old ex-miner.

'You don't happen to work?'

'Yes, I'm the night watchman at the big warehouse over there. Up and down stairs all night.'

Oh dear.

On my first visit to Irvine, arriving by train, the hotel favoured by the Tribunal Service was some distance away in the country. I took a taxi and although I tried to be discrete about my mission, the driver skilfully elicited why I'm in town.

'Don't speak to me about the benefits system,' he said.

As we went through the town, he pointed out agile persons who were on benefits for being unable to walk, and he contrasted their steady income with his own uncertain finances. I booked him for the return journey in the morning and he suggested that he would park outside the venue and signal 'yes' or 'no' as the appellants arrive.

Prestwick, with helpful buses, is a perfect place as a base for the local tribunal venues at Irvine and Ayr. I use a small bed-and-breakfast in Prestwick at the little crossroads in the middle of town, about a mashie shot from the railway station and the famous golf course's first tee. In Prestwick, to read the papers for next day's cases, I seek a pub and it has all that I require for reading – a quiet corner table lit by a good vertical light. But there is one blot on the horizon. I'm sure it is the pub bore, and he has spotted me. He comes over, ready to give me his Views on Life, and, like the Ancient Mariner, skilled in holding his audience, he first starts with flattery.

'You must be working on something interesting.'

The main thing is not to let dialogue start. I shake my head and avert my gaze. It's time for the nuclear option.

I pretend I'm a foreigner, and mutter

'No speak zee English.'

'Let's try French or Germany' he says.

I make an excuse and leave.

I'm up early at the B&B to get my *The Herald* and *Daily Telegraph* to enjoy with my breakfast. Next door there is a paper shop.

'Sorry', says the shop keeper, 'the *Telegraphs* are gone.'

No *Telegraphs* at eight in the morning? I ponder the matter. I've got it.

'There must be a party of visiting English golfers at Prestwick Golf Club' I suggest.

'Got it in one,' says the owner.

'OK, I'll take a *Guardian.*'

We have fraught cases in the morning and have to give one 'warning' about one appeal. These warnings arise when the claimant has got an award but is not content with its size, and they appeal to us. We might agree to an increase, but occasionally we can judge that the Department was in a generous mood or that new information suggests that the award was excessive. Instead of the appellant gaining more, we can take away their existing benefit. Hence, we give a warning.

This lady has an award for being unable to walk and even claimed that she cannot stand without another person's support. Now she wants an even better award. The Department has sent us a note saying that she is known to them, being the full-time carer for her father and she is paid for this 35-hour week.

She appears with a representative and we issue the warning. The representative knows the risk of proceeding, and they withdraw to confer. They send a message in saying that they have dropped their appeal; since we have taken no evidence, she keeps the existing award.

Later in the day, while waiting for the Glasgow train, I walk up the platform and look over into the famous golf course over the wall. The first hole is close to the railway and a modest slice puts the ball onto the line, leading to incidents of shots hitting trains and bouncing back, or even a ball being thrown back by helpful passengers onto the first green. I see a ball at the end of the platform; a nice ball, brand new, from one careless owner.

❧

Back to Dundee ...

As usual, we sit behind a large boardroom table, on which we spread our documents. These papers come to our home address in a large delivery envelope and we are warned not to leave the envelope on view. Unsuccessful applicants might like to know where you live. When turned down, we sometimes get a hint from the appellant that they made the claim because an undeserving person down the road was getting benefit. So, they might as well try. When they fail, they feel aggrieved. The greatest critics of the benefits system are working people on a low income. In the afternoon we are unsympathetic to a claimant involved in the drug scene who claims agoraphobia, being unable to leave the house. The reason, he explains, is that rivals will attack him if he leaves home. We judge that this is his problem, not the government's.

Next, a prisoner, just out after a long sentence. On release from the prolonged, enclosed life, they are still outside of society and institutionalised. Unwelcome in the community and vulnerable to old enemies, they also are unlikely to get work and depression follows. Although their crime is nothing to do with us, the length of this man's sentence suggests murder. It is a curious feeling being close to a murderer; they don't look any different.

∾

To Orkney again ...

No sign of that hostile air hostess. Perhaps she has left and joined the prison service.

Routine cases all day – fibromyalgia, depression and irritable bowel syndrome. At my general surgical clinic, I took an interest in these so-called IBS cases. Their dull, patternless pain leads to lengthy unhelpful investigations. I followed these patients with interest and they never got worse or better. I had the dark thought that perhaps they were using the puzzling complaint to gain something – to get attention, to regain lost love, or use it as a reason to opt out of life's burdens. It never occurred to me that the gain might be money, funds from the benefits system. Moreover, if my efforts to cure them had succeeded these patients would have lost income. A dark thought.

Back late to St Andrews, via Aberdeen airport.

To Kilmarnock, by train ...

The current television programme 'The Scheme' is about a sink estate in Kilmarnock and its reliance on state benefits. The programme has been well-received, but critics say it is 'poverty porn', using these people's problems as entertainment. Being my first visit and the venue is some distance from the railway station, I take a taxi and it turns out that the famous housing scheme is on our route and the driver takes me through the problem estate, as a tourist attraction

Only two of the four cases turn up for this morning session. If we were a business or a dental practice, we would be bankrupt.

Today, a lady claims improbably that she loses power in her left arm six times each day and she seeks benefits for this disability. We ask her briefly about driving, and, yes, she drives her car regularly. The ability to drive is an important test of arm power. since you steer the car, put on the brake and fill up with petrol. But a disability like hers should be reported to the Drivers and Vehicle Licensing Authority. Has she told the DVLA about her problem? No, she has not.

She is represented by her lawyer who senses danger and suggests an adjournment to discuss the case with his client. Shortly, they send word to us that the appeal has been with withdrawn. Either her problem is not that bad or she has a problem but wants to keep her licence. We have an ethical problem, since the public may be at risk. Should we report what we know to the DVLA, even though the case has not been heard? The jury is out on that.

A sad case follows; the boy, his mother and aunt appear. He has serious withdrawal problems after getting off diazepam (Valium) addiction. He lives alone but is agoraphobic, and spends most of his time in his bedroom, though in good spells he may be up and about in his home. His mother brings food and leaves it in his house for him. He never goes out. He does however still smoke cannabis and we have to ask how he gets it.

'Is he going out for the weed?'

'No' says his mother, blushing. 'I bring it in to him.'

She looks away, as if this has lost his case. She is wrong. We award the money. He has a disability.

The last appellant is a sex offender living in a distant town, ostracised by the community, and not allowed to approach young girls. There is no chance of being taken on by an employer and though keen to work, nothing has been offered. Do we automatically give him unemployment benefit? If so, does society approve?

Back late by train to Leuchars for St Andrews. We had a recent holiday in Greece and I mislaid a wallet containing my precious Fife bus pass. Boarding the bus to St Andrews, I tell my hard-luck story to the driver, an old friend, hoping he might let me proceed for free, but no luck. He does however promise to look out for any Greeks bearing a Fife bus pass.

To Kirkcaldy ...

On my first visit to Kirkcaldy, coming off the train I thought it best to take a taxi to the distant church hall venue unknown to me. I mentioned my destination to the driver, who seemed unhappy about the request, and I asked if he knew of it.

'Yes, I was married there' he explained.

Our first case is a reclusive paranoid schizophrenic seeking unemployment benefit. Refused benefit, one reason given in the Department's medical examiner's report is that the man played golf. From the moment he sat down and all we have read in the paperwork, this is unlikely and the reclusive appellant tells us the reason. He confirms that he never goes out, and told the Department's doctor that in the house he liked playing computer golf games. His general practitioner's letter speaks up for him saying

'I think it would be highly detrimental to this man, and the wider community, if he was pushed down a path towards seeking employment.'

The GP knows the whole story and we are glad to get such firm advice.

Award made.

At lunchtime, the newspapers have a benefits fraud case to divert us. The man claimed inability to walk. The investigators found that he was active in his local running club and had entered 54 runs including a 5-mile race. His membership of a gym showed he had used it up to five times a week. His 10 years of benefits earned him £46,000, and resulted in an eight-month suspended sentence. When we read about these, often spectacular frauds, we feel sorry for the doctors involved, misled by plausible cheats. Next time, it might be, or was, us.

If you make a fraudulent claim, there is some good advice. On Facebook, don't put on clips of holiday swimming or dancing. Since the tough investigators will try to get video evidence, there are some niche activities to avoid. If you work out of doors, you are vulnerable. Don't even think about it if you are a football referee. The Department cross-checks many databases, including the register of football referees, and they will send video cameras along to your next game.

The clerk tells us that one of the afteroon claimants, being overweight, has requested a special chair for the hearing, but we can't arrange for this in the church hall. The Clerk tells us that the appellant is outside in a car and he is huge, and our little chairs, even by putting two of them together, will not suffice. His sister is his representative and during this discussion, she is back and forth to the car.

The resourceful lawyer decides to deal with this claim today, if possible, by unusually conducting a tribunal in the car outside. Looking at the paperwork which shows poor mobility, and a quick look at him in the car, we return to the hall and decide to offer an award to this grossly obese man. We call on the sister to come back in and we make our fair offer. The sister says the award is not good enough. Having been flexible up to this point, all we can do is postpone the hearing and move it to a more suitable venue.

Coming back to St Andrews by train, there are always interesting encounters at Leuchars station. Some travellers are golfers now at the end of a long pilgrimage to the home of golf. You know which end of the earth they come from by the airline tags on their luggage and they may be uncertain about their hotel whereabouts, and I can help. Today I suggest to a young man that to reach his accommodation, we get off the bus early and walk up the famous 18th fairway. He expects gates and security guards, but there are none. This is not Augusta, I explain, as I point him to his hotel.

&

Shetland – to the islands again ...

There is no shortage of public money in Shetland because of the tough negotiations with the oil companies, and the road from the airport into Lerwick is noticeably good. We are staying in the hotel favoured by our organisation, but we know the food is poor and we decide to eat out. Looking into the dining room on the way out however, it is uncharacteristically busy with all the tables reserved. Seems odd. We think about it on the way to the town's best and only restaurant. Perhaps they have a new chef?

The penny drops. It is St Valentine's Day. A romantic lot, the Shetlanders.

After a day's work, having exhausted Lerwick's fine dining on the previous evening, we take the car to eat in Scalloway, the headquarters of the World War II 'Shetland Bus' which evacuated many from occupied Norway. The restaurant has excellent reviews and over white wine followed by delightful scallops dusted with black pudding, the chef/manager tells us the inside story of the Shetland hospitality sector and its strengths and weaknesses.

On the second day. I fall for the famous Shetland Joke. Asking in the newspaper shop for my daily paper, the reply was:

'Do you want today's paper or yesterday's paper?'

Odd question.

'Today's paper,' I say.

'In which case, you must come back tomorrow'.

Routine cases today. A recovering alcoholic has, after a long residence in an institution, been dry for three months. His addiction counsellor and psychiatrists both say that pitching him prematurely into the workplace will prejudice the fragile recovery. We agree, and restore his incapacity to work benefit.

$\approx$

To Edinburgh ...

On the train from St Andrews to Edinburgh, there are a group who might be soldiers or a band with hats and kilts? But no. It is the Tartan Army on its way to Wembley Stadium in London for the first Scotland-England match for decades. Not a drink in sight, confirming their reputation for good behaviour, but all is not what it seems. The ticket inspector explains to me that there's no drink allowed on the trains until 10 a.m. Travelling by train over the Forth Rail Bridge is always a thrill. To one side we see oil tankers making deliveries of oil and huge cruise ships travel under the bridge and dock at the Rosyth naval base on the other side. The Navy knew the Bridge well in a former day since, when passing under the Rail Bridge, the lavatory on a train above might be flushed. The great naval tradition was if you were hit, you had to buy the drinks that night.

Our cases involving fraud are rare, unlike the regular over-egging, but these occasional fraud cases are interesting. Video film may be produced and this adds variety to the day. Today our man, claiming to be unable to walk or do anything with his hands, was, at the time of the claim, working as a scaffolder. The film of him on the scaffolding was rather grainy, and his representative explains that the images are so bad that the grimaces of pain on the face of his stoical client cannot be seen. The rep adds that his client has good day days and bad days, and the heavy work on this good day was only possible with huge doses of painkillers.

His appeal fails. He must pay it back, but only from the date of the video. We have no evidence about events up to that point.

In these cases, proof is difficult. It requires video footage taken on different days to deal with the good days/bad days defence. To gather this evidence is expensive and it is not cost-effective to pursue fraud estimated at less than £12,000. Hence lots of low-level fraud is suspected, but goes unchallenged.

The next case involves an unhelpful general practitioner, and some GPs are hostile to the benefit systems. Our appellant is aged 74 and is obviously frail, but her benefit (Attendance Allowance) was withdrawn. The Department, to assess the case, had requested the usual report from her general practitioner, but had no response and when they made a telephone call to the doctor's surgery, the receptionist declined to help, informing them that 'my doctors spend their time caring for people'. A brief, reluctant report eventually came from the doctor stating wrongly that 'she can self-care'. Hence her attendance allowance was removed. She is in front of us, and with credible evidence from a kindly daughter, clearly there are problems. We restore the money.

❧

Off to Glasgow ...

For our session tomorrow, I get to Haymarket station in Edinburgh first then take the train to Glasgow. Normally you go through Falkirk but now there's a fourth railway route between Glasgow and Edinburgh and it wends its way through Middle Scotland including places like

Drumgelloch and Courtdyke which have brand-new stations and a fine gaelic names, but are unknown to travellers on the main line. We chug on to Glasgow.

In Glasgow, the local taxi drivers, shrewd observers of the scene, have a name for our office – Lourdes – because they deliver folk to the door who seem impaired, and later they emerge *sans* crutches and moving at speed.

Trouble with interpreters today. The Tribunals give interpreters to whose who cannot speak English, since if friends or family were used, they might change the evidence. Hence professional interpreters are involved, and they cost money.

Today we have an Italian appellant, unable to speak English, and he is provided with an Italian interpreter. Unusually, we also have a PO – a 'presenting officer' – from the Department who will defend the Department's decision not to award benefit. The POs formerly came more often, but there have been cut-backs. Having a PO helps give balance to the proceedings, especially if the appellant has a skilled representative. Without the PO we have to work hard to avoid slipping into an adversarial role.

We proceed slowly with the Italian's case. Exchanges back and forth through an interpreter are necessarily rather stilted and it is difficult to sense any nuances. But about halfway into the case, the PO asks our lawyer/judge's permission to speak. The PO, it turns out, is also Italian and states that the interpreter is favourably altering the appellant's evidence. This is a serious allegation, but immediate clarification follows. The interpreter turns on the presenting officer and attacks her for 'being disloyal to Italy'.

We were being misled. We close the case, reschedule it to be heard by others on another day and report the incident to our management.

Today we have a young lady who claims both poor mobility and poor manual dexterity which means she is unable to use her hands or cook. The legal papers describe a conviction for attempted murder of her partner, and, though normally a private matter, for once, we feel the nature of the assault might help us. For the attack, she explains, she used a knife.

Our clerk tells us that a letter from a future appellant has asked for the postponement of her hearing because she will be on holiday. Her claim for benefits includes inability to sit for more than 30 minutes. She helpfully gives proof of her planned holiday by sending an invoice for the return air ticket to Florida. We allow a postponement, since she booked the holiday before the tribunal was arranged. But the new tribunal will be interested to hear how she managed in the eight-hour flight to Orlando.

Back to Dundee for appeals. The V&A gallery at the waterfront is coming along nicely and with the ship 'Discovery' plus visitor centre, already nearby, the Dundee waterfront has changed remarkably, and makes an impact when viewed from the Bridge.

First up, a, middle-aged appellant on the methadone programme has lost his benefits. This scheme, not without its critics, replaces heroin with this less addictive or dangerous substitute, hoping to wean the addict off all opioids. 'I was the first heroin addict in Dundee,' he tells us nostalgically.

Next, a lady claims she is suffering from anxiety and depression because of neighbours' harassment in a drug-ridden community. The reason for her harassment and hence her mental state is that her son has joined the police, and having crossed the line, this is unacceptable to their community. We are sympathetic but decide that her causes for anxiety are real. She does not have a mental illness, as the regulations require.

We see a lot of crutches. If the appellant is using them correctly by leaning on them, we are sympathetic. If the suspicion is that the crutches are recent acquisitions for our benefit, we look at the case papers for evidence of earlier use.

We never see anyone with long-term use of a wheelchair denied benefit, and we presume that benefit is awarded routinely.

To the Moray Firth ...

To reach the Elgin venue by train, you can go either via Aberdeen or via the Spey Valley to Inverness, then along the Firth. It's difficult to decide which is the more enjoyable journey. I get to my Elgin hotel late and for eating late, the situation in the North is saved by the Chinese restaurants and takeaways. They have spread all over Scotland and, ever-available, they save the traveller from starving after seven o'clock. Their spread within Scotland awaits a historian.

Elgin is another of the many small Scottish towns whose centres have decayed, blighted by the rise of online shopping, high rates and periodic austerity. The once elegant Main Street and its solid stone buildings is largely boarded up and only charity shops thrive. But in Elgin's back streets, things are better. They have a real bookshop, and near it is the famous Gordon McPhail whisky shop and beside it, McCall of Elgin menswear who make kilts with a modern flair and they look prosperous.

First, a man with dementia. The medical assessment for dementia can include asking appellant to spell the word 'world' backwards. The appellant managed at the Department's assessment and for this and other reasons was denied disability.

After his case is over and he leaves, I try twice and fail. Time to retire. The young lawyer on the panel also fails.

Perhaps I can hang on.

I get the train and head home, planning to change in Aberdeen. But the news spreads that Andy Murray is doing well in the final of the US open, and I get off in Aberdeen and look for a pub with a television. Andy is still doing well, and I phone home and wait and watch, even after the last train going south has left. Andy wins gloriously about 1 o'clock in the morning. Nearby there is a grand modern hotel who offer me the usual Aberdeen price of £150, and the receptionist is unmoved by my offer of £50 for a few hours' sleep.

It is a warm night and when I retreat to think about it, I find we are beside the bus station. To my surprise, I see that a bus will leave at 4 o'clock in the morning for London, and moreover, the waiting area is quite a cosy place with benches and with only one homeless user.

Still flushed and triumphant at Andy's victory, I curl up reasonably well on a bench and catch the London bus. Changing at Dundee for St Andrews, I am home for breakfast.

จจ

To Greenock ...

It's an afternoon session only and being early, I visit the Museum and Library and browse the local history section. These shelves always have worthy books considered too arcane or uncommercial by the major bookshops. Lacking proper marketing, the books remain unknown.

Being early, I also stock up with essential shopping, particularly a need for shaving soap, but inside the chemist's shop, there is an odd scene. There is a group of five ill-looking young men who are chatting and are known to each other, and they politely make way for me.

The penny drops. They are on the methadone programme, and are attending the chemist for their agreed, fixed, noon-time measure of the green liquid. For their daily dose, they are ushered singly into the back shop.

Our tribunal assembles.

My old friend Sam Galbraith is from Greenock, now retired from the Scottish parliament, also does tribunal work here, helped by a reference from myself. The others on our panel regale me with stories of his blunt discourse.[*] He and his very talented brothers and sisters came from a local working-class family and the odd paradox is that the left-wingers like Sam and trade union panel members are privately critical of the benefits system, while the Tory right-wingers are more sympathetic than you might think.

As it happens, we have a methadone programme appellant with other problems, who has somehow lost his unemployment benefit, and we restore it. The chances of anyone employing a young man who must leave work to attend the chemist daily at midday are zero.

On the way back the train stops at Port Glasgow and an elegant, tanned couple come on. He tells me he is a property developer in Italy and he was puzzled at the low house prices in Port Glasgow.

He understands now.

* Sam Galbraith died in 2014.

Edinburgh Again ...

A young lady today reports pelvic pain, with pelvic inflammatory disease in the past, and reluctantly admits that she works in a 'salon'. She has 'clients' and can visit clients in the home. Her reluctance is because she claims inability to use her hands. When we make tactful enquiries about her profession, it turns out she works at an alternative health salon, giving acupuncture, massage and reflexology. No award.

Today we have a charismatic Edinburgh heroin addict, straight out of the novel *Trainspotting* and he is claiming benefits. For once, we pry into his financial affairs, knowing that heroin is not cheap. Shoplifting, he tells us, is his only income. He seems to want to talk and explains that you don't go back to the same shops too often. How then do you spread your daily workload, we ask?

'My drug dealer buys me a day ticket for the Edinburgh buses,' he tells us.

We occasionally have potentially violent appellants – PVs – and there is one on the list today. These are flagged up ahead as having caused trouble in the past, and the staff are on the alert. We have an alarm buzzer which will summon help, and in some venues, there is a back door in the tribunal room for escape if necessary.

But today our PV behaves well, and since it's our last case of the day, we employ a strategy to avoid final conflict. We tell him we will discuss his case and send out the decision by post. Even so, it's best not to leave the building too quickly, as he may wish to reopen the discussion outside.

❧

To Oban via Glasgow ...

The West Highland line to Oban is one of the great rail journeys of the world, rightly famous for the scenery. These trains proceed at a stately pace, people talk to each other and it has a quirky extra, namely the last place on the railways that you can get a smoke. The single track allows trains to pass each other only at the stations and at Crianlarich the ticket inspector announces ta 15-minute platform break while waiting for the train from the North. This brings joy to the smokers.

Our venue is a multi-purpose hall on the esplanade to the north of the town centre and in summer it is a favourite venue for Scotland's popular entertainers. The hall's billboards show that, last night, they had a visit from Britain's 'best known clairvoyant and mystic'. Our receptionist tells me there was a modest audience and only two of them managed to communicate with the dead. With this vantage point, overlooking the Bay, we can also see the appellants leaving and arriving. Since many claim to be unable to walk, this can be helpful.

Our first case is an appellant who moved from the city to live in a cottage in the Scottish islands. The papers show that no diagnosis has been made of her mysterious weakness and she claims not only to be unable to walk any distance but never ventures out without an escort. To assess her claim for benefit the usual Department medical examination was necessary and a doctor travelled by train, ferry and taxi to assess her, and his report is that her disability is unimpressive. To add to this, he was watchful. Missing the first ferry back, he got the next one and there saw the lady in question, moving at a fair pace, and when she left the ferry, without escort, she walked briskly uphill to a distant taxi.

She appears before us and is indignant. Her explanation is that her walk to her taxi was under 100 yards.

Was she alone, as the report says?

'My nephew was on the boat with me, but he had a migraine' she said 'and he hid away on the ferry.'

No award.

At the hearings, a familiar problem. A youngish man has had a stroke, a bad one, and he is in sheltered housing with much support. He has recovered some speech and power but the brain damage has had an odd effect, leaving him unnaturally cheerful and with little insight. At the medical examination, he told the Department medical examiner wrongly that he was fine. Today, he again perseverates, telling us everything is rosy. Fortunately, his social worker is with him and tells us the real story. He has a serious, life-long disability, and gets the money.

❧

To Edinburgh again ...

I have two days' tribunal work organised at short notice. Our office offers me an expensive hotel stay in Edinburgh but it is the Festival time and I decide to stay outside Edinburgh somewhere interesting and economical and get into Edinburgh by rail or bus. But where? Somewhere new.

So, I'm off to Linlithgow. Tonight, I need to find Sky television. There is a crucial football match tonight involving Glasgow Celtic who alone are flying the Scottish flag in European football. Walking down the main street, I like the appeal of the Football and Cricketers Arms (hereinafter referred to as the FCA).

Inside the FCA there is a comfortable snug side room with a television screen. I settle there with my paperwork and wait for the match, but as kick-off approaches, the room fills up. They all know each other and look at me with slight hostility, and soon their leader suggests that I move to the main bar. It turns out they are the FCA's chapter of the local Dominos League (hereinafter referred to as the FCA-DoL). I move out and the match starts, but the dominoes leader has not yet finished with me. To my annoyance he appears at the bar, obstructing my view and suggests that I buy tickets for their prize draw.

To get him out of my life, I give him the pound, and I get a ticket. After a struggle, Celtic score, winning at the last minute.

The FCA-DoL organiser now appears yet again with some news for me. I have won the draw and he proffers me the money. This is all getting surreal. To put all this behind me, I return the winnings to him, telling him it is a contribution to the funds of the FCA-DoL, and I then leave.

They probably talk about it to this day in the FCA-DoL circles.

'He was a tall, handsome, silent stranger. No-one knew who he was, or where he came from, but he transformed our finances.'

Next day in Edinburgh, we start.

A tough day ahead. A phone call had come in ahead from our first case, an appellant with fibromyalgia, stating that he has difficulty wiping his bottom and needs a trained person to assist him when at the toilet. The others turn to me as the best qualified. Fortunately, our man is having a good day.

Coming home, I get off the train at Leuchars station. But the bus to St Andrews pulls away from the station bus stop close by, just as we disembark from the train, and we have missed it. We are not pleased and grumble cynically about 'joined-up public transport'. Turning to a man beside me in the queue, I wax eloquently about sadistic bus drivers who drive away just when passengers are arriving off the train. He seems uninterested in my complaint, and, thinking he is hard of hearing I repeat it. He is unmoved. Perhaps he as a visitor and doesn't speak English, so I abandon my sermon. The next bus eventually arrives and we enter. The bus driver greets my companion in the queue in familiar terms and he responds. They are both bus drivers.

☙

To Inverness ...

A favourite long rail journey, second only to that to Oban. In Inverness, although the tribunal service will organise a hotel, they arranged this session at the last minute, and I found a bed-and-breakfast in a part of the town I do not know.* Heading back into town, with my papers, I pass through a cluster of shops with steel doors. Outside a pub, the tattooed regulars in football strips are smoking and their discourse uses a very limited four-letter-word vocabulary. I keep going, averting my gaze, but one of the men comes after me, unsteadily.

'Are you from the f*cking Council?' he opines.

Reluctant to get involved with any problem with his roof or drains, I keep going, outdistancing him, and reach safety in central Inverness.

Next morning, I take a taxi to the distant venue. I tell the driver of my adventures and he tells me that the area I blundered into is locally called Beirut. Beirut-on-Ness to be more precise, he says.

Our talented lawyer chairman has mastered a word dictation system and impressively dictates our judgements into his computer. To start dictation, the system needs the command 'Wake up' and after finishing dictation, to close it down you say 'Go to sleep'. Today we have a new

---

* Inverness gained 'city' status in 2000 acknowledging its recent growth and longstanding title of 'Capital of the Highlands'.

care member joining us, and at the end of the first case, the lawyer sharply says 'Wake up.' The new member takes it personally and blushes.

In the afternoon, we have mostly fibromyalgia and irritable bowel cases, plus a strange one. Our appellant tells us he has no feeling in his hands, adding that he can feel nothing below the middle of his forearms on both sides. Hence, he seeks benefit on the grounds of loss of manual dexterity. I put it to him that, if I stick a pin in your arms, will you feel it?

'No', he says, and I promise not to do so.

The claim is for Industrial Injury (to his neck) and for this benefit (unlike other disabilities) an examination is required. We move to the examination room, and I first look at his hands, then move to take his pulse at the wrist. As I detect the pulse, he recoils, protesting 'That hurt'.

I desist, and he gets no award.

He is truculent and I sense that, having been turned down, he may complain and allege he was injured during a rough examination by myself, and I ask the attending nurse to make a note of the events. Unsuccessful applicants do make complaints about these medical examinations to the General Medical Council and these claims have included claiming paralysis of the arm after taking the claimant's blood pressure. Although these claims are frivolous, dealing with them can involve tedious paperwork.

~

To Dumfries ...

The train journey from Glasgow to Dumfries goes via Kilmarnock, but the line uses old rolling stock and the train proceeds at a leisurely pace through the areas of Ayrshire suffering after the closure of the coal mines, then over the hills and down the lovely hidden Valley of Urr to Dumfries.

After a good night's sleep, I head down for breakfast before our tribunal session in the same hotel, and I narrowly miss catastrophy. When I sit down to breakfast, with my legal papers, I notice on the other side of the dining room, a group of 12 ladies in middle life at a long table and they are taking an interest in my arrival. I realise that this is a group of golfers from my wife's golf club in St Andrews; they must be having an outing here, 100 miles from home.

I go over and greet them, aware that they might think I was up to no good, being alone and so far from home. After these pleasantries, I move to our tribunal room in the hotel. The news is that the local lawyer has pulled out, and instead they have substituted a female lawyer from Aberdeen who I know slightly. A horror story now emerges. She too is staying in the hotel.

'Must've missed you at breakfast,' she says.

The blood drained from my brain. We could have been sitting together at breakfast.

The first case has cancelled and the second doesn't turn up. While waiting, we hear from our care member, who is active in the local constituency and he gives us the history of their local politics. Added to this, we talk about more fraud cases in the newspapers, including a man who claimed only 15 yards walking, but was secretly filmed as the proud lead drummer in the City of Preston Scottish Pipe and Drum band. He had got £7,300 benefit and the result was a suspended jail sentence. At least one doctor must have agreed that he was disabled.

The third and fourth appellants don't appear either, We have a pleasant lunch in the spa café and I get the gossip from Aberdeen

It's the last case on my last day. She has had four heart attacks and two coronary artery stent insertions and she says she can't walk 20 yards. Because the evidence is credible, and she is perhaps doomed, we give the award.

It's a nice ending to my career in the benefits service, I hope.

But it's not over yet.

When I leave for home, I find she is walking ahead of me, heading for the bus stop. I follow at a distance. Can she get beyond 20 yards? Do I even want to know? She does stop at 15 yards, or rather, 15 metres.

All's well.

We had by now moved to St Andrews.

CHAPTER 27:

To St Andrews

The move ... The town ... Pubs ... Golf courses ... Visitors
Historians ... Politics

ONE EVENING about the year 2002, Jean had suggested unexpectedly that we move to St Andrews when retirement came up in three years time. Such a bold plan had not occurred to me, but it was music to my ears. I had been visiting the town regularly for historical studies after I joined the Royal and Ancient Golf Club, and hence was delighted at her idea. I wrote it down that night, and fortunately she confirmed this proposal in the morning. As a swimmer, she was attracted to the famous West Sands at St Andrews, used for the film *Chariots of Fire,* and I judged it best not to raise the matter that the North Sea can be chillingly cold, unlike her more familiar West Coast waters. In the event, Jean swims there regularly, even when others avoid it.

For a move we had a window of opportunity ahead when our two boys would be off to university, and our Hazel could settle at school in St Andrews before her big exam years. We told her what would happen, and she accepted the plan. In good time, we began to look at houses in St Andrews. Conventional advice was to settle in the villas in the West End, but we returned several times to view a solid Victorian terrace townhouse with cosy small rooms on three levels close to the golf courses. A long strip of garden, as in a croft, lay hidden at the back and it had two out-houses, probably used for animals earlier. This solved a problem; my Partick Press could move into one. We bought the house.

Selling our house went well, just before a slump in prices. We had a single, quick offer from a strange man who aroused our lawyer's suspicions, but on these occasions, you can't be too choosy. He paid up, much to our relief, but never took up residence and headed for jail instead, not before ripping out our beloved conservatory and my vine-with-the-roots-outside. The house lay unloved thereafter for years; our children returned to visit occasionally, and wept.

One bit of luck, or rather two, were our St Andrews neighbours – a retired surgeon on one side and a retired academic on the other. The risk in St Andrews is having students next door; nice to have around, they keep the place young, but they can spoil your sleep, regularly.

Just before we moved, the owner let our house at the time of the 2005 Open Championship. Being only three minutes from the first tee of the Old Course, it was given as a base for the previous year's winner, Todd Hamilton, and after he stayed in it, he left us a signed memento. We regretted leaving our Aga cooker behind, a wedding present from Jean's mother, but the new house already had one. As ever, it keeps our small kitchen/dining area warm.

The move to St Andrews involved more than the usual challenge. Our belongings had, as ever, accumulated and box upon box of books from our large Kilmacolm home filled up our new house and also one of the bothies. My faithful printing engineer Harry Brooke moved the printing presses out of the old home and got them onto a big transporter lorry. In St Andrews a kindly traffic warden had put down cones and as the lorry's heavy crane swung the Arab machine onto the pavement, a senior citizen stopped by in admiration. It turned out he had learned his trade, as an apprentice printer, on an Arab, and this was a nostalgic moment. The two machines made it narrowly through the house and into the nearer bothy in the back garden. But, reluctantly, I soon gave up my letterpress printing. I was now in a hurry to publish and the University accepted my printshop intact. To get a book out, there was now no longer any need to find a publisher, a tedious business. With the rise of print on demand (POD) you can publish your own works promptly and without need to order hundreds and risk money upfront. But you need someone like my friend George to enter the text into the correct electronic format. These companies will also put your book on Amazon, free. Appearing on Amazon was a thrill, but you are not alone. Few notice the books, even there, unless you market them well.

Settling in, there were some challenges. My friend Alec, of the B&B just around the corner, had been unwell for a while and died shortly after we arrived. His daughter had helped run the business during his decline and she explained to me they had few friends in St Andrews, and would I mind saying a few words about Alec at the crematorium service later in the week? I was glad to do so. Next day, she came back and increased my involvement, explaining that since they had no church connections, and knowing my father had been a minister, she wondered if I would also take the service. I did so, and being 'to the manor born', the cadences came to me. I was one of the new cadre of lay celebrants.

The other event was our Hazel's first day at the new school. The choice in St Andrews was between the town's private, part-boarding school or the local state comprehensive, Madras College, around the corner, which was highly regarded. Madras suited our ideological outlook, and Hazel and her friends would all do well academically, and gained added social skills. Many of the local children spread out to success in the wider world and they return home in numbers at Christmas, bearing the news from afar.

However, Hazel's first day in fourth year rather shook our resolve. After a nervous wait for her to return home for lunch, she told us about her morning. A new class-mate, sitting beside her, offered Hazel her mobile phone, a novelty in those days. She then showed Hazel a picture of her boyfriend. Hazel made suitable noises.

We live in the centre of town, and having no industry, it remains untouched and compact because, as Cockburn said, it was 'Pompeiied' i.e. saved from modernisation. The shops are small and varied. In the town, everyone walks and your car as a handicap; there are also bicycles.

For those of us of a certain age, there is the bus pass for short or even longer journeys in Scotland and with it, starting from the small central St Andrews bus station, you can get to most places for nothing. It is a great success, and even encourages walking – walking to the bus stop and further walking when you get there. On the bus you escape the tyranny of the computer and the temptation to look for emails just in. I even used my bus pass in America when in Texas for a golf event. We were returning by bus back from downtown Dallas to our venue, and all the locals entering the bus ahead of us waved a variety of concession cards at the driver. My Fife card worked a treat.

Our sturdy Volvo estate went on and on, and clocking up a tiny mileage, the mechanics admired its robust construction at MOT time. But parked outside our house, it attracts leaflets, including 'Why scrap your car, when we will give you a good price?'

Outside our house there is a steady stream of students moving about between classes, which gives the town a youthful ambience. Another feature throughout the year are groups of four golfing visitors, friends sharing their trip of a lifetime to the home of golf. They move about the town, far from home and looking slightly lost, but savouring the surroundings. At graduation time, proud parents appear to join the celebrations and since everyone walks, mother's new dress is on display. After graduation, some rich students decline to take their excess belongings away and dump them in the charity shops. It means rich pickings for the locals.

When we reached St Andrews, I had some ready-made retired golfing companions, notably Robin Clark, our old surgical friend from Oban and Gibraltar days. Robin looked in the charity shops and found a formerly-owned R&A blazer for me. His small group of retired golfers made me welcome, and it included Michael Steel, the medical scientist, John Cubie, a Church of Scotland minister, and Bob Murray, a St Andrews accountant. Bob had been early into computing and kept up, and when he slowly developed renal failure, after golf, he could call up his recent blood tests results from the lab on his iPhone and discuss them with me. Also in our group was a man after my own heart, a retired professor of theology, who had been working on a book on the Old Testament's Book of Leviticus for as long as I had worked on my history of organ transplantation.

Senior golfers are a kindly lot and their golf enthusiasm continues. The race is over, and they are reflective and reject the idea that the latest expensive clubs will help your game. Robin Clark developed dementia and soon we had to collect him by car and get him to the first tee. On the course, his short game was better than ever and his putting became fearless. This was clear evidence, if anyone had ever doubted it, that the human brain interferes with our embedded God-given ability to play the game well.

≈

Jean played golf regularly after arrival and started at one of the all-ladies clubs beside the 18th hole. She then added the St Rule Club nearby, a ladies club with a golf (and bridge) section. Jean had a good year in 2008 notably winning the club Medal Finals played on the Old Course. She joined me in travelling to some golf history events, including a gathering near Prague that year, where, playing

Jean enjoyed being a scorer in local events and shown here at the 2018 Senior British Open with Peter Oakley, the 2004 winner.

in the older style, Jean was the Czech Women's Hickory Champion, and has an elegant trophy to prove it.

Daughter Hazel did well at the local Madras College school and then took a psychology degree at Edinburgh. During that time, she had holiday work in a St Andrews delicatessen and a local restaurant and

Our team on the Swilkan Bridge.

brought home many tales of customers, good and bad, like those who drink single malt whisky and Coca-Cola with ice. Then there was always folk looking to reduce the bill by complaining, so Hazel learned to check half way through with the defensive mantra – 'is everything alright?' After Edinburgh, studying psychology, and a nursing degree from Glasgow, she moved to London. Alistair took his medical degree in Edinburgh and realised, a bit like me, that there was no hurry to become a consultant, and meanwhile enjoyed himself entrepreneurially practising medicine in small and large hospitals in Scotland. With his love of surfing, the hospital at Wick, near Thurso, was perfect.

Duncan moved into digital marketing in Gibraltar, thus returning to his childhood holiday venue. He used the useful strategy of living in Spain and crossing the border daily. We soon visited him regularly, taking our time, taking any useful Ryanair flight out of Edinburgh at mid-day, then doing the rest by trains and buses over a few days. Ryanair's success changed travel in Europe at this time and it came from using small airports outside the cities which, as a wit remarked 'seemed to be in the hands of rebel forces but, if so, the food would be better.'

At the Royal and Ancient Golf Club, there are always visitors. Being a secret place, visitors are respectful and in awe of the mystique. We always remind them to bring a jacket and tie and I have both these essentials at hand for emergency use. One Ph.D. student, working on

the history of golf, turned up without either, nor did he have a shirt.
Our ever-helpful porters found one, since we have a fair collection
of items of clothing left behind by those overwhelmed by the
surroundings.

We have had golfing visitors to St Andrews from earliest times. An
early celebrity arrival was Vincenzo Lunardi, the pioneer balloonist who
in 1785 took off from Edinburgh, drifted over the Firth of Forth, and
descended near St Andrews. Locals scooped him up unharmed and,
taken to the town, the R&A promptly made him a member. He took 21
shots for the first hole, and like a seasoned golfer, blamed the score on
an injury sustained during his landing.

Among the visiting golfers, the town has always had its favourites.
Bobby Jones had a bad start, but the town forgave him and came to
love him. A local boy, Jock Hutchison, emigrated to be a professional in
America and when he came back, touring the town in a car with white
wall tires, he won the 1921 Open at St Andrews. Another Open winner,
John Daly is always welcome back, since the religious town feels kindly
towards sinners.

On the first tee of the Old Course, visitors can be overcome
with emotion. Even those who have run countries or headed armies
have stood on the first tee and trembled. Dwight Eisenhower, shortly
after commanding the victorious Allies in Europe, decided not to
hit from the first tee and moved away to start at the second. George
Bush, having coped with speaking to one hundred thousand people
in Prague's Wenceslas Square confessed that, on our first tee, he had
sweaty palms and a racing pulse. It's all so public. Anyone passing by
can, and do, watch.

When we have a visitor of note, the news spreads in town. When
Bobby Jones returned on a private visit, it was noticed and people
flocked to the links. In 2018, Obama arrived unannounced. Word
spread and, inconspicuously surrounded by security men in relaxed
clothing, the swelling crowd watched his left-handed swing with
interest. Also watching were snipers on the roof tops.

∽

In St Andrews we are, as it were, still rationed – with one each
of the essentials. One cathedral, one castle (both started c1158), one

University (1413), one famous beach, one small theatre, one cinema, one cheese shop, one nightclub and one luxury spa. One of the seven golf courses is more famous than the rest. There's a famous ice cream shop, a successful independent bookshop, and a drop-in hearing aid clinic at the excellent community hospital, which also has a highly-regarded end-of-life unit.

Only one of the earlier antiquarian bookshops now survives. Mrs Squires' famous Quarto Bookshop, now gone, had golf books old and new, and she liked her jokes. She had a paperback called *Tea aff the Bunker,* a tale of childhood deprivation in Dundee, and would tempt golf collectors with this hard-to-find work.* She had regular visitors, notably the world's most determined successful and thoughtful collector who would run a finger along the shelves as if, she said, it contained a computer chip. Another regular was a local man who arrived each morning about 11 a.m. and then made a vague request for a half-remembered title. His doctor had told him to walk half a mile each day, and this was the journey. The St Andrews charity shops are excellent and Jean gets quality paperbacks including interesting titles dumped by visitors from foreign parts. Previously-owned interesting golf balls, lost on the links, resurface in these shops and they have exotic logos from all over the world.

Our town has villages. The big ones are the university village and the golf village, and the music village is medium-sized. The botanic village, centred on the Friends of St Andrews Botanic Gardens, can get 50 members out on a cold December night for a talk on the flora of the Dutch East Indies.

The University village is recognised as the world's 'best small university in the best small town' and the students come from all nations. Its College bells ring on special occasions and we also have impressive church bells, tolling on the hour during the day. On Sundays, there is a Presbyterian silence about the place. That day, the students in their red gowns take a photogenic walk along the pier and have a rite of

---

* Margaret Squires' book *In Quarto* (2005) was based on her regular column in *Scottish Book Collector* magazine. She also tempted golf collectors with *Putting Up With the Russians.*

passage in the foam fight on Raisin Monday in autumn. In the second week in April, the Kate Kennedy student procession goes through town, celebrating people and events from St Andrews history. The student graduations follow in July, and some rich parents check into the Old Course Hotel. But parking can be difficult. The hotel Porter may enquire in the restaurant – 'Sir, if that is your helicopter outside, please move it.'

In the golf village, the facilities are lavish, and the clubs round the Old Course 18th hole resist any flashy modernity – there's no valet parking, or swimming pools, saunas or tennis coaches. Golf carts are few. The golf village has its rituals. Autumn sees the Autumn Meeting of the R&A with an 8 a.m. drive-in by the new captain. The 1892 cannon is fired as he hits the ball and the caddies, having researched the new captain's golfing ability, race to field it and the captain rewards the winner with a sovereign. It's all a bit feudal, but nobody minds.

There are six courses on the St Andrews Links, (plus one non-links out of town) and they belong to the town. Of these, the best known is the Old Course and because it is busy, and since play is often slow, we locals usually play on one of the other courses. Hence a round on the Old Course it is still a treat for us. The humblest course is the 9-hole Balgove, (Royal Balgove we call it), suitable for children and beginners but we seniors can arrive without booking and sprint round in one hour.

Local citizens need a Links Trust ticket to play the courses and the annual fee is about the same as the charge for a round on the Old Course. There are 17 other ways to get this precious annual ticket if you don't live in town.[*] One way is to be enrol as a student and cynically never finish your degree, or join the Army and hope to be moved to the Leuchars base nearby. If all else fails you should try to win The Open, or, perhaps easier, get a job with the Links Trust.

The Old Course is closed on Sundays signalling its many links with religion. It has the Valley of Sin, Hell Bunker, nearby Pulpit Bunker and the Elysian Fields. In golf you 'approach' the green as

---

[*] George Pepper's book *A Year at St Andrews* 2006 has much on golfing life in St Andrews, plus the full list of strategies available to gain the coveted Links Trust ticket.

you would an altar and coming back from the 12th hole, caddies give directions using the distant church steeples. When Hope Park Church's spire, seen from a distance, needed repairs, they got help from the R&A. Golfers sometimes leave instructions that their ashes are to be scattered on the course, or in the Swilcan Burn, and a minister of religion may occasionally be seen doing so on the iconic Bridge. More conventional burials are at the Cathedral and many great local professionals of earlier times have a gravestone there. Michael Tobert famously said that a team from our Cathedral graveyard could beat a team chosen from any other graveyard in the world.*

Golfers from afar, like the mediaeval pilgrims who reached St Andrews, may liken their golfing visit to a pilgrimage. Like those early pilgrims who slept overnight in their chosen shrine in the hope of spiritual and bodily healing, the golfing pilgrims wait overnight beside the Old Course Pavilion in sleeping bags. Come the dawn, if there are gaps in the starting sheet, they get them.

The Old Course hosts many events great and small. At less well-known amateur events there are no ropes, and you can follow the talented players on the course. From hole to hole they are as good as the famous professionals and differ from them only in one or two shots per round, usually putts. Jean likes to be close to the action as a scorer when major events come here. At the annual Dunhill Championship event, which mixes the professionals and celebrity amateurs, Dunhill's rich business pals are included and the scorers know the heroes and villains.

I like being a marshal at the Royal and Ancient Golf Club meetings. You have a few minutes chat on the first tee with the members and put faces to the names. There are some snappy exchanges. I noticed that a member's rain jacket had the logo of a famous New York baseball team.

'You follow them?' I asked.

'No, I own them,' he replied crisply.

It is a mystery that the east coast towns of Scotland with such golfing DNA and the unrivalled opportunity to play, does not produce

* See Tobert's *Pilgrims in the Rough* Edinburgh, 2000.

golfing heroes regularly. Some say that play on the hard links turf is poor preparation for tournament parkland courses, or blame our long winter or even that our social policy has annulled the stimulus of poverty.

☞

St Andrews is generously supplied with pubs. There is the Central Bar, of classic Victorian design with a central square mahogany servery, but others are small and quirky, like The Keys, dating from 1590, and a favourite with the caddies. Inside there is a plaque to 'Tip' Anderson, Palmer's caddie when he played in Britain. When here, Prince William and Kate had their favourite places for a night out, and all St Andrews knew where they were, but left them alone. Their minders were close by, having a low-key drink at the bar, with escape routes planned through the kitchens.

The Dunvegan pub and restaurant has a role as the 19th hole for the Old Course nearby, and anyone, even wearing spikes, is welcome. You can retire there with your caddie and catch up with your family and children. Everybody and anybody in golf has been through and, coaxed by former owners Sheena and Jack, they posed for a photograph. During great golfing events, the place is packed, with supporters from all nations, and the staff hold up tournament-style 'Silence Please' paddles when a crucial putt is being negotiated.

Our St. Andrews local is just around the corner. The cosy bar of the Russell Hotel, on The Scores terrace above the sea, is still in the hands of father (Gordon De Vries) and his son Michael, a trained chef. In the quiet winter, when they see our heads coming past the window, they pour our aperitif, and turn down the music, if on. Never dull, we like its varied clientele. There was a retirement home next door and old ladies' caring daughters brought mother in on her wheelchair for a gin and tonic. There are jet-lagged golfing visitors, curious about the town, ready to play next day and, and University departmental outings, with the professor holding court and the juniors listening respectfully and minding their manners. We watch – perhaps it is the Department of Philosophy's night out or even International Terrorism? Some music villagers dine here, as do important figures the the world of golf. We are careful with our candid conversations since you never know who might be listening. Later in the evening, Richard, the expert on the local paranormal, comes in after one of its spooky dark-time tours of the town, and his book on the topic, recording 200 strange local incidents, sells well.

In mid-summer the sun can set onto the little entrance patio of the Russell, a nice spot for people-watching on the Scores. One balmy night, we, unusually, had a second drink. A hotel guest asked me some good questions on the history of golf, and, pleased with my replies, inside he told the barman he wanted to buy us a drink.

'No, no,' said the barman, 'they usually only have one and they've had two already.'

We don't have Sky and use the pub for watching big golf events. During the Gleneagles Ryder Cup, a visitor plumped himself down sorrowfully beside us, turned away from Gleneagles, where they told him his ticket had been forged. To ease the pain, during the next commercial TV break, I marched him down to the R&A, an 8-iron shot away, to view the Open Championship Claret Jug. His iPhone pictures showing him beside the Jug went round the world to his pals. We were back in the pub in time for renewed golfing action.

The new laws on smoking in public places came in after we reached St. Andrews. This was a success for lifetime effort by activists, including Sam Galbraith, legislation opposed by the tobacco companies and libertarian politicians. Public opinion was ready for it and there was no problem. Even visitors to St. Andrews quickly got the message. Everyone thought it would be a problem at the hotels and at the Royal and Ancient Golf Club, since the many visiting golfers were smokers, often enjoying cigars, but even they accepted the new rules, and knuckled under.

We had a growing community of golf historians in St Andrews, supported by the British Golf Museum in St Andrews headed by Peter Lewis then by Angela Howe. In our group we had David Malcolm, who died in 2011, and his obituary in the *Guardian* spoke of the 'rigour and discipline of a scholar … readable and stylish prose … painstaking and dogged detective work.'[*] David could be blunt, and once started a noisy

---

[*] Co-authored with Peter Crabtree, their definitive *Tom Morris of St Andrews: The Colossus of Golf, 1821-1908* (2008), is unequalled for the quality of the text, typography and illustrations.

Tenth birthday meeting of the Literati, with a cake made by Jean.
Back row – Anthony Shone, John Pearson, Colin Strachan, Philip Truett,
Peter Lewis, Richard Williams, Georg Kittel.
Front row – Stephen Barnard, myself, Neil Millar.

argument with an American historian in the main room of the New Club, the dispute being over on the date of death of an early St Andrews professional golfer. To our distress, we heard David challenge the visitor 'to come outside'. But it was not for a fight, and instead David hauled the visitor off to the Cathedral graveyard to settle the matter.

Our numbers grew. Organised nationally as the 'Literati of the Links' we held our golf history meetings throughout the year. This helped to increase standards of writing and it served as a cooperative for sharing information and acting as readers for each other's texts. We were fortunate in having publication available in the British Golf Collectors Society's increasingly authoritative magazine *Through the Green* with its talented editor John Pearson. Books by the Literati gained many prizes and in St Andrews we had four winners of the United States Golf Association's Herbert Warren Wind Prize for the best golf history book of the year – David Malcolm, Peter Crabtree, Peter Lewis, and Roger McStravick. There was skilled local assistance for these efforts, since a feature of most of these books was the beautiful layout by our local designer Chic Harper.

By autumn 2014 my two personal Lost Causes were rising in the local and national agendas. The first was the long road towards Scottish independence and it was heading towards a denouement. The second was a more parochial matter, namely getting women into the R&A. Astonishingly, the stars are aligning, nae queuing up, since the vote on both matters would be on the same night, it being also our wedding anniversary.

In the R&A, when the new equal opportunity legislation arrived in 2012, reluctant consultation started and the leadership requested the opinion of the members by letter. Some letters were more equal than others. Hopeless though it was, I wrote in supporting the entry of women to the membership; it was turned down. The club have ways of dealing with members of the awkward squad like me. They put me on a committee.

But the mood was changing. Sponsors of The Open and distinguished visitors and politicians were staying away from the R&A's event. Stirring it up locally was the new Principal of St Andrews University, Louise Richardson, the first ever female Principal. As Principal, should have been an honorary member of the R&A, but they could not do so. She rebuked the club, but left it at that, and moved to Oxford shortly afterwards.

However, the leadership now realised that change was inevitable, and they consulted us committee members first. I re-sent my earlier letter. Support now seemed likely, if a postal vote, the first ever, was taken.

In the same year, 2014 came the referendum on Scottish independence. Even I was scared at the prospect that we would need a Scottish Army and Navy starting in the following week. This autumn vote was preceded as usual by the Edinburgh Festival, but unusually there were also the Commonwealth Games in Glasgow and then the Ryder Cup at Gleneagles. Scotland seemed to be the centre of the world, and we were also offered nationhood.

It was quite a week leading up to the referendum on Thursday 18th September. The crucial R&A meeting to discuss a postal vote on women's membership was also held that Thursday night and a two-thirds majority was not certain, since the opponents of the women's membership saw the danger. It went through, just, and there would be a vote. A long night followed, with television coverage of the referendum, and, come the dawn, Scotland had narrowly voted against independence. The Prime Minister David Cameron was up early and at 7 a.m., announced that Scotland was still in the Union. The Queen, he hinted was pleased. We gathered on the Links at 8.00 am. to see the R&A captain's traditional drive-in.

Soon after, the R&A postal vote was convincingly in favour of a mixed club. The Princess Royal and six distinguished lady golfers were promptly added to the membership, plus the new Principal of the University, again a woman. Applications by other golfing ladies started on the slow five-year process towards full membership. Shortly afterwards, there was the amalgamation of the Ladies Golf Union and the R&A, and the ladies' famous trophies entered the display cabinets of the R&A.

&

That's the story so far.

Envoi

A journalist asked Lee Trevino, the senior golfer, about getting old and he replied that 'three things happen to your golf – your drives get shorter, your putting gets worse and ...'

Trevino hesitated and added

'And I forget the third thing.'

But senior long-term memory can be good and my story started when we in Scotland were preparing for German air raids. In childhood there were still many epidemics to endure, and later I worked in the hospitals where the all-male staff, heavy smokers, did their best with the simple methods and technology of the day. Outside, the cities were polluted and the citizens deferent; male homosexuals were arrested and jailed.

Things have changed, slowly.

Autobiographies like this usually end with a lament that the country, and the world, are going to the dogs, and that the younger generations are not what they used to be.

That's not my view. Instead, I'm optimistic. I see a slow trend, with short-term difficulties, with a steady escape from the tyrannies of the past, edging us towards a better and fairer society.

❧

Printed in Great Britain
by Amazon